Wary Partners

Wary Partners

Diplomats and the Media

David D. Pearce

An Institute for the Study of Diplomacy Book

Congressional Quarterly Inc.
Washington, D.C.

Cover design: Ed Atkeson / Berg Design, Albany, New York

Printed and bound in the United States of America

Library of Congress Cataloging-in-Publication Data

    Pearce, David D.
    Wary partners : diplomats and the media / David D. Pearce.
      p.   cm.
    Includes bibliographical references (p.   ) and index.
    ISBN 1-56802-067-8 (cl : alk. paper)--ISBN 1-56802-066-X (p : alk. paper)
    1. Mass media--Political aspects. 2. International relations.
    3. Journalism--Political aspects. I. Title.
    P95.8.P43   1995
    302.23'0883522--dc20   95-15761
                                                       CIP

For my parents,

Duane and Mary Jean Pearce

Contents

Preface

"By and large, the Foreign Service and the foreign policy establishment don't think in public relations terms," says former secretary of state Lawrence Eagleburger. "Too many of the people I've seen working with the press at the State Department are fundamentally afraid of them. They're not prepared to be straight and honest, and this kills you over time. We have a terrible tendency to be disingenuous or fluffy or fuzzy or not answer the question." [1]

This book is an attempt to help address those problems. Over the past twenty years I've worked both sides of the briefing divide, as reporter and as diplomat. I came into journalism as Senator Sam Ervin kicked off his Watergate hearings in 1973. I covered revolution in Portugal and civil war in Lebanon for UPI, and I worked on the *Washington Post* foreign desk during the Iran hostage crisis. After traveling to China for a National Geographic book project in 1981, I entered the Foreign Service in January 1982. Since then, I have held assignments as vice consul and political officer in Riyadh, Saudi Arabia; watch officer at the State Department Operations Center in Washington, D.C.; country officer for Greece; Arabic language student at the Foreign Service field school in Tunis, Tunisia; chief of the political section at the U.S. embassy in Kuwait (before, during, and after the 1990-91 Gulf War); and special assistant for Middle East and South Asian affairs in the Office of the Under Secretary for Political Affairs. After completion of a one-year Una Chapman Cox sabbatical leave to write this book, and a year of Farsi language training, I took up an assignment in 1994 as consul general in Dubai.

During the years of this two-phase career, the chasm of distrust in government-press relations has steadily widened. Although not surprising, it is nonetheless unfortunate. The American people are no better served by dysfunction and gridlock in government-press relations than they are by dysfunction and gridlock in executive-legislative relations.

There is no magic formula here for changing deeply ingrained attitudes. Institutional shifts, if they happen at all, come slowly. But this book will review some of the practical problems, organizational dynamics, and professional issues reporters and diplomats face in their day-to-day dealings. Part I will offer a capsule summary of changes and trends in diplomacy and the media; then Part II will address specifics—setting ground rules, understanding reporters and their organizations, preparing for a meeting so it will be productive for both sides, and then a few thoughts about conducting the meeting. Finally, the book will look at some of the diplomat's organizational considerations, whether in Washington or at a post overseas. And while the focus is on the specific case of diplomats and the press, the dynamics and lessons learned may have parallels in many large organizations, government or private, that have regular contact with the news media.

The lacunae doubtless are many. I have only scratched the surface of a rich subject and would have liked more time. I interviewed about seventy-five diplomats, reporters, and media analysts, but wish I could have met and talked to many more. This number does not include dozens of incidental "corridor" conversations, many phone contacts, and multiple follow-up discussions with some sources.

I plunged into the professional literature on both sides, but wish there had been even more time to read and explore. My biggest surprise was finding how lean the pickings were on the practical dynamics of contacts between diplomats and reporters.

I did most of the legwork for the book in the fall of 1992 and the first half of 1993. For the descriptions of news organizations and press dynamics, I relied on personal interviews with journalists, supplemented by a reasonably substantial body of written material available on the subject. I also drew on my own experience: M.A. in journalism from Ohio State University; broadcast writer for the Associated Press in Columbus, Ohio; sports editor of the English-language *Rome Daily American* in Rome, Italy; AP radio stringer in Rome; correspondent for UPI in Brussels, Lisbon, and Beirut; copy editor on the metro and foreign desks of the *Washington Post*; and writer-editor in the book division of the National Geographic Society.

Diplomats, especially working diplomats, are not particularly easy subjects: they prefer anonymity, they choose their words carefully, and their offices lie behind locked doors and security guards. When compared with the never-ending navel gazing of journalists—whether on changing patterns of news coverage or the ethics of citing sources, whether in books or journalism reviews—the literature on the nuts-and-bolts media concerns of diplomats is slender indeed. Even the best treatments, such as David Newsom's *Diplomacy and the American Democracy*, usually handle the subject as a small piece of a larger whole (which it is), and focus more on the *why* of press contacts than the *how*. Consequently, I have had to compile themes, rules of thumb, and practical lessons drawn mostly from primary sources, private lore, and interviews.

Much of the material in this book is derived from personal interviews, as in the case of the quote from Secretary Eagleburger. I began by meeting a range of State Department and U.S. Information Agency (USIA) colleagues. Interviews were conducted in person for the most part, over the telephone when necessary. Usually I would take notes, with the permission of the person I was speaking to, for later dictation, transcription, and printing via computer. I supplemented this body of raw material with myriad "corridor" contacts and other casual encounters. At the end of the day I would jot down any such gleanings for later use. I have not stated time and place when quoting from each and every one of these many conversations, and unless otherwise indicated the reader may assume that they are the source of the book's many quotations not cited in the notes.

I made clear up front to those with whom I spoke that I was working on a book and wished to have as much material as possible on the record. Nonetheless, many of those still working—especially less-senior officers—did not wish to be quoted. Others did not want critical remarks attributed. Retired officers were, on the whole, more relaxed and willing to be quoted.

So were journalists. I tried whenever possible to find reporters who had covered foreign affairs overseas and in Washington. Having started my career in journalism, I had a good base to start from, and drew on numerous contacts from my days with UPI in Beirut and at the *Post* in Washington. I found reporters honest critics of both their own profession and that of the diplomat, and a rich source of illustrative anecdotes and tales.

With diplomats, I sought the views of officials at all levels of the State Department and USIA. I spoke to officers with expertise in every major geographic area, from policy makers on the sixth and seventh floors to the Spokesman's Office to the public affairs officers to the various country desk officers.[2] USIA officers in particular provided many valuable insights and were unstintingly generous with their time. These public affairs officers serve not only on detail to the State Department, but as embassy press spokesmen overseas. They have the often difficult job of brokering the relationship between press and embassy.

As a Foreign Service officer who looks ahead to many more years in this business, I believe it is vitally important that we improve the quality of our dialogue with the press and public on foreign affairs. Success or failure will turn on the perennial question of trust.

Acknowledgments

Since 1973 it has been my good fortune to work with many talented journalists and diplomats, and it is the gift of their knowledge and experience, more than anything else, that has shaped this book. I am indebted to former Under Secretary of State David Newsom, USIA Counselor Donna Oglesby, Brookings scholar Stephen Hess, and Mark Foulon, a talented diplomat who left the Foreign Service to work for Senator Bill Bradley, for taking the time to read and provide early feedback on my drafts.

I owe a special debt of gratitude to Doyle McManus, a close friend since 1976, when we both toiled for UPI in Beirut and shared a house in the old waterfront neighborhood of Ain Mreisseh. Doyle, who has been both a Washington correspondent and foreign correspondent for the *Los Angeles Times*, read every draft chapter and made a great many helpful comments on both substance and organization.

Many other senior diplomats and journalists were extraordinarily generous with their time and thoughts. Ambassador Thomas Pickering, to take but one example, gave me two interviews when he was very tightly scheduled on the eve of his departure to head our mission in Moscow. Likewise, Don Oberdorfer, the former State Department correspondent for the *Washington Post*, freely spun out a great store of invaluable comment, anecdote, and analysis.

Needless to say, although many persons are quoted and many helped in the preparation of this book, I did not always take every piece of advice or use all material gathered. Thus, the responsibility for any defects in the substance or organization of this book must rest with me, not with any contributors or readers. Nevertheless, to all who contributed, whether directly in contacts for this project, or indirectly by guiding me through two decades of work in journalism and diplomacy, I am grateful.

Three institutions made this book possible: the Una Chapman Cox Foundation, Georgetown University's Institute for the Study of Diplomacy, and the U.S. Department of State. Quite simply, the research could not have been done without the support that the Cox Foundation provided during my 1992-93 stint as a sabbatical leave fellow. Both the Cox trustees and Executive Director Alfred L. Atherton Jr. encouraged the project from the start.

The Institute for the Study of Diplomacy told me early on that it saw the book as a useful addition to its publishing program. I am much indebted to ISD director Hans Binnendijk and to his successor Casimir Yost for their backing and to the Martin F. Herz Memorial Fund for making that support possible. As part of its mission to further education in diplomacy, the Institute has produced a series of studies, drawn principally from U.S. experience, on the varied roles played and objectives pursued by diplomats serving in embassies abroad. Beginning in 1990 these works, including this book, constitute the Martin F. Herz Series on United States Diplomacy.

Above all, ISD director of publications Margery Boichel Thompson has been with me every step of the way—encouraging, coaxing, and cajoling—in short, patiently steering me through every shoal in the book production process. Her sound advice and encouragement lifted me up and kept me going time and again, whatever the difficulty.

My sabbatical leave year to write this book stemmed from a Department of State effort to encourage midcareer training for U.S. diplomats. I know I benefited enormously from the chance to step outside the usual career path to read, study, and reflect on what I was doing. I hope similar opportunities will continue to be made available to others as well. The opinions and views expressed in this manuscript are solely my own and do not necessarily represent those of the U.S. Department of State.

This book is dedicated to my parents, Duane and Mary Jean Pearce, whose love, sacrifice, and example have sustained me always, no matter how far from home I have strayed over the years. It never would have been completed, though, without the help of my wife, Leyla, who not only put up with the aggravation as I worked on the project in nearly every spare hour for over two years, but also assisted in a million other ways to make it work—whether reading, organizing, or helping me with transcriptions. I owe much to her patience and assistance. Not least, with apologies, I want to thank two terrific kids, my daughter Jenny and son Joey, who not only tolerated me through all this, but also let me unfairly monopolize the family room.

Chapter 1

Diplomatic Sources

You often say my work is coarse. 'Tis true,
But then it must be so—it deals with you.
—MARTIAL

When the two journalists arrived at the young diplomat's house, the officer's wife left the room and he closed the door.

"What I am about to tell you," he said, "will mean the end of my career."

It was 1967, during the civil war in Nigeria. Younger officers in the political section of the United States embassy in Lagos believed the ambassador had suppressed information about alleged massacres of Ibos.

Stanley Meisler, one of the journalists, was covering the war for the *Los Angeles Times.* He had received a note from a junior Foreign Service officer (FSO) at the embassy asking that he and the *Washington Post* correspondent come to the officer's house for drinks. According to Meisler, the young FSO told the two correspondents about an incident involving a number of Ibo prisoners taken by the Nigerian military.

The Nigerian soldiers reportedly commandeered a boat belonging to an oil company and told its American operators to take them and their Ibo captives to an offshore island where there was a prison. En route to the island, however, the soldiers killed all or most of the Ibos. This incident greatly upset the Americans, who told others about it. They asked to leave the country and were sent home. "There was actually very little of this in the war generally," Meisler said, "but this incident did occur."

After hearing the story from the young FSO, Meisler raised it with the ambassador, who said the embassy was looking into it but the Americans involved were gone, there was no way to find evidence, and he wasn't going to report a rumor to Washington. When Meisler filed his story, he included the strife in the embassy as part of it.

"On top of this," Meisler said, "the ambassador did an outrageous thing. He asked everyone in the embassy to say [in writing] when they had talked to me last and whether this incident had been discussed. Of course, the junior officer who did it lied and said he hadn't seen me." Another very junior officer, however, wrote that he was present at a meeting with Meisler and the political officer but that the issue had not been discussed. "This young guy felt so humiliated about this," said Meisler, "that when I showed up in Nairobi two years later, he showed me a copy of the note."

That FSO in Nairobi never explained his next act, which was to hand Meisler a file of embassy cables. "Once a week," the correspondent said, "I would come to his office and look over the file. He never said why, he never even said he was doing it. I would just come in and sit, and he'd hand me the file, and I'd sit in the corner taking notes. It was a great help to my coverage because Nairobi was a centrally located embassy and got a lot of cables from other posts in the area."

Meisler concluded, "I can't imagine this kind of thing any more. Back then you had the feeling that the Foreign Service and the press had the same agenda. It might not be the same as the ambassador's, but we in the press and the young FSO wanted the world to know and understand Africa."

Postscript: Meisler said that, to the best of his knowledge, the officer who told him the story of the Ibos was not found out, but about a year later he decided to resign from the Foreign Service. "I always presumed that situation had something to do with it," he said.

★ ★ ★

In 1990 the United States and the Soviet Union were engaged in sensitive negotiations on the text of a joint statement of principles for political settlement of the Afghanistan crisis. At one point a newspaper reporter called on the U.S. special envoy to the Afghan Resistance, Peter Tomsen, and produced a copy of the draft accord, asking for comment. Ambassador Tomsen was taken aback, because the draft was classified and its distribution extremely restricted within the U.S. government. He asked the reporter where he had obtained the text, but the journalist declined to say.

Because of diplomatic drafting conventions, however, Tomsen immediately realized when he examined the document that the source was the Soviet embassy. He pointed this out to the correspondent, explaining that the two sides were at a difficult spot in negotiations, and the Soviets obviously were trying to use the reporter, leaking the draft in order to build pressure in favor of their own position.

It happened that this reporter and Tomsen had known each other well when both were posted overseas. The correspondent therefore took the diplomat's point at face value. He still wrote a story, and referred to the draft accord, but he did not publish the text. Thus, the correspondent got a good story and the special envoy, as a result of the contact, managed to limit potential damage to the U.S. negotiating position. "If you don't have good relations," Tomsen said, "you can't do something like that."

* * *

There has been a world of change, in both diplomacy and journalism, since Stan Meisler and that young FSO became caught up in the dramatic events of the Nigerian civil war in 1967. With communications advances, the media have become relatively more powerful and the public aspects of diplomacy have increased in importance. At the same time, many reporters and officials believe relations between the two sides have come to be marked by an unhealthy degree of distrust. Most date this from the war in Vietnam and the Watergate scandal.

Nonetheless, good media relations are part of good diplomacy, and the fundamental rule remains: both sides need to play straight. Successful diplomats, especially those at senior levels, realize this and put serious thought and effort into public affairs. Media appearances are a central part of the job of any secretary of state, and every assistant secretary knows that when he or she goes to Capitol Hill to testify, the agenda is likely to be determined in large part by what is in the *New York Times* and *Washington Post* that day.

Senior officials also realize that the media are important message multipliers—the fastest, most efficient way to communicate, not only with the general public, but with foreign audiences and key domestic constituencies like Congress, public interest and ethnic groups, the business community, and the rank and file of government agencies. In short, communicating with the public is as much a part of the diplomatic job today as reporting, analyzing, and negotiating.

Unfortunately, however, it is also the part foreign affairs professionals do least well. Most career diplomats would rather face an angry demonstrator or the harangue of a hostile foreign ministry official than a probing reporter. Diplomacy, after all, is traditionally a confidential business, and reporters want to spill the beans.

More than thirty years ago Bernard Cohen concluded a fine study of the press and foreign policy by suggesting that the relationship between the press and policy officials is a political competition. The "problem," he said, is not how to create an information environment in which officials can pursue policies efficiently, or how to create better access for journalists to critical decision-making processes. "More centrally," he noted, "the problem is how to influence the terms [on] which this political competition is waged, so that it loses some of its zero-sum character. . . . We are interested both in effective foreign policies *and* in democratic procedures for reaching them, and what we should be asking from the press and from policy officials are attitudes and approaches that increase the area of compatibility between them."[1]

We haven't gotten very far in the three decades since Cohen wrote those words; indeed, things are probably worse. Still, I would like to think it is time for the pendulum to swing the other way. I believe this can be done without compromising professionalism on either side.

PART I

The Nature of the Job

Chapter 2

Opening the Closed Shop

You don't need a weatherman to know which way the wind blows.
—Bob Dylan

On the seventh floor of the great square mass that is the Department of State in Washington, D.C., an armed guard sits outside an unpretentious door with a small glass window. Inside, beyond the guard, and behind a cipher lock, is the bustle of the State Operations Center, where watch teams of Foreign Service officers liaise twenty-four hours a day with embassies around the world. They sift incoming cables and news service reports, cutting "alert copies" for top State officials and designated action offices.

The center of the scene is a Senior Watch Officer (SWO), who directs the action from a large console equipped with computer screen and numerous telephone buttons. Behind the officer is the Geochron, a distinctive blue clock-map whose bell-shaped illumination charts the passage of global day and night. The SWO has the number of every embassy in the world, as well as the home and office number of every key official in the department. He has a drop line to the secretary of state and a drop line to the White House Situation Room. This is where the first word of a foreign crisis usually hits, perhaps in a 3 A.M. phone call from an embassy. This is where the U.S. response often begins.

Suspended from the ceiling in the middle of the room is one of the most important foreign crisis management tools at the disposal of the U.S. government: a color television monitor tuned to the Cable News Network (CNN). That monitor, facing the watch team in the heart of the State Op Center, is a totem of potent forces shaping American society and, with it, the conduct of U.S. diplomacy.

"CNN makes it very difficult for anyone to get a private jump on anyone else," said CNN Vice President Stuart Loory. "We have leveled the playing field. The public is getting what is seen at the State Department Operations Center or the White House Situation Room."

A More Public Diplomacy

"Diplomats are a closed shop," mused Marvin Kalb, longtime CBS News diplomatic correspondent and director of Harvard University's Joan Shorenstein Barone Center on the Press, Politics and Public Policy. "They see themselves as having a special responsibility for the security of the country. That's all true—and it's dated as well. The role of diplomats today is significantly different."

Since the days of the Greeks, the practice of diplomacy has evolved in tandem with the evolution of political systems, and the forms of democratic diplomacy have been in flux since the nineteenth century. In his classic 1939 work *Diplomacy,* Sir Harold Nicolson wrote that "to my mind democratic diplomacy has not as yet discovered its own formula." The British diplomat predicted a long process of trial and error "to adjust this infinitely delicate piano to the sturdy fingers of a popular electorate." He also noted that "when, during the course of the nineteenth century, the old theories of diplomacy appeared to be adopting new shapes, it was in fact not the diplomatists who were undergoing a change of heart but the political systems which they represented." Nicolson cited three factors that exercised a special effect on the methods and theory of international negotiation: "a growing sense of the community of nations; . . . an increasing appreciation of the importance of public opinion; and . . . the rapid increase in communications." [1]

Those same factors are still at work today and, happily, they continue to shape the practice of diplomacy. In the post-World War II period, the conduct of foreign relations—for hundreds of years the almost exclusive province of foreign offices and their envoys abroad—has moved steadily out from behind closed doors and into the public arena. Inevitably, public communications intruded more and more on diplomats' work. "Diplomacy, generally, became more public, more open," said former under secretary of state David Newsom. "Diplomacy is no longer the realm of monarchs and their ministers, working in secret. Diplomats and foreign ministers are responsible now to parliaments and publics."

The Art of Suasion

Edward R. Murrow, the renowned CBS broadcaster who served as John F. Kennedy's U.S. Information Agency director, once observed that the real art in diplomacy was not simply moving information or policy guidance thousands of miles but moving it "the last three feet in face-to-face conversation."[2]

This is still true—whatever the changes, the essence of diplomatic work remains the art of suasion, whether in private or in public. What is different is that it is no longer enough for diplomats to practice their skills only in private. Effective envoys must have both the core traditional skills of reporting, analyzing, and negotiating *and* public communications skills. They must recognize the need to reinforce traditional activities by coherently transmitting information and policy messages across the media spectrum to key audiences. This requires some knowledge of the media environment in which they work, as well as effective internal communications.

It is almost a commonplace to hear or read that ambassadors have lost their importance due to greater personal contact among world leaders, who meet each other regularly and talk on the phone. "Making the points that need to be made every day in our relations with countries can't be done by fax," said Ambassador William Clark Jr., a veteran Asia hand. "It's true that it's easy enough for the president to call the prime minister. But the fact is, he doesn't have time to do that—so you'd better have people out there who are [making these points]."

Thus, the substance of diplomatic work—the effort to reconcile differences and achieve policy objectives through diplomatic interactions—changes little over time, but the tools and methods of diplomacy can, and do, evolve. The development of better, faster, and more invasive technology for transmitting and receiving information has given added impulse to the increasingly public conduct of international relations. In the twenty-first century publics will have ready access to a great deal of information, and this will profoundly affect the conduct of international affairs. Not only will the information media play a central role in the formulation of public policy, but the efficacy of diplomacy as a tool of policy will depend to a large extent on how well diplomats adjust to that reality.

Whether briefing on background overseas, speaking for the record, or drafting the daily press guidance in Washington, public communications skills bulk large at all stages of the foreign policy process and in the practice of diplomacy. "You can't operate in the United States without broad public support," said Phyllis Oakley, who served as spokeswoman for Secretary of State George Shultz. "But you must go out and build that support. It doesn't just happen."

Public communications skills are especially essential for the senior policy maker, but they are no less important for the desk officer who writes the guidance, or the diplomat overseas doing a routine background briefing. A deputy assistant secretary does not spring fully formed from the mind of Jove. From an early stage in their careers, U.S. diplomats should be developing communications skills, including regular contact with the media, as a core ability.

"We are not taught about the press as an instrument of foreign policy execution, and that is crucial," said Ambassador Alexander Watson, assistant secretary of state for Inter-American Affairs. "You have to have an appreciation of the role the press plays in the decision making of whatever body you are concerned with—whether it is a foreign government, the U.S. government, the U.N. Secretariat, or a guerrilla force. You also have to have an awareness of how [that organization] treats the press, whether as a source of information or to disseminate its own view. You have to *use* the press, and when I say 'use,' I don't mean cynically, in the sense of hoodwinking. I mean use it in the sense that it's an instrument that is there for you."

This means that setting media policy is a central element of foreign policy leadership. Whether in Washington or at a mission overseas, management must establish clear guidance for media contacts and attend carefully to the coordination and implementation of those contacts. Access to the media should not mean a breakdown in discipline, or a proliferation of anonymous policy criticism. It should mean not losing any opportunity to gather information, to explain U.S. policy, or to inform the U.S. public about the implications of foreign events that can have an impact on their lives.

The political leadership is accountable for its policy decisions to Congress, the press, and the public. It is therefore vitally important that those decisions be clearly articulated, so that accurate information flows down through the machinery of government and out to the public. Public diplomacy goals and objectives, as well as the means of achieving them, should be carefully considered so that all members of the organization understand what the policy is and what their piece of the message is. The senior, most accountable officials carry the policy to the general public through television, press contacts, and congressional testimony, while those with specialized knowledge flesh out detail for influential elites through background briefings.

Besides bearing the heaviest burden of public accountability, the State Department leadership bears the primary onus for strategic thinking about foreign policy-related media issues. This means thinking about how policy will be explained as it is being developed, and not treating it merely as a public relations problem that comes after all important decisions have already been made. It also means a constant effort to anticipate issues and follow through to get reliable information down to the bureaucracy and out to the press.

The information flow should work the other way, too, because effective anticipation depends as well on good bottom-up communications. This is hampered if the rank and file, who have the day-to-day expertise and detailed background on issues, do not work from a solid conceptual understanding of what U.S. policy is and what it is trying to achieve. The most valuable asset of any government official is a correct understanding of his political leadership's mindset.

A Dab of Trust

Some analysts are skeptical that an elite mode of policy making can last in a television-educated American democracy. "We're trying to find out what the public needs to know in order to be participants," said Dan Amundson, director of research at the Center for Media and Public Affairs in Washington, D.C. "We swing from oversimplifying and overtrust in government to antagonism and believing the government lies. And we're likely to go back and forth in this way until we figure out a rule for how this relationship should work."

Even if the rule has not been figured out, however, a few outside limits are discernible. Foreign policy formulation will always require some degree of specialized knowledge—of language, culture, and historical circumstance—in order to best serve the national interest. Taxpayers fund the development of such expertise and expect it to be brought into play. Confidential discussions between governments will also continue to allow more room for negotiation and compromise than competing public declarations and press statements. And it will remain important that diplomats be able to move their message those last three feet.

But no policy, however brilliant the concept or informed the analysis, can long stand if it fails the final test of public accountability. In any case, government officials will surely recognize—if they ever doubted it—that the "foreign policy elite" includes the press and that public suasion is just as important a part of their job as private suasion.

In short, the institutional self-image of the State Department could stand an update. "We view ourselves as practitioners of quiet diplomacy and analysis, reporting to our government directly and discreetly, and that's *all*," noted Alexander Watson. "The culture is to be discreet, talk to people, and then work in our offices preparing little reports of classified information. It's a very archaic view of diplomacy, but still the prevalent one. Foreign Service people are not used to being major players in the political game. You learn, you report, you make a few recommendations, then your job is done. And if that's your outlook, it means you're not prepared to see the press as something with a huge impact."

The inherent tension between reporters and diplomats cannot and should not be done away with. Freedom of the press, in our system of government, is *intended* as a check on officialdom, in order to, in the words of Thomas Jefferson, "put it out of the power of the few to riot on the labors of the many."[3] The *intent* is to regularly inconvenience policy makers, despite the difficulties this sometimes might entail for orderly and coherent administration.

William Macomber, in a 1975 book on diplomacy called *The Angel's Game*, wrote that the root of the problem of government-press relations in foreign affairs "is that a properly functioning press deals with disclosure and exposure at all times, while the diplomat deals in these terms only in end results. In his dealings along the way to these results, the diplomat has learned that not only are the best results obtained through confidentiality and privacy, but that often results can be obtained in no other way." He added, "It is a very real and very important conflict in diplomat-press relations, which neither side can responsibly lose sight of. It means that if both are doing their job, neither will be fully comfortable with the performance of the other."[4]

Even so, healthy skepticism need not become acrimony, and tension, inherent in the relationship, need not be exaggerated. The wheels of both institutions turn on the axle of public confidence, and each needs a dab of trust to grease its turning. Each should recognize the professional requirements and constraints of the other. Reporters have information and direct input to public opinion. Diplomats have information and policy insight.

"Neither side can do it by itself," said Don Oberdorfer, the *Washington Post*'s longtime diplomatic correspondent. "A start might be to avoid things that exacerbate the problem. For government officials, this means avoiding untruths and half-truths. For the press, it is to avoid the automatic assumption that what you hear are lies, and to avoid denouncing government officials unless clearly and provably required."

The guiding purpose of most reporters covering foreign affairs is not to sabotage U.S. foreign policy or get government officials in trouble. It is to get the facts of a story, get sufficient context to make sense of those facts, and then write an informative story. This means the diplomat's briefing will often be only a part of the reporter's tableau. In the same way, the guiding purpose of most diplomats is not to hide the screwups of government from legitimate inquiry. It is to advance the foreign policy interests of the United States. That means there will occasionally be limits on what any diplomat can say without compromising those interests. Between these poles there is a great deal of leeway, and nearly always enough for diplomats to provide reporters with the grist for a story.

There is no such thing as a risk-free briefing. Every time a diplomat sits down with a reporter, he or she must make a judgment about whether that individual will respect the ground rules and handle responsibly the information provided. There will be times when the diplomat is not pleased with the resulting story. The only way to avoid this, however, is not to brief at all, and this is to serve incompletely. The potential gain usually outweighs the risks, and the latter can be minimized by learning a little about how journalists work, by remembering a few simple rules of engagement (for example, the Bohlen Rules—see chapter 10), and by learning to be professional about procedure (that is, setting ground rules up front and knowing the difference between "background" and "off the record"; see chapter 7).

To be sure, opening up the closed shop of diplomacy is much easier said than done. No one knows this better than Richard Boucher. As State Department deputy spokesman and spokesman in the Bush and early Clinton administrations, Boucher spent many hours trying to coax releasable information from reluctant department officials.

"We have a strong interest in explaining our policy and getting our views out," he said. "Not only do we need to answer to the U.S. public, but also we need to keep Congress, the [press] commentators, and anyone else with an interest in the issue informed. The real problem is the bureaucratic culture. We hide things even when we don't need to. Everybody who writes press guidance should do just one briefing. They'd learn fast enough about the need to have decent answers to questions."

Chapter 3

Media Democracy and Media Diplomacy

The camel's dung points to the camel.
—Arabic proverb

As the influence of the press on public opinion and foreign policy making has grown, the business of briefing reporters has grown in tandem. Nowhere is this more evident than in the evolution of the State Department's noon briefing over the past four decades.

In the 1940s Secretary of State Cordell Hull would call about a dozen newspapermen into his office every weekday at noon for news conferences. James Reston of the *New York Times* was one of them. "All sat on his three black leather couches and listened to his Tennessee mountain stories and his wayward accounts of the war," Reston wrote in his memoir *Deadline*. "We were not allowed to quote him directly, but were permitted to publish the gist of what he said after it had been cleaned up for respectable consumption." Reston observed that "in those anxious days before television transformed both reporting and politics, officials didn't have to hire a hall to meet the press."[1]

Inevitably, briefings grew in size and came to be conducted not by the secretary, but by his spokesman. In the late 1950s the spokesman conducted daily briefings around a long table seating fewer than twenty reporters. "It was a clubby atmosphere," recalled *Washington Post* correspondent Don Oberdorfer, "dominated by reporters of the wire services, a few major U.S. newspapers and prestigious overseas outlets such as the *Times* of London and *Le Monde*."[2] By the 1960s the briefing was in a special room equipped with podium, background map, and microphone. In the 1970s, when Hodding Carter held the spokesman's job, television entered the chamber.

14

"The Carter administration's decision to permit a live television feed from the daily State Department briefings is usually called a watershed dividing the history of briefings into two epochs," wrote Brookings Institution scholar Stephen Hess. "Diplomats and print journalists blame the cameras for luring the crowds that have turned the briefings into a circus, for making the briefers less frank because of their concern about being on TV or more simplistic because of their desire to be on TV, and for making the questioning more combative, longwinded, and bizarre." [3] However, Hess added, it was probably the growth in the *size* of the briefings (especially after the 1979 hostage crisis), even more than the presence of television, that contributed to the decline in their substantive utility for reporters.

The gradual transformation of the noon briefing from background for a select few with the secretary of state to on-the-record for many with his spokesman brought with it a transformation in the work of U.S. diplomats. Every working day, every geographic bureau in the Department of State is tasked to prepare Q's and A's for the spokesman. The Bureau of Public Affairs responds to questions from reporters, and the guidance, prepared both before and after the briefing, is converted into cables and dispatched to diplomatic posts all over the world.[4] "They're producing instant policy," Hess said in an interview. "We have an official U.S. government line on every issue that's in the A-section of the *New York Times* every day."

Whatever the benefit of a daily ration of policy guidance, the daily press briefing has moved center stage in day-to-day work at all levels of the State Department. It has become, in a word, bureaucratized. "People resent it," the public affairs officer of one geographic bureau said. "The problem I face in general is that most of my officers believe that somehow the daily press briefing forces them to make policy before its time, before it's ripe. They see press work as a nuisance, but they are forced to come around because of the power of the spokesman."

Former spokesman Richard Boucher expressed some frustration with the bureaucracy's output:

> In general, what I found is that the higher you go in the policy process, the more responsive people are. There are various levels in the building. The first level is How do I get rid of this task and get on with my real work? The second level is How do we get away from this question? The next level up is How do we explain what we're doing so that it makes sense? And the fourth level is How can I honestly answer this question so that it advances our policy goals or moves us toward them? This generally corresponds to bureaucratic levels, going up from desk officer to office director to deputy assistant secretary to seventh-floor principal. It corresponds to how often an individual himself has to answer questions. The seventh floor generally sees interaction with the public as part of the policy process—for example, appearing before the

press or on a podium, or doing testimony before Congress. I'm only half joking when I say the way to get people to do a better job is to get them to do a briefing just one day.

Thus, State Department press operations have grown in size and complexity. But bigger has meant more bureaucratic, and more bureaucratic often has meant more anodyne. Reporters, yearning for meat and potatoes, are not satisfied with the thin gruel of official guidance. Diplomats, meanwhile, yearning for a bit more deliberative space, dread the intrusion of the media elephant in the policy shop.

Vietnam, Watergate, and CNN

Although the importance and centrality of government-press relations has grown steadily over the past twenty years, the quality of those relations has steadily deteriorated. I found among both diplomats and journalists a pervasive sense that the dynamics of the relationship have simply gotten out of whack, although distinctly less so overseas than in Washington. "The antagonism has gotten more acute," a serving senior career officer said. "There has been a breakdown in confidence in government. There's cooperation between the two sides overseas, but back here the bureaucracy is the target. An FSO is not an FSO here; he is a policy problem, just a jerk who serves the people badly, covers up the errors of the U.S. government, and lies for a living. In that context, it's hard to see what basis there is for a relationship." This bleak assessment, while not universal, accurately reflects the view of some State Department officers. It is matched by a correspondingly bleak view of government officials on the part of some reporters.

Former *New York Daily News* editor Michael O'Neill has written, "Thanks mainly to Vietnam and Watergate, journalism's traditional skepticism toward government was converted in the 1970s into a combative relationship. All young reporters were imbued with the idea they had to attack officials and challenge policies or lose their press cards. The feeling is less intense now, but it has not disappeared; the methods and sometimes even the motives of government are questioned automatically." [5]

Adds Don Oberdorfer, who retired from the *Washington Post* in 1993 after thirty-eight years in journalism, "It's gone too far, on both sides. Many reporters, especially the new generation, view government with deep suspicion. The going-in assumption is that what public officials say is not true. And I judge that on the other side, there is a great deal of suspicion of the press. One thing I find disturbing is that a generation ago, when I started out, there seemed to be more people in government who considered giving out information an important and legitimate part of the job, and without any particular 'spin.' "

Because government officials don't volunteer much, Oberdorfer noted, reporters must seek out information and explanations that go beyond the official line. To do this, individual correspondents engage in what he termed "personal transactions" with individual public officials.

Experienced reporters know they must tread carefully with such information transactions because there are many considerations involved besides informing the public. The persons providing information may be interested in gaining favor with an important journalist or news organization—and thus present themselves as more knowledgeable on a given subject than they really are. Some sources might shade their account to make themselves look good with the boss or out of concern about how other parts of the bureaucracy will react. Others will hedge their accounts out of genuine concern that the resulting story will undercut whatever policy or goal they are trying to promote or accomplish.

"You have to be more skeptical," Oberdorfer said, "any time someone is giving information in the service of some particular cause."

Seen from the reporter's point of view, then, the growth in the influence of the press has brought with it a correspondingly greater danger that self-serving government officials will attempt to exploit the "personal transaction" format. Because the press today is much more powerful than a generation ago, Oberdorfer observed, "there is a greater temptation to use it. The game is more open, there are many more players. Many would like to use it for their own ends."

By the same token, diplomats feel that the media cuts them less slack than it used to. "I remember going overseas in 1973, when I was assistant secretary for African affairs," said former under secretary of state David Newsom. "I could sit down with reporters and say, 'This is how the situation is at the moment, but we don't want to say anything about it yet,' and that would be respected. Five years later, a diplomatic reporter said to me, 'Don't ever tell me anything now you don't want printed. It's no longer my decision; my editor makes that decision.' That is, the reporter could, and probably would, try to persuade his editor, but he could not guarantee the outcome." Newsom attributed this not only to greater distrust, but also to intensified competition, as, for example, from television.

Newsom also felt that one of the effects of Vietnam was that the tolerance of the press for a "no comment" had been substantially reduced. "If an official says he can't comment for more than forty-eight hours, the press will think it's a cover-up, or the administration is in disarray, or the official is stupid, or some other pejorative conclusion. The pressure to say something is greater than it has ever been."

Reinforcing that pressure is the relentless march of information technology, whose progress gives a further nudge each year to the momentum of events. The bigger the crisis, the greater the pressure that builds on harried decision makers—and the greater the risk of hasty action and error.

Former secretary of state Lawrence Eagleburger, reflecting on changes in foreign relations work, cited Vietnam for intensifying the adversarial relationship between reporters and officials, and CNN for stepping up pressure on officials to react to foreign events more quickly:

> There is no question, in my mind at least, that Vietnam changed everything. It gave a big boost to the issue of questioning authority, government, and the government spokesman. The era of investigative journalism changed the rules of the game. It's not that it was completely hands-off before but that the foreign policy establishment was given more leeway.
>
> Second, and more important, is the whole impact of CNN. We have yet to understand how profoundly it has changed things. The public hears of an event now in real time, before the State Department has had time to think about it. Consequently, we find ourselves reacting before we've had time to think. This is now the way we determine foreign policy—it's driven more by the daily events reported on TV than it used to be.

The Cultural Onslaught: Dallas *in the Sahara*

Consider the effect of television, satellites, and computers:

• From 1960 to 1990 the U.S. population rose from 179 million to 249 million. In roughly the same period, the number of television sets in American homes rose from 47 million to 170 million and the amount of time American households devoted to watching television surged from two hours to seven hours a day.

• Cable television was serving 61 percent of American homes by 1992. While domestic expansion had slowed, the international market, still in its infancy, had only begun to be tapped.

• In early 1993 the Cable News Network reached a watershed: for the first time, it had more viewers outside than inside the United States (65 million households outside against 62 million inside). CNN executives expected the gap would steadily grow.[6]

Consider also that in many countries the state no longer monopolizes television, even when it is a state monopoly:

• In late 1992 the destruction of a mosque led to Hindu-Muslim religious rioting in India. The government-run network carried neither the initial vandalism nor the ensuing violence, but the effort to suppress the news backfired because satellite dish owners tuned to BBC television coverage of the event.[7]

• Also in 1992 the Thai government censored local broadcasts of clashes between prodemocracy demonstrators and soldiers in which scores of unarmed civilians were killed. But satellite dish owners videotaped BBC and CNN reports, which gained widespread distribution, stirred public indignation, and contributed to the fall of the government.[8]

Just as significant, however, is the tremendous social impact abroad of the entertainment programming that is pumped daily into the international television system—in effect, the United States is invading other countries with a weapon far more powerful than troops and tanks. "As the millennium approaches, American popular culture has never been more dominant internationally, nor more controversial," wrote John Rockwell in the *New York Times*. "Serious money is involved; this is America's second biggest export after aircraft. But just as some Americans have doubts about our pop culture—its propensity to celebrate violence, sexual stereotyping, and sheer lowest-common-denominator crassness—those doubts multiply abroad, especially when the imports are seen as a threat to local cultural identity."[9]

Despite USIA's efforts, the image of America abroad is not George Washington chopping down the cherry tree; it's Madonna, Michael Jackson, and MTV. At the end of 1983 a large nomadic tribe in the Sahara, the Tuareg, reportedly put off their annual migration for ten days in order to avoid missing the last episode of *Dallas*.[10] As this was being written, viewers in Lebanon could watch Arnold Schwarzenegger at the movie theaters, while Lebanese television featured U.S. programs like *Fresh Prince of Bel Air* and *The Bold and the Beautiful* and music in demand included Guns 'n' Roses, Nirvana, and Def Leppard. In China viewers watched *Dynasty* and *Growing Pains* on television, even as *The Terminator*, *First Blood*, and *The Deer Hunter* played in the cinemas, and audiocassettes in demand ranged over such favorites as Red Hot Chili Peppers, Michael Jackson, and Madonna.[11] Commenting on the Chinese appetite for U.S. television, Michael Jay Solomon of Lorimar Telepictures observed, "It's scary because we're going to change the way these people act and feel and think."[12]

In the Middle East, an area where I have spent much of my career, it is not our political ideals that alarm many but the dilemma posed by what the government of Iran has dubbed the "cultural onslaught." Take the case of satellite dishes. By early 1994, to the consternation of the Iranian government, dishes had sprouted by the thousands on rooftops all over

Tehran and other Iranian cities. They were no longer the province of the wealthy: groups of low-income Iranians had started to pool their funds to buy shared dishes, and the prospect was that in the near future the dishes would become less expensive and smaller—that is, accessible to more people and even harder to control. Alarmed by this trend, the interior minister solemnly declared in April that "President Hashemi [Rafsanjani] does not want our Islamic culture to be a target of offensive material via satellite." [13]

But authorities seemed uncertain how to cope. A decade earlier the effort to outlaw videocassettes had backfired, leading to a booming underground rental market for illicit tapes, including pornographic films. [14] At first the government announced its intent to confiscate all satellite dishes, but then backed away when this raised a firestorm of criticism— including from clerics who ridiculed the idea on the grounds it would not only increase the allure of the forbidden fruit, as happened with videocassettes, but would also prove impossible to enforce. On videocassettes, the government decided in February 1994 that if it couldn't stop the onslaught it would open state-backed video rental shops and thus at least channel some of the demand toward programming deemed to be unoffensive to Islamic cultural values. In the same way, even as some voices in Iran's ruling establishment pressed for enforcing a ban on the import, manufacture, distribution, or use of satellite receivers, others argued that the effective answer to invasive satellite technology lay less in state controls than in more innovative and appealing indigenous programming. The tendency, in other words, was to address the problem from both the supply and the demand side.

"Satellites are a global phenomenon and should be treated as such, not through crackdowns," wrote the Tehran daily *Abrar* ["Rightly Guided"], which is affiliated with an important faction of the ruling clergy. "Technology is advancing so fast that maybe next year dishes as small as 35 centimeters [14 inches] in diameter will fill the market. What can we do then?" [15]

Governments, in short, are finding they have less control over what people see and hear. The United States, with a powerful pop culture married to an invasive delivery technology, is sometimes greatly feared, not for its political gospel, but as an infectious social influence that others find destructive of traditional ways and values. "The globalization of television," wrote John Naisbitt and Patricia Aburdene in *Megatrends 2000*, "is explosive and controversial because it conveys deeper values the way literature does. Entertainment, through the medium of language and images, crosses over the line of superficial exchange and enters the domain of values. It goes right to the ethos of a culture, addressing the fundamental spirit that informs its beliefs and practices." [16]

This clash of cultures and values will affect the sociology of international relations, and thus the work of diplomats, well into the twenty-first century.

Media Democracy, Media Diplomacy

In a globe-encircling electronic culture, then, the impact of the media—and especially of television—on both domestic policy formulation and international relations is a fact of life that needs to be understood by diplomats at home and abroad. We live in a media democracy and, increasingly, we practice media diplomacy.

At home, the media not only tell the government and public what the other is doing, but help set the policy agenda, provide the forum for debate, and then evaluate government performance. "The media now serve as the main, and in many cases the only, source of information for citizens about what is happening in the government and the primary mechanism by which government learns what is happening in the public—two traditional functions of political parties," wrote Gary Orren in the prologue to Martin Linsky's 1986 Harvard study, *Impact: How the Press Affects Federal Policymaking*. The press, he said, not only has a large role in setting the policy agenda, but performs "the quintessential partisan task of scrutinizing and evaluating government performance." [17]

A month before the 1992 presidential election, *Washington Post* columnist Richard Harwood cited figures showing that 72 percent of network election coverage was monopolized by a few reporters and commentators, compared with 15 percent of air time for quotes from voters, political experts, and other sources, and 13 percent for sound bites from candidates. "What these numbers mean," he said, "is that journalists—not the politicians and not the people—dominate the conversations of democracy." [18]

Abroad, because of the speed of communications, the media have assumed a larger intermediary role in international relations. The statement made in Beijing that once could have waited a few days for an answer now requires a same-day response in Washington. First impressions from abroad are formed by CNN, other broadcast reports, and then print journalism. These, in turn, have an impact not only on the public at large, but on Congress, the executive branch, and other key foreign affairs constituencies.

While the beastliness in the world is not new, seeing it live, up-close, and ugly is. Policies can no longer be presented to the public in the abstract. They are constantly measured against images on television—images that are instantly available, around the clock and around the globe. The most potent force shaping this trend is CNN, with satellite-delivered international service to about 130 million viewers in 140 countries and territories worldwide.

Chinese and American leaders alike felt the full impact of live television during the violent June 1989 Chinese crackdown on prodemocracy demonstrators in Tiananmen Square in Beijing. The emotional impact on American viewers of that event set back nearly two decades of gradual improvement in China's public image in the United States. When former president Richard Nixon visited Beijing shortly afterward, he told Chinese leader Deng Xiaoping "that there had never been a worse crisis in the relationship between our two countries and that it was up to China to take steps to deal with the outrage of the civilized world." [19]

Similarly, in the spring of 1991 televised pictures of Kurdish refugees streaming into Turkey from Iraq—preferring death by hunger and cold in the mountains to the ruthless mercies of Iraqi president Saddam Hussein—caused the Bush administration to reverse a decision not to provide aid. Thus, whether it is a clash in Beijing, or Russian leader Boris Yeltsin facing down coup plotters from atop a tank, or Berliners pulling down their hated wall, the power of live television imagery can swiftly raise the political temperature of any decision-making environment.

"Foreign Policy on the Fly"

CNN Vice President Peter Vesey, who heads the network's international service, observed that CNN had changed the form of diplomacy on major issues. He said, "The process of diplomacy and the process of government are being demystified by the growing awareness that what happens in Tokyo affects prices in Paris, which affects policies in the U.S., which makes Argentina's businessmen look northward. People want to know more. My advice would be to feed that trend positively and not hold back. It is useful for viewers to know what George Bush and Saddam Hussein are thinking at the same time."

The issue for policy makers, who must look beyond the immediate, is how to cope with the constant pressure this puts on the necessary pause for decision. "Live television doesn't change the policy," said former chairman of the Joint Chiefs of Staff Gen. Colin Powell, "but it does create the environment in which the policy is made." [20] As the pressure to respond faster grows, the lag time for reflection diminishes, and this presents a real quandary for public officials. The need to pause and analyze is inseparable from responsible decision making. The policy maker needs a decent interval, and staff support, to sift facts, marshal sober analysis, review policy options, scrub them down with experts, and reach sound decisions.

"Diplomats," said former CBS correspondent Marvin Kalb, "are now in a race against time, and sometimes against their own interests. This is an imperative of communications."

Richard Boucher, State Department spokesman during the Gulf War, spelled out what this meant in practical terms. "The technology for the collection and transmission of information has grown faster than our ability to analyze and act," he said. "During the Gulf War, Saddam Hussein could make a speech and have it carried on CNN at 11 A.M. (7 P.M. Baghdad time). Then I would have to react at twelve o'clock. That's damn hard. Foreign policy cycles are not the same as media cycles. You can't do foreign policy on the fly."

Another issue is the data overload on the irreducible few senior officials, human beings all, who bear the responsibility for deciding policy. However gifted they might be, they remain men and women of finite capacity.

"The difficulty of getting high-level attention to issues really worries me," observed Hermann Eilts, former ambassador to Egypt and Saudi Arabia. "People are so busy they have other people who do the issues for them. They just don't or can't read those embassy cables and reports. All this is accentuated by CNN, which serves a very useful purpose; but the danger is that people will be content with that. By the time an embassy message gets in with the analysis, the president or secretary of state has found something else to be busy with, so it goes to the desk officer. He may try to get it up to the secretary or president, but it's hard."

The flip side of this is that, in times of crisis, some decisions sometimes begin and end at the top, skipping the ranks of various regional experts altogether. Tim McNulty of the *Chicago Tribune* relates that at 7 A.M. one morning in February 1991 during the Gulf War, President Bush gathered his advisers to discuss television reports from Baghdad of an alleged Iraqi "peace initiative." "We've got to get an answer out there fast," the president reportedly told his advisers. "Everybody in the world is going to say 'Take them up on it.' If it's not adequate, we've got to know."

Within the hour, President Mubarak of Egypt was calling to say the proposal should be ignored. Meanwhile, the British were in contact to ask what the United States intended to do, and the French foreign minister had weighed in with a recommendation that the United States consider the offer. A CBS morning news correspondent declared that "this war, for a lot of intents and purposes, is over." With only television reports to go on, a Bush adviser called Saudi Ambassador Prince Bandar bin Sultan to ask how the Iraqi leader's statement read in Arabic. Bandar reportedly read an untranslated partial text and then declared that it was full of conditions and failed to meet the requirements of the relevant U.N. resolutions.

The president told his spokesman to issue a White House statement rejecting the Iraqi offer. "Within two hours," McNulty wrote, "the proposal delivered by satellite was shot down by satellite." He quoted a participant as saying, "The course of action was set. There was no talk of cables back to embassies or phone calls back to heads of state. In most of these kinds of international crises now, we virtually cut out the State Department and the desk officer. Their reports are still important, but they often don't get in here in time for the basic decisions to be made."[21]

The story of the Iraqi "peace initiative" was but one battle in the intense public affairs contest that accompanied the ground and air campaigns of the Gulf War. In this case, however, the direction of basic strategy and policy had already been set and decision makers were operating within an established framework pegged to various U.N. resolutions. In such a situation, with the policy firmly in place, a strong argument can be made that time-sensitive decisions on spot tactics can and should be made by a small leadership group, just as described by McNulty.

In other cases, however, particularly when television reports on international issues come streaming in *before* the political leadership has decided what its basic policy should be, a less ad hoc approach is required. It is conceivable that there might be relatively little coverage, or that the nature of the event—such as an international economic crisis or the suspected diversion of nuclear fuel to a weapons program by North Korea—does not readily lend itself to portrayal in pictures. In this case, policy makers may have the relative luxury of making a decision in an environment relatively uncluttered by powerful images.

More often than not, however, dramatic television coverage will supercharge the decision-making climate. The reporting of a crisis, especially one that is serious enough for the commitment of U.S. troops to be a potential issue, presents a particular problem because it tends to generate a public opinion bell curve—with a sharp upside as horrors and atrocities are revealed, stirring public concern, discussion, and calls for action. The downside comes in an equally sharp drop-off of support for sustaining a troop commitment, once made—especially if casualties occur with no clear interest at stake and no clear exit in sight.

This makes it vital for public officials, despite media pressures, to carefully sort out interests and possible courses of action and resist the impulse to act prematurely. What constitutes a decent interval for policy choice will differ from Somalia to Bosnia to the Persian Gulf. But the key to flattening out the bell curve is to pause, reflect, decide—and then explain, so that any limits on action are understood on the front end, and any commitment made can be sustained on the back end. That means there will be times when the best answer to a question will be a polite variant on "no comment," which, however unsatisfying, is infinitely preferable to rushing out an ill-considered policy.

Part of the "pause and reflect," to be sure, should be a careful regard by the political leadership for public attitudes, as measured in polls, press coverage, and congressional consultations. In the end, however, the political leadership must make a considered decision and then lead, not follow, opinion. "The trick," wrote *Washington Post* columnist Jim Hoagland, "is to keep principle, communication and leadership in balance and not to back away from hard choices abroad simply because they are unpopular or hard to explain." [22]

The crux of the matter is not whether the public can *handle* images and difficult choices; plainly, as a group, it can. More to the point is whether the public has all the *information* needed to make informed judgments.

"If you could inform the people well, television democracy has many advantages," said Dan Amundson of the Center for Media and Public Affairs. "But if policy is swayed by stories of starving children, without background, then you'll get policies that jump from one thing to another."

When I worked at UPI, we had a common sense rule: "Never underestimate the intelligence of your reader; never overestimate his fund of information." Information must include analysis. It is not enough for either government or the press to simply rain facts and images on a benumbed public. Consumers have a right to expect both officials and reporters, who have access to the expertise after all, to do a little sifting and sorting. People want to know not only what happened, but what it *means* for them. They may suspend judgment on day-to-day policy management, but they will definitely draw conclusions about the *results*. The public is not unlike the owner of a football team: he may not intervene with the coach on the play-by-play, but he'll fire the son of a gun at the end of the season if he loses too many games.

In no area of government is the nexus between media coverage and policy tighter than in the coverage of foreign affairs. "If you have a brilliant policy," said senior Foreign Service officer A. Peter Burleigh, "and you don't explain it to the media, public, and Congress, you may find yourself with a brilliant policy that has no support." [23] Diplomats thus have more need and more occasion than most public officials to meet the press.

Although foreign affairs professionals will not always be able to harmonize the differing rhythms of media coverage and diplomacy, they must learn to recognize and work with them. On some issues—possibly most—traditional diplomatic channels will remain primary. But on important, high-profile matters, when the public perceives it has a stake, the public aspects of diplomacy will take on great importance. For the diplomat, this means there will be times when it is more important to provide Washington with timely input for press guidance before the noon briefing than to finish the classified reporting cable on the meeting with the foreign minister.

The Harvard study cited earlier, product of a three-year research effort by the Institute of Politics at the John F. Kennedy School of Government, found that "senior officials in foreign policy were at the high end of press activity" and "foreign policy was the area with by far the highest potential for press influence." It was also the area where senior federal officials surveyed believed the press had the biggest overall impact and officials themselves felt they had the "lowest success rate in their press relations." [24]

To be sure, it is not easy to work to the long term while speaking to the short term. But to do the job well, clear lines of communication through the media to the public are essential. These, in turn, depend on productive relations with the reporters who are the intermediaries in the process. Such relations work best when each side understands something about the dynamics of the other's job.

Chapter 4

Desks and Deadlines
Print Media

*If I've regretted my silence once, I've regretted my words
a thousand times.*

—ARABIC PROVERB

Given the impact of the media on both domestic and international affairs, nearly every diplomat has wondered at one time or another in a career, or has been asked by foreigners, "Why doesn't the U.S. press pay more attention to international developments?" The answer lies in how the print and broadcast media operate. Their methods and organization stem from the need to heed the interests of their readers and listeners. Diplomats who understand something about this will have sharper instincts about communicating. They will know that the printed word can deliver complexity, but only to limited audiences and specific market segments. They will realize that television can effectively reach a mass audience, but that it prizes emotion and its format often imposes practical limits on complexity. They will understand that the news business, no less than the business of diplomacy, is constantly in flux.

Behind every reporter is an organization and an editorial process. Each has its own audience and internal requirements. To deal with them, the diplomat should understand something about their filing deadlines, the kind of information they need, the varied formats their reporters must work to, and how their editors and producers fit into the processing of information gathered by correspondents in the field.

Briefers who have this in mind before they brief can prepare better. If they have it in mind during the conversation, they will make better use of the reporter's time and their own. Their expectations will also be more realistic. They will know they can talk to a print reporter at length on background, but that this will be less help to the television or radio journalist who needs a talking head for a few seconds on camera, a pithy quote for a concluding stand-upper, or a forty-five-second audio spot.

A newspaper reporter might have the space to properly explain a fine point of politics or economics, but he has no mass audience. Broadcast journalists have less space, but a substantially larger number of people will hear or see their work. Some reporters have a great deal of control over the stories they file; others, such as newsmagazine correspondents, may be contributing only one element of a story that will be blended in New York or Washington from various sources.

"Very often, the reporters themselves are okay, but the problems come with editors and producers," a former director of the State Department's Press Office cautioned. "Very often they don't care for the facts. All they care about is circulation and ratings: the ten-second sound bite or the headline that is not a good summation of the story."

Just as often, though, the risk of oversimplification or distortion can be minimized if the briefer is conscious of the format constraints under which reporters and editors work.

The Wires: Deadline Every Minute

Any discussion of media organizations must begin with the wire services. The international services—Associated Press (AP), Reuters, United Press International (UPI), and Agence France Presse (AFP)—are the front lines of journalism. Their reporters get little recognition outside the profession, but their stories are enormously influential, providing a constant flow of news to thousands of print and broadcast outlets around the globe. [1] (CNN, which will be discussed in more detail later, now shares this frontline role with the wires.) "There are only two forces that can carry light to all corners of the globe," Mark Twain wrote. "The sun in the heavens, and the Associated Press down here." [2]

Wire service reports are sometimes the first word the U.S. government receives of foreign crises, and the State Department Operations Center monitors wire copy closely. When I served there as a watch officer in 1984-85, the first we heard of the assassination of Indian Prime Minister Indira Gandhi was via a wire service report. Similarly, late one evening in 1978 when I was in Beirut as a UPI reporter, Israel invaded Lebanon. I called the home of the political counselor of the American embassy looking for quotes and comments on the breaking story. He, in turn, called the ambassador, who called President Elias Sarkis, which was how the president of Lebanon first heard that his country had been invaded.

When the first American news agency, the Associated Press, was formed in 1848 (United Press came on the scene in 1907), American newspapers were a disputatious and opinionated lot. A cooperative, the AP had to serve members with very different views on domestic and foreign issues, and this requirement profoundly affected the evolution of newswriting style and American journalism. To satisfy different clients and members, stories had to be factual and nonpartisan and thus was born the cult of "objectivity" in newswriting.

To serve a varied market, the agencies developed the "pyramid" style of newswriting: stories written to be cut from the bottom so that the same item could run either at length in a big paper or as a single paragraph in a small one. This put tremendous emphasis on the "lead" paragraph and created, in wire service slang, an incentive to "needle" stories, or make them as sharp as possible.

In a 1966 book, *The Artillery of the Press: Its Influence on American Foreign Policy*, James Reston described the impact of this new style:

> This solution to a technical problem had results that nobody in the Associated Press or United Press International intended and certainly nobody in the State Department wanted. For it tended to sharpen and inflate the news. It created a tradition of putting the most dramatic fact in the story first—the hot angle—and then following it with paragraphs of decreasing importance. Thus it encouraged not a balanced but a startling, even a breathless, presentation of the news, featuring the flaming lead and the big headline. This was adequate for the news of wrecks, murders, or football games, but was a limiting and distorting technique as news of foreign policy became more important and more complicated.[3]

The importance of this legacy cannot be overstated. Every reporter, no matter what the news organization, must think in terms of the "lead" (and good briefers must thus think ahead of time about what "lead" they want a news conference or briefing to produce). Reporters will pick the most interesting or important aspect of the story and put it first. According to this formula, descriptions of fighting and violence usually take precedence over political developments, because conflict is more dramatic.

Despite the format-induced incentive to dramatize, the ideal of most wire service reporters and editors is to write simple, clear, and accurate copy. At UPI this was epitomized in the maxim that we were writing for the "Kansas City milkman."[4] Wire service journalists develop their writing skills under relentless deadline pressure, and many distinguished print and broadcast reporters have come from their ranks. The wires are, in effect, the spawning grounds of journalism because nothing beats wire service training for development of clear writing, respect for factual accuracy, and brevity.

News agencies produce copy on two twelve-hour cycles, an A.M. cycle extending from noon to midnight, and a P.M. cycle from midnight to noon. It might seem an oxymoron for the A.M. cycle to run in the evening, and the P.M. in the morning, but they are so named because A.M.

newspapers are put together in the evening and P.M. newspapers in the morning. Although the number of P.M. newspapers has dwindled steadily since the advent of television, agencies still prepare their reports on two twelve-hour cycles. At the beginning of each, they send subscribers a "budget," or menu of one-paragraph summaries of major stories coming up during the cycle.

In Beirut, for example, we would write an A.M. story of about 400 words in the early afternoon. This was called a "night lead," and would be given a new top as necessary during the evening with a "first night lead" or "second night lead" updating the item. Shortly after midnight, a "day lead" would go out for the P.M. cycle, to be freshened in the morning with a "first lead" or "second lead" recapping new developments. Because of the need to "cycle" a story this way, it can be exhausting work to be the lone wire service reporter on a long-running crisis story.

Wire service correspondents measure their performance in "logs," or play reports indicating which agency's story was preferred on various issues. The following are UPI logs from the week ending 12 June 1976, a period of vigorous UPI-AP competition:[5]

• IDAHO FALLS, Idaho—30,000 persons forced to flee when dam crumbles and water floods 300 square miles. 13 [UPI]-6 [AP] in Sunday AMs. (The *Chicago Sun-Times* and the *New York Daily News* phoned kudos for UPI's coverage.)

• BARNESVILLE, Ohio—Once-powerful Congressman Wayne Hays, now target of two investigations into charges he put mistress on federal payroll, in coma from overdose of sleeping pills. 6-18 in Friday AMs and 1-12 in Friday PMs.

• MADRID, Spain—Conservative-dominated Spanish parliament refuses to end persecution of political parties. 0-8 in Wednesday PMs, but 5-1 in Thursday PMs.

When I ran the UPI Beirut bureau in 1976-79, it covered virtually the entire eastern Arab world except Egypt, which was handled by our Cairo bureau. We were two full-time U.S. reporters, assisted by four full-time Lebanese journalists. Our office was in the building housing Lebanon's premier newspaper, *An Nahar,* and we frequently tapped the expertise of its editors, reporters, and columnists. Besides monitoring various Arab radio stations and news agencies, we fielded reports from stringers around Lebanon and in Damascus, Amman, Kuwait, and Saudi Arabia. This mixture—U.S. and local staff, supplemented by monitoring and stringer reports—is a fairly typical news agency operation.

I could file stories directly to UPI customers on the "regional" wire for Europe, the Middle East, and Africa. For the main U.S. "A-wire," however, the copy went first to New York, where editors reviewed the piece and decided where else in the world it would go and with what priority.

Often, when the copy arrived in New York, the cables desk would rewrite the lead paragraphs and chop the story dramatically before putting it on the "A-wire," the prime national news wire. The truncated, rewritten version would then go to newspapers and broadcast outlets, where it was usually cut again. It was thus possible, even likely, that the two-paragraph briefs appearing in many newspapers across the country under the BEIRUT (UPI) dateline might not contain a single word actually written by UPI in Beirut.

"Need Matcher Sappest"

Pyramid stories and competitive angling are a fact of journalism at all levels, not just in the wire services. If there is a big breaking "spot" story, the pressure will be on for as sharp a lead as possible. If it's not a breaking item, the reporter will still be looking for the best possible angle, in order to compete successfully within his or her own organization in the eternal clawing for space. The bigger the story, the more intense the pressures on the reporter.

The best lesson I ever had in this was during the November 1976 entry into Beirut of 30,000 Syrian troops of the "Arab deterrent forces." The deployment was the biggest international story of the day because it was hoped—vainly, it turned out—that the bloody Lebanese war was finally coming to an end after two years. I was the lone UPI staff correspondent in the city.

On Sunday, November 14, Syrian troops fanned out through the Lebanese mountains, descended to the suburbs of Beirut, and stopped just short of entering the city proper. I filed a story reporting that they had come down to the city's edge, but made clear they had avoided entering the heart of the city. My AP colleague saw a Syrian colonel lead a group of men into town, apparently to reconnoiter. Since they passed within the city limits, he wrote that the Syrians "entered Beirut." This was a much better story, but I had seen no such thing and thought the overall deployment pattern was pretty clear. Soon our Cyprus bureau, through whom I communicated via telex with New York, began to get "rockets" (callback messages from the cables desk). The messages all pointed out that AP had Syrian troops actually entering the city and ended: "Need matcher sappest" (meaning "We need a matching story as-soon-as-possiblest").

I felt AP had needled the story, and was annoyed that my own desk was pressuring me to do the same. Fortunately, all the phone lines to

Beirut were out, and the brunt of the calls and messages fell on my colleague in Nicosia, Doyle McManus, with whom I was in telex contact. Doyle informed me of the messages, but I was adamant. I had been up since before dawn traveling all over the Lebanese capital and had put a great deal of effort into determining exactly where the Syrians had deployed. It was obvious to me that they had come down to the suburbs and stopped, deliberately *not* entering the city. To the consternation of the cables desk, I firmly refused to change the story and, as they no doubt anticipated, we lost the play handily.

Early the next day, November 15, the Syrians actually entered Beirut in what was by then clearly a two-phase deployment. I wrote the "entry" story, and we fared better in the logs. The same folks in New York who had pressed me so hard to change my story the day before now crowed that we had been right from the start.

The fact is, though, it is cold comfort for a reporter to be right and lose the play on a big story, or to not make it into the paper because he soft-pedaled his lead when his colleague in Bonn goosed his. It happens from time to time, and those are the breaks of the game; but no one wants to be a habitual loser, even a principled one.

Newspapers: "Validating" Coverage

A pet peeve of wire reporters is that often their desk does not consider a story a story until after the *New York Times* or *Washington Post* has validated it. This well-founded grouse reflects the influence of the *Times* and the *Post* in the coverage of foreign affairs.

The secretary of state's morning press clips, prepared each day by the Department of State's Bureau of Public Affairs, are must reading for senior officials in the department.[6] The *New York Times* and the *Washington Post* have traditionally dominated the space. Other newspapers culled include the *Los Angeles Times* (increasingly well represented in recent years with the advent of a Washington edition), *Wall Street Journal*, *Washington Times*, *Baltimore Sun*, and *USA Today*. In addition, the newsmagazines are regularly excerpted, as are key regional newspapers, especially those that maintain foreign bureaus, such as the *Boston Globe* and the *Chicago Tribune*.

A foreign correspondent for an opinion leader like the *Times* or the *Post* is usually in the "must brief" category. First, what he or she writes might have an impact not only on key government readers, including members of Congress, but also on editors making coverage decisions at other news organizations. In addition, because their copy is distributed on "supplemental" news services such as those of the *Washington Post/Los Angeles Times* or the *New York Times*, the stories in these newspapers are often carried in leading foreign outlets as well as hundreds of other dailies in the United States.[7] Most important, newspaper correspondents work to a format that allows for elaborating complexity, and those working for leading newspapers are usually well-paid journalists of proven ability. Thus, the reporter for a leading daily not only has the right audience, he or she is more likely than most to have the skill to tell the story right and the space in which to do it.

A newspaper's stable of foreign correspondents at any one time typically might include a mix of old hands and others who, although not new to the newspaper, are new at operating overseas. At the *Washington Post*, a beat on the metro desk—an ideal course in the ways of the newspaper and its audience—is often the first stop for future foreign correspondents, and not infrequently the first stop for returning foreign correspondents. Foreign assignments are also seen to some extent as a way of "seasoning" rising stars. Thus, after a foreign assignment or two, many reporters return to Washington. Some of the *Post's* best-known reporters and editors have traveled the metro-foreign route to beats on the national staff.

Post Deputy Foreign Editor Edward Cody noted that the newspaper's editors are inclined against correspondents staying out too long, lest they lose touch with the paper. In a similar vein, former foreign and national editor Peter Osnos, now a vice president of Random House, said, "On assignments, I think three or four years is about right. There is a tradeoff between expertise gained as opposed to losing your perspective."

Once overseas, the name of the game for correspondents is, quite simply, getting into the paper. This means filing a good, competitive story to survive the daily spawn of byliners vying for limited space. To some extent, however, the fate of the file depends on factors beyond their control, including the general news climate, the day of the week, and the dynamics of the newspaper's editorial process.

If the reporter is writing a major breaking story, and the editors expect it, and it gets filed on time, chances are he or she will get in the paper. But if the piece is not the top story in the world, it will be in tough competition for space. A single major event—domestic or foreign—can quickly relegate a carefully developed dispatch to the hold file or the "bust spike."

In the teeth of a big competing story, an experienced reporter will often consult the desk and hold off filing a dispatch in order to have a better shot after the other event subsides. Diplomats who have announcements to make, or policies to explain, are also competing for space (and broadcast time), and should think the same way if they wish to maximize the impact of what they have to say.

How the Desk Works

Behind every correspondent abroad is the foreign desk back home. Each operation is slightly different, but typically the desk for a large newspaper might include a foreign editor, a deputy, a slot editor, and several copy editors.[8] Ordinarily, the foreign correspondents' files arrive early in the day and are put together with related wire copy (reporters in Asia, the Middle East, Europe, and Africa are all five hours or more ahead of EST; only those in Central and South America are slightly behind and file late). The work of the desk begins in late morning or early afternoon, when the foreign editor and his staff scan the day's take and prioritize material. Around 5 P.M., the executive editor calls the foreign editor and other key department heads (for example, metro, national, business, sports, pictures, layout) to a page one meeting. The various section heads review their wares and pitch their most competitive stories for page one. In a rough-and-tumble free-market competition, decisions are then made on what gets in and how the items will be played. The meeting breaks up, pages are laid out, headlines and story lengths are assigned, and the foreign desk slot editor sets copy editors to work fitting stories to assigned space and writing headlines.

Thomas Friedman described this process at the *New York Times*, detailing what happens when he leaves a diplomatic briefing overseas and files his story:

> The story goes from me to the foreign desk. They decide if it has merit and deserves to be in the newspaper. If so, it will be "top-edited," that is, the lead will be looked at. The foreign editor or one of his immediate assistants—we call them the backfield—will decide if the lead is in the lead or whether the fourth paragraph is the lead. Then the story goes to the copy desk, for copy editing, printing, and headline writing.
>
> If it's a possible page one story—a "frontable" story—there's another layer: it goes through the news desk. If it's a frontable story, there is a 5 P.M. meeting. All of the editors—for the metro, national, science, foreign, and Washington sections—meet with Mr. [Max] Frankel, the editor-in-chief, to discuss page one. The foreign editor would say, "Well, we have Friedman from Pakistan. He had a briefing there and says we're going to do a new arms deal with Pakistan."
>
> At the end of the meeting they take out a white page and they draw up a front page. They might say, "Well, the Friedman story is pretty good, maybe we'll make it the off-lead."[9] After the meeting, the foreign editor comes back to the desk and says, "We have two stories on page one: Friedman from Pakistan and Jones from Moscow." The backfield then does the top-editing, it goes to the copy desk, and then to the news desk.
>
> At the five o'clock meeting, there may have been some questions about my story, in which case they'll call me in Islamabad and ask me the questions from the meeting.

I asked Friedman whether it was standard procedure for the desk to call a reporter back if it changes his copy. "We usually do call back at the *Times* if it's a substantial rewrite. In fact, they often make *you* do it." (Most other major newspapers also try to contact their correspondents if the surgery is major.)

On some issues, a foreign correspondent's file may receive inserts or adds. If, for example, a reporter files from Baghdad about U.N. inspections of Iraqi missiles, related material may also be generated from the U.N. in New York or from Washington. If space does not allow separate bylines, all three filings may be combined in one item under a single dateline, with a tag line at the end noting contributions from other reporters. The top of the story may also be substantially rewritten to include the new information.

A correspondent could file a story of thirty column inches, but the layout editor, when he gets his dummy news pages with advertising blocked in, finds he only has space for twenty-five inches. Of this, another six inches will go to the inserts from New York and Washington. Thus, only about nineteen inches of the thirty-inch original file is used, and the leading paragraphs may be recast.

The Friday Night Hole

Since most news is generated Monday through Friday, the pressure on space is greatest for Tuesday-Saturday papers. But from the reporter's point of view, Saturday is not a good day to appear, since Saturday newspapers tend to be lightly read, and key audiences may not see, act on, or react to the information. As a corollary, slow-news weekend days mean somewhat less competition for space in the well-read Sunday and Monday papers. Every foreign correspondent knows that a good file sent Sunday has a better shot at Monday page one than other days of the week and Sunday has long been a favorite filing day for Middle East-based reporters, since the Arab world rests on Friday and Israel on Saturday.

Some lessons—at the risk of stating the obvious—are:

1. If the briefer has information of some kind to release, but *doesn't want it to have much impact,* he should issue his statement or give his briefing on Friday night, Eastern Standard Time. (Note: The official should have no illusions about fooling anyone with this. Reporters will recognize the stratagem and be unhappy with it, even if they can't do much about it.)

The State Department bureaucracy, oblivious, has raised this to an art form—not from a sophisticated intent to avoid headlines, but as a function of the time it takes for bureaucratic waves to lap policy shores. "We have a wonderful habit of disgorging everything at seven o'clock on

Friday night," former spokesman Richard Boucher remarked, with evident frustration. "People have had all week to work on something. On Monday they get the tasking and on Tuesday they draft it. Then it's cleared around and goes to the bureau front office. It goes upstairs at five o'clock Friday night and at seven o'clock the decision comes out. It's too late for the Saturday newspapers, too late for the Friday evening newscasts, and by the time the Sunday newspapers are being prepared, it's a day old. So it falls in a hole."

Therefore, unless it is *intended* that all that hard work on the Afghanistan statement fall in a hole, the prudent briefer will go home Friday night, and keep the item for Saturday, Sunday, or Monday release.[10]

2. On the other hand, if the statement, announcement, or briefing is intended for *maximum play*, it should be released early enough in the day—preferably by midday—to allow reporters time to write and file their pieces, or maximize their chances of getting scheduled for evening newscasts; alternatively, it should be released on a slow-news weekend day, when there is less competition for space and air time.

3. The important thing is to try to think like an editor. Nothing happens in isolation. At all times it is vital to consider what *else* is going on and the pressures this will generate on news organizations. If a statement must be issued urging moderation on the warring factions in Nagorno-Karabakh, or condemning human rights violations in Sudan, the official will not want to release it the same day that Israel invades Lebanon or the Chinese crack down on prodemocracy demonstrators in Tiananmen Square (unless, of course, the idea is to bury it).

In the real world there is often little control over timing. But if it is the height of the summer silly season, and the TV news has run three straight features on the president's cat, the Afghanistan statement that would pass unnoticed in November might just catch the eye of a bored foreign editor.

Newsmagazines: No Day Like Thursday

Notwithstanding the groping of the newsmagazines for new graphics and editorial personas, they remain a major vehicle for getting analysis to a mass audience.[11] Indeed, this is one of their greatest strengths: they work to give readers the "so what" for news of the week gone by. With color, quotes, and background, they try to supply an extra dimension to what readers learned on television or in the newspaper.

The major differences between this medium and others are filing schedules and format. Magazine correspondents file once a week.

Typically, editors try to close the "book" not later than Friday night, with production and distribution Saturday-Sunday, and new issues on the stands Monday. Changes can be made up to Saturday if needed, but major late-breaking makeovers disrupt production schedules and are thus expensive.[12]

Newsmagazine reporters will try to get most of their information gathering done in time to write and file by Thursday. A file sent Thursday afternoon from Moscow or Jerusalem will arrive at opening of business Thursday morning in New York. Thus, the magazine correspondent will love you Monday through Thursday, but not on Friday. If you offer to brief after deadline, you might as well not offer at all.

"I used to have what I called my 'Thursday feed' with Larry Eagleburger," *Time* correspondent Bruce Van Voorst said. "His secretary, Millie, would give me ten or fifteen minutes with him. No bull. Specific things. It was marvelous. Once, I was in with him during the final days of the pullout from Saigon. The secretary stuck her head in the door and said, 'Saigon is on the line.' I got up to leave, but he told me not to bother, and proceeded to discuss lots of details about the evacuation of Saigon with me in the room. Then, afterwards, he said, 'Now, Van Voorst, goddammit, protect me on that.' Larry knew who he could trust, and I'd burn in hell before I'd betray that trust."

The need to provide readers with an extra dimension on the news lends itself to a fairly dramatic writing style. Since they are repackaging news that will be several days or a week old by the time it is read, the newsmagazine correspondents file vividly written pieces, rich in color and detail. For many years, the tradition was that correspondents would send rather long files to staff writers in New York, who would then use them as grist for finished, all-source stories, usually under the New York writer's byline, with the various contributing correspondents listed in a tag line at the end. Although this is still done, since the late 1980s even *Time* has broken out of the style it pioneered, moving toward more writing from the field, with foreign datelines and bylines figuring more prominently.

Invariably, the correspondent will file far more than the magazine can use, and what finally appears is usually a tiny fraction of the material submitted by contributing reporters. The edited file is played back to correspondents on Friday, along with any questions editors or researchers may have developed. The reporter then reviews it and sends back comments and corrections.

Newsmagazine reporters traditionally have faced more draconian rewrites than newspaper correspondents. This comparative lack of control over files is worth bearing in mind when briefing, because a diplomat's throwaway line may be the only thing that survives when the rewrite expert in New York wraps the file in with other material.

A little forethought can help magazine reporters enormously. Official guidance is of scant use; reporters need color and meaning. If the diplomat is briefing on a summit, he should describe the inside of the conference room, the mannerisms and facial expressions of the participants, and the kinds of guns the security guards carried. Political jokes are always good copy, and so is a capsule summary of any relevant history. Tell them, for example, that the prime minister delivered his speech in the same drawing room where a crazed artist gunned down his father twenty years ago. If the bullet holes are still in the walls, say so.

Increasingly, newspaper writers are after this kind of detail as well. Both magazine and newspaper reporters will sometimes ask for help with a "tick-tock"—a detailed reprise of just how a series of events occurred.

Whatever the format, just as wire service reporters are important because they "lead" coverage and set the initial tone for a story, so too newspaper and newsmagazine correspondents are important because they play a key role in "validating" the coverage of others and setting the news agenda. Diplomats should remember that good print reporters invariably gather more information than they can use in their own stories. This makes them important not only for the access and influence with public opinion that their institutions represent, but also as sources of information in their own right.

Chapter 5

Desks and Deadlines
Television

> *Governments need to know that electronic services,*
> *especially television, eliminate or dissolve representative*
> *government. TV ends representation at a distance and*
> *involves one in the immediate confrontation of an image.*
> —MARSHALL H. MCLUHAN AND BRUCE R. POWERS

The great strength of television news is its immediacy and the drama and emotion of its images. The medium is less effective, however, at informing in depth, an issue that has often been at the center of the debate over how best to organize and present television news.

"I used to boast of being the only producer left who assembled pictures first and then had the scripts written," wrote Reuven Frank, former president of NBC News. In a memoir looking back on a distinguished career in television journalism, he lamented that "the word people had won" and that television news had evolved in a way that played not to its strengths, but to its weaknesses. Television, in the view of Frank, one of its pioneers, is at its best in complementing and illustrating other news sources, not substituting for them: "When television news accepted that its mandate was to be a primary news source rather than the *complementary* one it had been when it began, it was obliged to report important stories that were not available to the human eye or the camera lens: negotiations, tax increases, the clash of beliefs, economic trends—the list is infinite." [1]

The flagship news program for all three television networks is a twenty-two-minute evening newscast. (Most viewers think it's a thirty-minute newscast, but eight minutes of that time is given to commercials.) In this format, which is divided into several segments by commercials, a *long* piece is two or three minutes. A short international item might consist of no more than fifteen seconds of video agency film, voiced over by the anchor. That means the on-camera appearance of any

39

news *subject* will be correspondingly short. A Harvard sociologist who examined the recent history of the sound bite found it had shrunk from 42.3 seconds on average for presidential candidates in 1968 to 9.8 seconds in 1988.[2] How much can be said in 9.8 seconds? About twenty-five words.

Beyond pictures and compressed format, another element inherent in television news reporting is the tendency to write stories in the form of portentous minidramas in which a conflict is raised in the body of the piece and then resolved, with fitting gravitas, in the correspondent's exit line. As far back as 1963, when Reuven Frank was executive producer of the NBC Evening News, he wrote a memo to staff on story structure: "Every news story should, without any sacrifice of probity or responsibility, display the attributes of fiction, of drama. It should have structure and conflict, problem and denouement, rising action and falling action, a beginning, a middle and an end. These are not only the essentials of drama; they are the essentials of narrative." [3] Needless to say, not every news story conforms to this neat structure, but the model remains.

Impressions can be powerful and enduring—a starving child clinging listlessly to his mother in Somalia, or the death embrace of a young couple cut down by snipers in Bosnia. But complexity cannot as easily be bent into a few short lines of script. The impulse to dramatize, to prop up the straw man and then knock him down, makes it tempting to simplify. In addition, program organization, however skillful, sometimes conspires against comprehension. Items in a newscast, if presented too quickly, are hard to absorb in detail. In a quick-change format, there may be little repetition or explanation or time for things to sink in between items.

Ambassador Charles Redman, who served as department spokesman under Secretary of State George Shultz, remarked on this when I discussed this project with him briefly. Contrary to general belief, he said, he had found it hard to get a message to people via television. Unless the message is repeated over and over again on television, as on a recurring issue like the Iran-contra scandal, it does not sink in.

Redman's point was that what remains in viewers' minds from network news programs the night before is usually little more than a generalized impression, often drawn more from a picture than from words (hence the power of television to outrage, on an issue like famine in Somalia or civil war in Bosnia, but not to inspire specific policy responses).

It is not that the spoken words are not there or do not count. They are, they do, and a great deal of skilled effort goes into their preparation. But they ride a twisting, eye-catching helix of pictures and graphics. "After words are written, pictures are matched to them, relevant or irrelevant, that day's or last year's, but pictures," said Reuven Frank. "In editing rooms they're called 'wallpaper' or even today's TV 'eyewash,' but news could not function without them." [4]

The impact of the print media and that of television are markedly different. Newspaper reporters are fond of pointing out that an entire evening newscast, reduced to a transcript of words on paper, typically runs less than twenty-five double-spaced pages, or less than appears on a single page of a daily newspaper. Television journalists rejoin that this is true, but the statistic, by focusing on the number of words, takes no account of the most significant aspect of television news: the message of the *pictures*.[5]

What the foreign affairs professional needs to keep in mind is simply that television is unmatched as a purveyor of experience and impression, but more limited as a vehicle for transmitting nonvisual information and complexity. Although these are admittedly very general considerations, they govern the particulars as well—both how television journalists gather their information and how government officials interact with them.

Dynamics of Coverage

Far more than print media, television coverage is a team effort. The correspondent for any story is but the tip of a news-processing iceberg that includes producers, cameramen, soundmen, and a host of other technicians. The logistics, and the expense, of moving all these people around and transmitting pictures can be considerable. A network correspondent and crew flying into a remote foreign location, say Somalia, may carry 800 pounds or more of luggage, including edit packs, cameras, lights, sound equipment, satellite communications equipment, and other gear. The sheer unwieldiness of it all, and equipment dependency, can be a limiting factor.

"In a lot of cases we must make deals with the devil," said CNN Vice President Stuart Loory, citing the expense and trouble of setting up equipment. "We have to be concerned about this. In the Gulf War, for example, we had to make our accommodations with the Department of Defense or the Saudi Ministry of Defense or whatever jurisdiction had control so we could get our equipment in to provide that live capability. To put up a satellite dish in the desert, you need Saudi and DOD permission. They say, sure, but under these conditions—for example, no talk about incoming missiles or where they land. In essence, we agree not to tell the whole story."

Regarding Gulf War coverage in general, he said, CNN and others gave up the ability to go anywhere they wanted, tacitly agreeing to go where they were taken. Those who broke away, like CBS's Bob Simon, found themselves in "big trouble." That marked "a big change from Vietnam, when DOD helped correspondents, and it started with Grenada." Loory doubted whether CNN and others in the news business who chose to participate in those arrangements in the Gulf had really done a good job of working with the Defense Department in setting the ground rules.[6]

On routine foreign coverage, after the correspondent shoots the story, he or she will review the pictures with the producer and write a story to go with them.[7] If the piece speaks of a leader addressing a crowd or his troops, it must have a picture illustrating it. If there are demonstrations or riots, they must be shown—or, at a minimum, there must be shots of destroyed and damaged property in the aftermath. If the correspondent quotes an expert expressing concern about the economic situation, the remarks should be on film, preferably in English.

Reporter and producer send a short proposal, describing the story and pictures, to New York via computer-modem phone link or telephone. If it is from Somalia, seven hours ahead of New York, it would normally still be morning when the proposal arrives on the other end. The evening news team begins its day by reading in, reviewing not only the proposals from its own correspondents, but wire service reports from around the world and items in the major newspapers. Because of the time difference with Europe, Africa, and the Middle East, the team will also have a good sense of what pictures are available from the major video news agencies and consortia, such as Reuters Television (formerly Visnews), Worldwide Television News (WTN), and Eurovision (a film-sharing forum for major European broadcasting organizations).

At a story meeting, the executive producer of the evening news and his assistants decide to put Somalia in their lineup and ask the correspondent in Mogadishu to send the script. Of the twenty-two minutes or so available on the evening news, five to ten minutes might typically be allotted to foreign coverage. Since the U.S. troop deployment means interest in Somalia is high, it could get substantial play—a minute and forty-five seconds.

The field producer—who coordinates among correspondent, tape editor, crew, and New York—passes on the correspondent's finished script to New York for review, where it is edited if necessary and then returned to the field. The producer also ensures that the pictures are cut and edited to fit the story properly. The correspondent does an audio track for the pictures, and a "stand-upper" for the on-camera segment. If there has been fighting somewhere that must be mentioned in the story, but the crew did not get pictures, the producer may leave a blank segment on the tape so that London or New York can cut in film acquired from one of the video agencies that did manage to get pictures.

The last step is the satellite feed; the satellite is called "the bird" and sending the film is "birding" it. If the crew has its own portable dish, or "flyaway" (which is increasingly the case, as when CNN correspondent Peter Arnett reported from Baghdad during the Gulf War), an uplink is established at the time specified by New York. If there is no portable satellite communications gear, the producer goes to the satellite ground station of the local television system (if it is functioning) for the feed. Failing that, he ships the film by plane to the nearest transmission point. (During the civil war in Lebanon, Beirut-based correspondents frequently flew to Amman or Cyprus to bird film. I remember this well, because Larry Buchman—an ABC News stringer who was a colleague and codenizen of the Commodore Hotel—died when his chartered Arab Wings commuter plane crashed at Beirut Airport. Buchman and all on board perished trying to get film of a Yasir Arafat interview by Barbara Walters out to Amman for transmission.)

New York books the satellite time in coordination with local broadcast authorities and tells the field producer what time the feed will be. The tape goes into a fancy VCR (at the ground station or in the portable unit) and is sent when the uplink is established. The logistics of birding film can be tough when local authorities don't want to cooperate—the ground station is their chokepoint. Unless the TV crew has its own flyaway, the locals can still defeat a story they couldn't prevent reporters from covering by cutting it off at the pass, when it is being birded through *their* facilities. Since satellite times are booked and paid in advance, missing the bird due to transportation problems, lazy or inept local station employees, political obstruction, or any other reason can be costly. The producer often must devote a great deal of attention to sorting out these things while correspondent and crew are out shooting.

If the crew has no "edit pack," it might send rough-cut film and sound to London or some other intermediate point for processing. This pushes up filing deadlines even further, since time must be allowed for London editing. Other factors that can affect a deadline are the need to insert captions for pictures and translate any non-English segments.

If the network has no crew on the scene, it might elect to take pictures supplied by Reuters Television, WTN, or another organization or international consortium whose film it has access to, such as the BBC or Eurovision. The network can then either write its own story for the acquired footage, to go with a voiceover by the anchor or a correspondent in London, or run the report of the film agency reporter (not often done by the networks, although such reports regularly run at length on the Public Broadcasting System's *MacNeil/Lehrer NewsHour*).

What is important for U.S. officials to know about these logistics is that television news is produced by a team. Several senior diplomats had unpleasant memories of doing interviews that were then edited and run over images from other material. One official, for example, recounted a documentary program that showed file footage of dead bodies being piled up as a backdrop to his words outlining U.S. policy on South Africa. Ambassador Thomas Pickering recalled one occasion when a well-known journalist came with a film team to El Salvador to do a documentary on the war. "They focused on a single question about government bombing, and my answer reflected accurately what we knew of government bombing at the time. But it was juxtaposed with some old file footage of government planes bombing villages and peasants talking about the results of the bombing. It was a total montage."

Pickering drew several lessons from the experience:

> Number one, it is best to do something like that live if possible. You don't have individuals dickering with the footage and chopping up your interviews into little pieces. They have no way to manipulate what you say when it is live. The next best thing is live to tape, for example, with a credible program like MacNeil/Lehrer, which can be fairly trustworthy. The worst thing is to do a rambling interview, on tape, for a film or documentary, because then they can just take bits and pieces.

Correspondents and Producers

A trend in coverage that has nettled some network journalists is the rising power of producers. The relationship between field producer and correspondent has always contained the seeds of conflict. Many producers are not only good organizers and logisticians, but skilled reporters and writers. Sometimes they fill in on the air for correspondents on leave or take up the slack by reporting when a story gets too big for one person to cover. But this cooperation can turn into competition.

The friction appears to have become increasingly acute in the 1980s, and especially since the change in ownership of the three networks in 1986. To old guard journalists, the new power relationship in the field is less a function of budget calculus than a value shift at corporate headquarters. They feel responsibility to shareholders has displaced too big a piece of the space occupied by public trust. Just as their print colleagues grumble that marketing values have gained ascendancy over editorial judgment (see chapter 6), so do many broadcast veterans feel that presentation and packaging of news have taken precedence over news gathering.

"In all the cost cutting imposed by the new proprietors at all three networks," wrote Reuven Frank, "most of the cuts came out of getting the news and almost none from the costs of presenting it. News bureaus were closed as anchormen's salaries rose; cameramen were laid off while stage settings became more elaborate and graphics devices more complicated and expensive."[8]

On the ground, correspondents saw a change in the authority and clout of the producer, and in the relationship between the producer and the correspondent. "The producer has effectively gained control over the flow of information," said former NBC foreign correspondent Henry Champ.[9]

The same point was made by Liz Trotta, who worked for both NBC and CBS, in her book *Fighting for Air*. "At CBS particularly, the new producers—often referred to as 'video kittens' if they happened to be women—moved in on the correspondents, determining the thrust of a story and often setting out to prove whatever hypothesis they had already formed. In 'setting up' a future story, such as a series, the producer did the ground work and thus shaped the story from the start." Trotta also cited the power of the editing-room producer to determine whether the correspondent's stand-upper made the air and the increasing role of field producers in directing camera crews, doing interviews, working out story lines, and even writing scripts. "Because I was accustomed to working alone with a crew," she said, "the ascendancy of the producer brought me into a series of clashes."[10]

Champ observed that the current schooling of television correspondents reflects the emphasis on presentation. New correspondents, he said, do not carry the same baggage as the older generation and are more inclined to settle comfortably into the new producer-correspondent relationship. "Take my son, who works for the Canadian Broadcasting Corporation. He graduated from Carleton University in Canada, the top journalism school in the country. He spent lots of course time in studios, working on programs and shooting film. This is not what prepares or teaches one about journalism; it sets and hardens over the concept of working with the machinery, that is, with the producers, editors, and others who have a foothold in news dissemination."

A classic case of presentation sidelining substance was the rigged crash test of a General Motors truck shown on *Dateline NBC* in November 1992. Although the correspondent reportedly objected to the executive producer about including the tests in the broadcast, they were not only left in, but climaxed the segment.[11] When GM investigated, held a press conference showing the conflagration was staged, and filed a lawsuit, NBC admitted misrepresentation and apologized. Said Reuven Frank: "This is the worst black eye NBC News has suffered in my experience, which goes back to 1950."[12] In early March 1993 NBC News President Michael Gartner, who initially defended the broadcast as "fair and accurate," resigned. On March 19 NBC fired three producers—the executive producer of *Dateline NBC*, the senior producer for the program, and the producer of the GM segment.

At a time of change and transformation in the television industry, then, an important issue for many broadcast journalists is preserving news standards. "Power has gradually passed, over the years, away from the correspondents and newscasters into the hands of producers, accountants, lawyers, and management, people who are bottom-liners, budgeteers, legalists, not news people," said former CBS correspondent David Schoenbrun.[13] Similarly, after CBS cut the news budget 10 percent and announced the firing of more than 200 employees in 1987, anchorman Dan Rather wondered in a *New York Times* op-ed piece: "Do the owners and officers of the new CBS see news as a trust . . . or only as a business venture?"[14]

To put this in some perspective, it must be said the networks still commit huge resources to covering the news,[15] and given the considerable format constraints they work under, they do a very good job indeed. When they commit resources to major stories, or focus on a special issue, they can produce excellent television viewing. But even conceding the current commitment of resources, money, and talent, and that the new corporate owners have not been entirely remiss in looking for economies, there seems to be a concern that goes beyond this: that the citadel of news integrity is under siege from the partisans of hype. The *Dateline NBC* caper, in this view, is the fruit of an unhealthy emphasis on dramatic presentation. This, in turn, stems from the push of the network news divisions for profitability, symbolized by the 1990s trend toward "magazine television" infotainment. "Though many network executives dismiss the incident as an aberration," *Time* magazine concluded, "it is symptomatic of the pressure to make stories that sizzle."[16]

CNN: "Our Kicks Are Not the Same"

CNN shares many of the same basic format considerations of the television networks, but there are important differences, especially in the amount of time available to correspondents. The networks come on morning and evening, with occasional special reports during the day for big events. CNN is there all the time.

For foreign correspondents at the networks, the holy grail is the evening news. CNN's Stuart Loory recalled running into a CBS correspondent in Geneva in 1985, during the first Reagan-Gorbachev summit. Loory asked the reporter how things were going. "Terrific," he said. "I led the Evening News with a minute-thirty-five last night." Loory said that summed up the network foreign correspondent's life perfectly: ups and downs, with success measured by the number of seconds on the evening news.

"Our kicks are not the same," he said. "We get on immediately, if possible live, and as much as we can—in some length, and in some amount of depth, if you equate depth with telling the story as it's developing." Loory acknowledged that CNN had been criticized for not being analytical enough, but said the network had given extra attention to special reports and in-depth reporting in recent years to overcome that perception. The CNN predilection to go live and at length is known at the network as the "live philosophy" and is a major distinction between it and the networks.

From the point of view of the foreign affairs professional, the important thing to know about CNN is not how it fares in comparison with the other U.S. networks, since all are important vehicles for reaching a mass audience in the United States. What really sets CNN apart from the networks—and makes it of unique importance as a factor in international relations—is the elite nature of its *worldwide* audience. "The audience of CNN worldwide tends to be people at the very top of business and the financial community, heads of government, intelligence, and national security, and journalists," said CNN International Vice President Peter Vesey. "We have affiliations with over 200 broadcasters around the world and 340 affiliates all over the United States. It can be said that we have perhaps the most elite circulation of any news organization in the history of mankind."

CNN receives about eighty to a hundred items a day—pictures and film obtained from its own sources or purchased from various services and from its affiliates. The CNN World Report unit communicates with broadcasters around the world and monitors about twenty different newscasts, including China TV, as well as feeds from Hong Kong, Italy, Portugal, Russia, Taiwan, and elsewhere. No other news organization has the same extensive, twenty-four-hour, global capacity to send and receive news, although the BBC began to compete head-to-head in 1991—especially in Europe and Asia—with the launching of its World Service Television (WSTV).

"A Diplomatic Party Line"

CNN's vice president for international news gathering, Eason Jordan, is in charge of coordinating coverage by some thirty correspondents and thirty crews working out of about twenty international bureaus. He takes exception to the notion that the day of the "legendary foreign correspondents" is past, citing CNN correspondent Mike Chinoy in Beijing, who speaks Chinese and "whose idea of travel is to go to Hong

Kong and Taiwan," and Moscow correspondent Steve Hurst, who speaks Russian and has covered his beat many years.

Jordan acknowledged that some journalists felt the old days were better but dismissed this as both romantic and unpragmatic. "The difference between now and the days of Edward R. Murrow and William Shirer is that back then, people covered London and Berlin. The world is not that small any more, we have to cover much more. We very much want to have correspondents who know the story extremely well. But we have nineteen bureaus and we need to send people to 200 countries and territories." [17]

Under Jordan are three senior international editors: a director of coverage, responsible for same-day news coverage; a director in charge of planning and futures; and a director responsible for special projects, such as half-hour specials (when this book was being researched, a special assignments unit under former ABC producer Pam Hill was doing this long-form reporting). The international assignments desk is staffed with twenty people twenty-four hours a day, seven days a week. The director of coverage supervises four editors who handle separate, clearly defined areas. On the day I visited, one was shepherding three correspondent teams in Yugoslavia, another was doing Russia and Somalia, another was responsible for all of the Americas outside the United States, and a fourth covered all of Asia.

During the Gulf War, CNN became a part of diplomacy. A Saddam Hussein speech would be carried on CNN, and State Department Spokesman Richard Boucher would respond at his noon briefing. The U.S. ambassador to the United Nations used CNN as a vehicle to get U.S. views on issues to other U.N. members. The Kuwaiti government-in-exile gathered regularly around the CNN monitor at their hotel eyrie in Taif, Saudi Arabia, high up the Red Sea escarpment, to follow the latest news. Not only were the Iraqi government and the State Department Operations Center tuned in, but so were the Russians, the Egyptians, and other key actors. It was, in analyst Lewis Friedland's fine phrase, "a diplomatic party line." [18]

Eason Jordan commented, "We were very cognizant that people on all sides were watching us, and we went out of our way to be responsible in our presentation."

Strengths and Limitations

Television is a team effort. In their individual dealings, diplomats should remember that the correspondent or producer they speak to does not have the last say on a finished piece. A long, rambling interview to tape is therefore a roll of the dice. A live interview is the only way to be sure of content and context.

In broader terms, just as every good television journalist is acutely aware of the strengths and limitations of his medium, whether the issue is covering the Gulf War or covering the State Department, so too should public officials be. "Fleeting, disjointed, visual glimpses of reality, flickering on and off the screen, here today and gone tomorrow, are not the 'information' on which sound judgments on complicated international problems are to be formed," said diplomat and author George Kennan in a letter to the *New York Times*, commenting on the role of television in galvanizing public and congressional support for the 1992 U.S. military intervention in Somalia. "Television cannot consult the rich voice of prior experience, nor can it outline probable consequences, or define alternatives, or express the nuances of the argument pro and con." [19] What it *can* do, with extraordinary power, is convey striking images, in real time, to a mass audience.

Furthermore, whatever the drawbacks of relying too heavily on television coverage as a basis for policy development, and whatever the format contraints, television will remain an essential medium for policy makers who wish to get their message to the widest possible public. In order to have a substantive policy effect, however, television—no less than any other medium—must have a substantive message on which to focus. In other words, officials should avoid becoming so entranced by the power and immediacy of television that they forget that good television is no substitute for either good thought or good policy.

"Increasingly during the 1980s," White House Communications Director David Gergen has written, "government officials have shaped their policies with an eye toward generating positive and timely television coverage and securing public approval. What too often counts is how well the policy will 'play,' how the pictures will look, whether the right signals are being sent, and whether the public will be impressed by the swiftness of the government's response—not whether the policy promotes America's long-term interests." [20]

Similarly, Ted Koppel of ABC News, in testimony before the House Foreign Affairs Committee, addressed the impact on policy of live pictures, saying that "absent a clearly enunciated foreign policy by [the] executive branch, television will have more of an impact, but so will Congress, so will newspapers, so will anything else." If there is an information vacuum, he noted, whatever is available will fall into that vacuum.

The first thing [an administration] has to do is create a foreign policy. Then it has to worry about how it's going to sell that policy to you folks here on the

Hill, to our colleagues in newspapers, to the American public. And frequently in selling it to the American public, it determines that television is the most efficient means of doing that. But I would not confuse the creation of a television policy with the creation of a policy. I think all too frequently over the last five or ten years, administrations have created terrific television policies and have forgotten about creating foreign policies to begin with.[21]

Chapter 6

Patterns of Coverage

All is flux, nothing stays still.
—HERACLITUS

News follows its market, and the market for news is changing. As change affects reader, viewer, and advertiser preferences, so too does it affect patterns of foreign coverage and editorial priorities. Both print and broadcast journalists have been laboring, as never before, under the pressures of businesses and professions altered by technology and economic shifts.

Modems, portable computers, and satellite phones allow reporters to go anywhere and not depend on telex, telephone, host nation satellite ground stations, or leased circuits through the local PTT (post, telegraph, and telephone office) to transmit stories. For television crews the formidable logistics of moving correspondent, crew, filmedit pack, cameras, lights, and satellite phones are getting easier. Every year cameras get smaller and satellite transponders better. What now takes a day to set up will take only a few hours in the future.

"It's infinitely more sophisticated," said Random House Vice President Peter Osnos, a *Washington Post* reporter from 1966 to 1984, who served as Moscow correspondent (1974-77), foreign editor, and national editor. "When I was in Moscow, if I wanted to place a phone call to my home office, it was a major production. Now the Moscow bureau is just another extension on the Washington switchboard. Back then I didn't know what was going on in the world outside. I had to pay Reuters fifty rubles a month to get a drop copy of their wire to keep up. Now the correspondents sit at their desks and tap into not just the wire services, but the internal communications of their own newspapers. These things have to make a difference."

Many veteran correspondents see a downside as well, though. A common complaint is that improved communications and travel have combined with economic pressure to make coverage more superficial. Rather than maintain expensive bureaus overseas, news organizations have tended increasingly to dispatch reporters abroad from home offices or hub bureaus—on so-called "parachute" coverage. Unfortunately, this can lead to less informed horde reporting of crises.

"The greatest single tragedy in current journalism," *Time* correspondent Bruce Van Voorst declared, "is the demise of what I would call the 'legendary foreign correspondents.' These are the people who know their beat and have been there a long time. Ten years ago, when there was a war in the Middle East, about a dozen of us would show up. Look at Desert Storm. It was covered by a band of incompetents—anyone who could afford the ticket. A newspaper that wouldn't think of sending its sports editor to cover a local concert doesn't hesitate to send a municipal reporter to cover a war."

Added another veteran foreign correspondent, "This is what had swamped, and wrecked, the Pentagon pool system in Panama [when U.S. troops invaded] in December 1989—it was a nearby, easily accessible miniwar that drew hundreds of correspondents, even from local TV newscasts, who had no business being there."

Mixed incongruously into the stampede are star anchormen for the networks, whose on-scene presence is believed to add luster to both reporting and ratings. "With the new mobility," notes AP's Paris-based special correspondent, Mort Rosenblum, "correspondents clustered in big bureaus are off at the bell. Between airport, event, and satellite feed, there is little time for what it all used to be about: knowledge." He adds, "Today, reporters go abroad with higher standards, more education, and better tools. In the end, however, few competent, calmed-down professionals stay with the story long enough to understand it. Plenty of them exist, but few have the luxury of staying with their story. Complexity still does not sell papers."[1]

The number of correspondents posted abroad fluctuates constantly; so does their deployment.[2] Broadly speaking, the number of serious, full-time foreign correspondents working for U.S. news organizations declined after the Vietnam War, but rebounded in the 1980s. By the beginning of the 1990s, trends were mixed. While major newspapers had maintained and expanded bureaus, smaller ones had cut back or resorted increasingly to parachute coverage. CNN was expanding its international coverage, but the three major U.S. broadcast networks had, in varying degrees, cut back the number of bureaus, entered into sharing arrangements, and otherwise consolidated overseas operations. AP still had a strong overseas presence, but UPI, on the ropes financially through various ownership changes in the past decade, had reduced strength dramatically. Newsmagazines had retrenched, but still kept fairly sizable and experienced foreign staffs. (The number of foreign correspondents listed on the *Time* masthead, for example, dipped from 47 in January 1970 to 33 in January 1980 to 28 in January 1990. In April 1994 the number was 22.)

The *Washington Post* correspondent, for one, still writes for a government/elite readership with a high interest in foreign affairs. "Foreign news has a strong claim on space at the *Post*," according to *Post* deputy foreign editor Ed Cody. "We get an average of about nine and a half columns a day, and we can easily go up when we need to. Foreign news is by far the most expensive news coverage, but for a city like Washington you cannot *not* have it." Cody says the *Post* more than doubled the number of its foreign correspondents from twelve in the late 1970s to twenty-five in the early 1990s. (Parallel increases were also registered by the *New York Times*, the *Los Angeles Times*, and a few major regional dailies with a tradition of foreign coverage, like the *Chicago Tribune* and the *Boston Globe*.)

By contrast, *USA Today*, the flagship of the Gannett newspaper chain, is more typical of trends in the newspaper industry as a whole. It has a broad readership with less appetite for detail. The newspaper regularly dispatches correspondents abroad on temporary assignment, and editions of the paper are published in Hong Kong, Singapore, and Switzerland. But no permanent foreign bureau serves Gannett's 80-plus daily papers, 50-plus periodicals, 10 television stations, and 11 radio stations.

"It Has to Make Your Toes Curl"

As this book was being written in 1993, coverage of news from abroad seemed to be getting both better and worse, both more sophisticated and more superficial. This reflected technological developments, increasing differentiation in the news marketplace, and economic change in the media industries. There is a lively discussion among journalists about the impact of media conglomerates, technology, and shifting consumer preferences on their profession and on how they do their job.[3] Since these trends have affected international print and broadcast coverage, the journalists' professional concerns are worth a thumbnail review.

Most striking, perhaps, is the strong feeling among print journalists that sinking circulation numbers have led to an important power shift in the newsroom away from what might be termed "old-fashioned news judgment" toward serving up entertainment and advertising to targeted market segments.[4]

"The design and marketing people are in the ascendant over the editorial people in the desperate move by newspapers to find a niche to win and hold readers," said George Krimsky, former head of AP World

Service's news department. "The attention span of readers is shorter, and people spend less time now on newspapers. So to give readers as much as possible for the time they have available, newspapers are producing sectioned, zoned, packaged products in which there is something for everyone. People want something quick, and they want it to be interesting and provocative, if possible. It is not enough to be important: it has to make your toes curl."

One formula for giving TV-acculturated readers what they want is to make newspapers more like television—shorter stories, more pictures, and more color. The premier example of this is *USA Today*, which dubs itself "McPaper." Reporter Paul Taylor of the *Washington Post* says, "The running joke is that if *USA Today* continues to be a journalistic trendsetter, the Pulitzer Prize will have to include a new category—'best investigative paragraph.' "[5]

The three major newsmagazines have felt the same pressures and have undergone major graphics surgery since the mid-1980s. All are now more visual—shorter articles, more pictures, more headlines, more color, more graphs, and more white space. "People who listen to two-second sound bites are not going to be inclined to read nine-page cover stories," commented *Time*'s Van Voorst. "Now the cover stories are four to five [magazine] pages." It also should be noted that foreign affairs covers are firmly established as losers at the newsmagazines. The classic example of this was the 1985 Reagan-Gorbachev summit in Geneva. *Time, Newsweek,* and *U.S. News and World Report* all made it their cover story—and for all three, it was the year's worst-selling cover.[6]

As a group, journalists are notorious handwringers, but even discounting for this, there seems to be a genuine tinge of malaise among newspaper reporters. "The smell of death permeates the newspaper business these days," said *Post* media critic Howard Kurtz, who feels the job isn't as much fun as it used to be and "some fine people are drifting away from the business." Kurtz cites the case of Bill Walker, who quit to join Greenpeace after working for the *Sacramento Bee, Denver Post,* and *Fort Worth Star-Telegram.* "I belong to an entire generation of burned-out, fed-up, pissed-off reporters," Walker said. "I could not spend the rest of my life producing the shallow, sensational, trumped-up trivia that passes for news today."[7]

What happened?

Newspapers in Transition

For one thing, as television's influence has waxed, the readership of newspapers has waned:

- From 1970 to 1990 daily newspaper circulation in the United States stayed fairly flat at about 62 million, but this represented a decline in real terms because the number of households increased by 48 percent in the same period.[8]
- The trend away from newspaper readership seems particularly pronounced among younger readers. A 1990 study indicated only 30 percent of Americans under thirty-five had "read a newspaper yesterday"—compared with 67 percent in 1965.[9]
- People tend not to read the paper after work any more; they watch television. Thus, as television consolidated its hold on the evening news niche, afternoon newspapers began to die. In 1975, 57 percent of newspapers sold were afternoon editions; in 1990 the figure was 33 percent.
- Competition among newspapers also declined: at the turn of the century 500 U.S. communities had competing daily newspapers, almost all in the hands of proprietors with no other media holdings; with the rise of newspaper chains and television, the number of cities with two or more dailies owned by separate companies had fallen to 66 by 1970, and by 1990 there were only 43 (half of them served by papers with joint operating agreements, that is, separate editorial staffs, but joint business, advertising, and printing facilities).[10]

Advertising, the lifeblood of newspapers, has shifted increasingly to television. In 1950, 36 percent of all advertising money went to newspapers, and 3 percent to television. In 1970 the newspapers' share dropped to 29 percent, and then in 1990 to 25 percent; television's portion rose to 18 percent and then 22 percent in the same period.[11]

For most of the country's roughly 1,600 dailies, declining ad revenues have meant smaller newsholes, that is, nonadvertising space available for news stories.[12] It is axiomatic that newspapers will accord local news precedence over national or international items, especially when space is tight and times are tough. The foreign newshole, always tight, was tighter than ever in the early 1990s because of declining ad revenues.[13]

Readers/viewers/consumers have a finite amount of time and more media than ever vying for their attention. They want less information and more knowledge, that is, more analysis explaining the meaning of events. Even at leading dailies that pride themselves on their international coverage, swift communications and the proliferation of available information have made "combined" stories a fairly common phenomenon. At the *Los Angeles Times* the process has been dubbed "triangulation."[14]

"On certain major stories," explained Stanley Meisler, a noted Africa hand and *Los Angeles Times* correspondent since 1967, "we might have foreign correspondents on the spot who would send information back to the *L.A. Times*, who would then give it to the brilliant specialist in the Washington bureau, who would then talk to his sources and put together a story—the net result of which is a much more informed version of what is really happening. The trouble with this, apart from the fact that the sources are mainly State Department with a couple of professors thrown in, is that it negates the whole point of having a foreign correspondent—that he give you the view as he sees it in the country."

Meisler added, "When the memo came out explaining this, several foreign correspondents protested to the foreign desk. But this is all over the place, not just at the *L.A. Times*."

"Triangulation" echoes in some respects the old *Time* magazine editing approach, in which correspondents filed from various points to a New York editor who combined their input into a single, all-source finished piece. (Ironically, the newspaper trend toward writing that mimics newsmagazine style coincides with a countervailing trend in the newsmagazines themselves since the late 1980s toward more individual pieces signed by field correspondents and a less dominant role for rewrite experts.) But even if the blending of dispatches has become somewhat more common in the desking of newspaper copy, the phenomenon of editors believing that reporters in Washington know more than reporters in the field is hardly new. During the Vietnam War, when reporters like David Halberstam of the *New York Times* sent copy suggesting the war was not going well and the *Times* got a different reading from its Washington bureau, the Washington version often got the most prominent play.[15] (This is not unlike what happens when diplomats report from the field and their perspective does not square with that of Washington analysts.)

Reinforcing the point that genuine local expertise has been devalued, Meisler said he felt the significance of datelines had been diminished. He recalled covering the United Nations in 1991 when U.S. hostages were released in Lebanon. Meisler was the rewrite person, getting information from several sources, including the wire services, and his byline was on all stories. "If we had a file from a correspondent or a stringer in Damascus or Beirut, the dateline would be where the stringer was. So it would read 'Stanley Meisler and Marilyn Raschka in Beirut,' or 'Stanley Meisler and Nick Williams in Damascus,' even though I was writing the story and I was in New York. My good friend, *L.A. Times* board chairman Bob Erburu, called the newspaper's editor, Shelby Coffey, because he was concerned that they would be sending a man my age around to all those places! There was a tag line at the end of the story saying Stanley Meisler was at the U.N. and Nick Williams was in Damascus, but who reads that?"

This fudging of datelines has an echo in television news with the networks' use of film purchased from video agencies and voiced over by anchormen or hub bureau correspondents. Just as broadcast correspondents harbor reservations about voicing over film of events they have not reported themselves, so too Meisler felt it made newspaper reporting more superficial if reporters could "just grab the wires" to do their stories. "On a daily basis, we don't get to the heart of what's going on as much," he concluded. "There is more and more spot coverage. You don't have to think too much, and it tends to be hyped. Everything is momentous. I think it is TV-driven."

Owners and editors would dispute the notion that standards are slipping, and in many ways the profession has improved a good deal since I got my first job with the AP in 1972. Reporters are better educated and better paid; women and minorities are better represented in the newsroom; and communications applications have been put to use throughout the industry with great ingenuity. In short, the tools and raw material are better than ever.

But the dynamics of corporate ownership, argues former *Chicago Tribune* editor James Squires, mean that the free press is in danger of disappearing. "In the starkest terms, the news media of the 1990s are a celebrity-oriented, Wall Street-dominated, profit-driven entertainment enterprise dedicated foremost to delivering advertising images to targeted groups of consumers," he argues. "Journalism, the mirror through which the society has seen itself, has been drastically distorted, its practice commercialized and appropriated for a decidedly different purpose." [16]

Media critic Howard Kurtz sees greater scope for salvation. He feels that the chief ill of newspapers is that they have become unplugged from their readers. The solution is less "dumbing down" of newspapers and more "detailed, compelling reports on controversial subjects that simply can't be found elsewhere." Kurtz acknowledges this flies in the face of the short-term bottom line, but argues the wisdom of the investment over the long haul. [17]

I will not hazard a prediction on the ultimate evolution of newspapers, but I confess to liking Kurtz's prescription. The strength of newspapers lies in their ability to inform, not entertain. One way or another, newspapers are likely to adapt and survive, and there will continue to be a market for them.

Even if fragmentation of the market is occurring, this should not be supposed to be a bad thing. For readers interested in foreign affairs, for example, satellite publishing and syndication have already produced a distinct benefit. Newspapers with good international coverage—such as the *Los Angeles Times, New York Times, Wall Street Journal,* and

Washington Post—are now available for morning delivery in major cities throughout the country or via syndicated news services to many regional and foreign news organizations. This means not only greater availability to those who actively follow international affairs but a longer reach for those news organizations in shaping opinion on foreign policy issues. Similarly, the *Wall Street Journal* is available nationwide to members of the business and financial community.

Shock Time for Television

The 1980s were also shock time for the television industry. Since the 1960s the three major U.S. networks—ABC, CBS, and NBC—had seen audiences and advertising revenue grow steadily. But in 1981, when the cable television industry was effectively deregulated, the tide began to turn.

Only a tenth of U.S. homes had cable service in 1980, but in little more than a decade the figure climbed past 60 percent—at the networks' expense. Aggregate prime-time audience for the three majors dropped from 85.0 percent in 1980 to 62.4 percent in 1990-91. Costs continued to rise, but revenues were down. By 1990 the cable industry's revenues of almost $18 billion were double those of the three networks.

The ownership of all three networks changed hands in 1985 and 1986. In March 1985, Capital Cities Communications acquired ABC: in December, General Electric announced it had gained control of RCA, parent company of NBC; and in September 1986, investor Lawrence Tisch of the Lowes Corporation took the reins at CBS. Not surprisingly, the new business-minded corporate owners all wanted to know how CNN could put on far more news than they did for a fraction of the cost. Ken Auletta, in his chronicle of network television in the 1980s, *Three Blind Mice*, provides the following account of a dramatic 1986 meeting between NBC News President Larry Grossman and GE Chairman and CEO Jack Welch:

> Since Tom Brokaw was gaining on Dan Rather and the network was pulling ahead in prime time, Grossman said now was the time to put more, not fewer, resources into News. "S-s-s-hit!" shouted Welch, whose slight stammer was more pronounced when he was upset, as he pounded the table. "Ted Turner puts on C-C-N-N-N for twenty-four hours a day for only $100 million! Ted Turner makes $50 to $60 million. We do three hours of news. We spend $275 million and lose $100 million." [18]

Squeezed by rising costs and declining revenues and indisposed to treating their news divisions as sacred cows, the new bosses imposed economies. One of the results was that expensive bureaus in cities like Paris, Bonn, Cairo, Hong Kong, and other capitals were closed.

Television reporter Henry Champ spent two decades as a correspondent for the Canadian Broadcasting Corporation and NBC, with assignments in Vietnam, Hong Kong, Tel Aviv, Toronto, Frankfurt, Warsaw, and London. "When I first went to Europe with NBC in 1982," he recalled eleven years later, "there were fourteen full-time NBC correspondents covering the area—four in London, three in Frankfurt, two in Rome, two in Paris, two in Moscow, and one in Warsaw. Now there are three in London, none in Paris, Frankfurt, Rome, or Warsaw, and two in Moscow, for a total of five."

There were domestic cuts, too, including a decision by CBS in 1993 not to assign a correspondent to the State Department full-time, putting Pentagon correspondent David Martin in charge of both beats. Austerity budgets mean the three networks have tended to husband their powder for big, costly events like the Gulf War and Somalia. To be sure, when they focus on an issue or event, all three still produce good television reporting. Unfortunately, however, they are less inclined now to field overseas correspondents on secondary items and features. Instead, they rely more heavily on film from other sources, such as Worldwide Television News (WTN) and Reuters Television, often with voice-overs for the acquired footage supplied by anchormen or journalists in hub bureaus like London.[19]

In a related cost-cutting move, the networks have also sought film-sharing and bureau-sharing arrangements with other international broadcasters. In March 1993, for example, ABC News announced a partnership with the BBC that called for sharing of correspondents and production crews, as well as joint coverage planning. Similar alliances are bound to proliferate in years to come as the networks concentrate bureaus in key spots and continue to look for ways to reduce the expensive logistics of acquiring pictures.

"Of the kinds of material we generated in 1982," Champ said, "virtually everything would be an NBC-originated story. Every correspondent's film would have at least 80 percent NBC film. We wouldn't put the story out with someone else's footage—not that there was any great objection in principle; it's just the way things were done. There was slight use of Visnews for material from Africa, for example, or for a train crash in Spain—incidents like that, not enough to send a correspondent for, but when you might want fifteen seconds of footage, with the story read by Brokaw."

The problem with heavier reliance on agency film is quality control and truth-in-packaging. The network correspondent doing a voice-over in London may be a first-rate reporter. But he or she is writing a script for something that hasn't been covered in person and voicing it over film and images that the reporter has not been able to measure against first-hand observation for accuracy and context. It's secondhand coverage, and it rides on audience trust built up by years of firsthand reporting.[20]

As noted earlier, what disturbed broadcast correspondents most about the new corporate ownership was not just budget cutting, but the perception of a value shift. Executives saw money to be made in "cross-over" programming, that is, news shows with entertainment value ("infotainment"), whose profits went straight to the network, with no percentage siphoned off to Hollywood production companies. "The new owners," wrote Ken Auletta, "speeded the trend to hold news to the same ratings standard as entertainment shows."[21] News was a commodity, subject more than ever to market dictates. Many broadcast journalists shared the feeling of their newspaper colleagues that the calling had become too commercialized.

Despite the upheavals, and the likelihood of even more to come in a fast-evolving communications industry, the networks remained powerful forces in American journalism in the early 1990s, spending about a billion dollars a year in news coverage and commanding 60 percent of the viewing audience during their newscasts each night. But their news divisions had also become more vulnerable to the cost-cutters and the inroads of entertainment values.

CNN: Bucking the General Trend

At CNN, meanwhile, things were moving in a different direction. On 1 June 1980 CNN signed on as the first twenty-four-hour news network, serving 1.7 million cable TV households in the United States. By early 1993 this had jumped to about 130 million, with over half the viewing audience outside the United States in 140 countries and territories worldwide.

Within the United States, especially since the 1990-91 Gulf War, CNN has made significant inroads on the still-dominant position of the network news programs. It has been the network of choice for many viewers during breaking events, although the networks still dominate the evening news slots. It has also changed the way people watch TV news, and therein lies an important distinction between it and the three networks.

Despite low ratings, CNN is immensely successful. The key is its twenty-four-hour format: the news programs of the networks provide morning shows and a twenty-two-minute evening headline service, but CNN is accessible anytime. "At any given moment," writes analyst Lewis Friedland, "less than 1 percent of the American viewing audience is watching CNN. During any week, however, about 25 percent of the viewers will have checked in with CNN. In contrast, viewers watch the Big Three nightly newscasts in numbers ranging from 11 to 15 percent every night." [22]

What many viewers do not realize is that CNN has three major components: CNN, Headline News, and CNN International. CNN is the flagship U.S. report; Headline News is a set-piece, cyclical recap of current news; and CNN International is the special programming mix beamed abroad via satellite—the program U.S. embassies receive worldwide.[23] On the morning I spoke to CNN's Stuart Loory in Atlanta, he had three monitors going on the credenza opposite his desk—one for each of the three services. At one point, there was a report on CNN on women and the various benefits of estrogen, an update on fighting in Bosnia-Herzegovina on Headline News, and State Department correspondent Ralph Begleiter conducting an extended interview with Secretary of State Warren Christopher on CNN International. Loory commented that the Begleiter interview, run at length on CNNI, would likely appear on CNN or Headline News in shorter format.

From operating losses of $16 million in its start-up year, 1980, CNN moved to profits of $167 million in 1991, with income not only from cable subscription fees and advertising but also from sales to broadcasters of CNN material as supplemental video. As the networks cut news costs and reduced employees, CNN hired more, moving from 200 in its early days to more than 2,000 in 1993. Most important from the standpoint of trends in international news coverage, as the networks were closing bureaus overseas, CNN was opening new ones.

"CNN is bucking the general trend among the other networks to cut back," said CNN's Eason Jordan in April 1993. The network had opened four new bureaus (Amman, Bangkok, New Delhi, and Rio de Janeiro) in the eight months preceding our conversation, he said, bringing its total to nineteen international bureaus. In early 1994 a Johannesburg bureau raised that number to twenty. This contrasted with nine radio TV bureaus for ABC, four for CBS, and eleven offices listed worldwide for NBC.[24] "Ted [CNN founder Ted Turner] wants to have a bureau in every country on earth," Jordan said. "We'll see about that, but for sure we'll be expanding." [25]

The Body Electronic

A final word is in order about the way news organizations relate to one another, because that, too, is an important consideration for anyone briefing media representatives. Within the media, constituent parts have somewhat specialized roles.

The wire services are like a central nervous system, often alerting the press as a whole to the first signs of trouble. They lead other organizations and set the initial tone of coverage. For a majority of U.S. newspapers and radio stations, and hence a majority of U.S. readers and listeners, the wires are the primary source of foreign news. Wire service correspondents work under a great deal of deadline pressure and usually stay current in any breaking situation. They often have command of much more detail than they can use themselves. Thus, in addition to "leading" other news organizations, they have the added virtue of being excellent sources for diplomats.

Radio is immediacy. Domestic radio stations in the United States function as the public's primary hour-to-hour alerting service and provide public affairs feedback via talk shows. Ninety-nine percent of American households have radios, and the commercial radio stations—there are more than 9,000 of them—reach millions of Americans in their cars every hour. Abroad, especially in remote areas, radio is often the only source of information for many people. Domestic radio stations are often a government's primary means of communicating its policies, especially to remote areas.

Radio is also variety. It is short-format network and wire service radio spots;[26] and it is long-format programs on National Public Radio (NPR), Voice of America (VOA), and the British Broadcasting Company. It is also independent broadcasters, religious programming, pirate radios, and government-controlled outlets.

At embassies overseas the most frequent radio contact is likely to be the visiting VOA or BBC correspondent, whose in-depth work often goes beyond spot reporting to the agenda-setting job of picking up and validating stories and influencing opinion leaders. Indeed, in many countries overseas, especially where the government imposes tight controls on information, BBC and VOA broadcasts are *primary* sources of independent news. Diplomats should be mindful as well of the audiences for various local or regional radios: a timely interview with the Radio-TV Portugal or Radio France International might be the best way to get a message to Africa.

Newspapers and newsmagazines tend to play a validating role—blessing and elevating wire items by their own coverage, adding analysis, and putting issues before opinion leaders. Stories in the *New York Times, Washington Post, Los Angeles Times,* and *Wall Street Journal* have substantial impact not only with the Washington foreign policy community, but in setting the agenda for other news organizations. Reporters for these organizations will seek well-organized backgrounders with quotes, color, and context.

Even though the three major television networks often follow the wires, radio, and newspapers on breaking foreign stories, they are unmatched in their ability to concretize that story with pictures and put it before a mass audience. They consolidate the public agenda. Both the mass audience and the on-the-record nature of television normally require high-level handling, by designated officials in Washington or, less frequently, the ambassador in the field.

CNN to some extent plays multiple roles. It shares with the television networks the ability to translate a story into powerful images and then convey them to a mass audience. It competes with the wires and radio in the early-alert function. But the ability to go live and at length (and, increasingly, in depth) also gives it an important piece of the up-front influence with opinion elites that has traditionally been the realm of print media. Most important for the diplomatic practitioner, the network can quickly deliver a message, not just to a U.S. audience but to viewers and opinion leaders all over the globe.

Every print and broadcast news organization has its own audience and dynamic. Although reporters for the various media work within the same general framework of what constitutes news, they respond to different organizational requirements and deadlines. Intelligent briefers will distinguish carefully among reporters and remember when speaking to one that they are in fact speaking to a whole organization.

PART II

Terms of Engagement

Chapter 7

Ground Rules

There is no friendship without a quarrel first.
—ARABIC PROVERB

"There is no such thing as off the record," one veteran foreign correspondent said. "Sooner or later, if you say it, it always comes out. If you don't want to read about it, don't say it. Nobody can quote what you don't say."

If that is the first rule of ground rules, the second is not to forget them. It is the diplomat's responsibility to establish terms, not the journalist's. "Ground rules for attribution should be established at the beginning of conversations between Department officials and reporters. Normally, government officials take the initiative to determine ground rules," says an October 1990 memo from the State Department's Bureau of Public Affairs. "Ground rules can be mixed—information on background, some on the record—but each time, it must be made clear at the outset. The discussion should proceed only after both parties are clear on exactly how the reporter can use or attribute information." [1]

Syndicated columnist William Safire would put the onus on the correspondent: "The reporter has the responsibility to make the rules clear. Everything is on the record unless specifically restricted." [2] In fact, many of the best and most experienced reporters will go out of their way to seek clarification even when the official neglects to do so, but this is a professional courtesy, not, strictly speaking, a professional requirement.

"One thing I've learned is that you need to protect people from themselves," *New York Times* correspondent Tom Friedman said. "Sometimes people forget to say it's on background. Other reporters might say, 'Well, he said it,' but I'm a firm believer in protecting people from themselves, because you always need to go back to the well."

Another correspondent with over two decades of experience overseas and in Washington told me he would camouflage his sources at times in order to protect them. "I might say 'a senior official in the State Department,' when it's at the Department of Defense. This is just a device to protect someone, and I will even lie to [the news organization this correspondent works for] on my expense accounts in order to cover the source. If the matter ever goes to court, the court could discover from business files what I refuse to say as a matter of professional principle. You don't mislead on quality, but rather on location. The point is, I'm always alert to the consequences of what I write."

Experienced briefers maintain a healthy skepticism about ground rules. These rules are the only tool for establishing the terms of the dialogue with a reporter, but they are by no means a precise instrument. In the interviews for this book, I often asked diplomats what they would like to have known about the press at the beginning of their careers that they had had to learn the hard way. Understanding ground rules, and how to set them, was nearly always at the top of the list. So is keeping in mind that they may be stretched or broken.

For their part, reporters find few things more aggravating than to pick up an interesting tidbit and then have the source try to stuff it back in the bottle by saying it was off the record.

"Reporters assume on-the-record unless told otherwise," said Mary Curtius, State Department correspondent for the *Boston Globe* and a former Middle East correspondent for both the *Globe* and the *Christian Science Monitor.* "With most diplomats, it's not a problem. They say at the beginning, 'This is on background, attributable to Western diplomats,' or whatever it is. Nothing is worse than having someone say at the end, 'Oh, by the way, you can't use any of that.' "

Don Oberdorfer, longtime *Washington Post* diplomatic correspondent, said it is ridiculous if the State Department does not teach diplomats ground rules, as appears to be the case. "Officers say 'off-the-record' when they mean 'background,' and the press constantly has to correct them. Most officials have only a dim idea what ground rules are, and there is no reason for that. If FSOs can learn the intricacies of how the Sri Lankan parliament works, they can certainly learn the ground rules for day-to-day intercourse with reporters. I tend to give officials the benefit of the doubt when they talk first and say afterward that what they said is 'off-the-record.' But that's silly, there is no excuse for that."

Understanding "Limits"

When I was a reporter in Beirut, I learned well the proverb at the head of this chapter that there is no friendship without a quarrel first. It is an idea that has some relevance as well to the relationship between diplomat and reporter.

In the Middle East, the concept of *hudud* (pronounced hu-DUDE), or "limits," rules both interpersonal and interstate relations. The idea is that there are certain limits or bounds for appropriate behavior—and these are governed by status, ability, and circumstances. Thus, in Beirut it is common to say in Arabic of an impudent or rude person, "He doesn't know his limits." If there is any uncertainty on the part of one person about another with whom he must deal, there will be a testing and probing process, which results either in one side establishing dominance or in a clash because one has pushed the other to the limit of his tolerance. In this way, a mutually agreed "limit" is established. Hence the proverb. (Hence also, incidentally, the Israeli concept of "red lines" setting limits of acceptable Syrian military activity in south Lebanon.)[3]

In the same way, it is vital for diplomats and reporters to understand at the outset of any discussion what the limits are. The problems come when one side or the other is not clear about this. If there is going to be a quarrel, it is best to have it before the briefing, not after.

"Don't be bashful," Deputy Assistant Secretary of State David Mack advised. Mack, who served as ambassador to the United Arab Emirates from 1986 to 1989 and as deputy assistant secretary of state from 1990 to 1993 in the Bureau of Near Eastern and South Asian Affairs, is a leading expert on the Arabian Peninsula and Persian Gulf affairs. As such, during and after the Gulf War he did many on-the-record and background sessions with both U.S. and foreign journalists. "In the beginning you should be very businesslike. Don't hesitate to say: 'Wait a minute, everything I say is on background, only diplomatic sources.' You've got to say this up front."

On the Record

> **On the Record**—*Information may be quoted directly and attributed to the official by name and title.*[4]

Whether in Washington or overseas, there is no more sensitive or important issue than speaking to the press on the record. In Washington, the principal on-the-record activity is the noon briefing, which is conducted by the State Department spokesman with input from the entire bureaucracy. In addition, senior officials may grant on-the-record interviews and make other public appearances. Most of this is done at deputy assistant secretary level and up, and coordinated through the Press Office in the Bureau of Public Affairs.[5]

Former spokesman Richard Boucher explained the rationale simply: "You don't give your own opinion on events without vetting it upstairs, at the policy level. That is, you don't talk about it unless and until you're sure it's policy. I have no objection to responsible people talking on a subject they understand. The problem is when people are flogging their own agenda."

Similarly, at an embassy, guidelines about who speaks on the record should be made clear to all employees and all agencies in the mission. There was a general consensus among State Department and USIA officers that this ordinarily should be strictly limited to the ambassador and the public affairs officer, or PAO. At one geographic bureau I visited, the public affairs officer was at some pains to stress this point, noting that the Agency for International Development (AID) director at one of the posts in his region "was trying to upstage the ambassador."

On-the-record appearances overseas with major U.S. media must be cleared with the Bureau of Public Affairs, but there are gray areas. Fast-breaking crisis situations periodically arise when U.S. ambassadors come under sustained and intense media attention. Each case is different, but when this occurs the department may decide to give individual envoys freer rein to pursue an on-the-spot public information strategy. Examples of this are Ambassador Edward Gnehm Jr., in Kuwait after its liberation from Iraqi occupation in 1991, and Special Envoy Robert Oakley during U.S.-assisted relief operations in Somalia early in 1993.

Since such situations are, in effect, exceptions to the normal chain of command from ambassador to mother geographic bureau (and Bureau of Public Affairs) in Washington to seventh-floor policy makers, the bureaucratic ambiguity they entail can generate tensions. Perhaps the best-known example of ambassadorial tap dancing was Thomas Pickering's high-profile dealings with the media during the Gulf War. Stanley Meisler, who covered the United Nations for the *Los Angeles Times* during Pickering's tenure, reported that a senior State Department official groused that "Pickering would get from A to D all right. The problem is, he wouldn't go through B and C." In other words, some in Washington were ill at ease not with the U.N. envoy's performance on policy grounds, but rather with his autonomy. Meisler felt there was an added element: "Pickering was too much of a star."

Philip Arnold served as PAO at the U.S. mission to the United Nations during the war. He noted that Washington tended to be extremely restrictive about talking to the press, but events frequently broke quickly and prior coordination was not always practical. "It undermined our position if we didn't speak to the press, so we did an enormous amount of backgrounding up here at the U.N. Pickering did a lot of ad hoc speaking to television and reporters when he came out of meetings.

It wasn't an interview, it wasn't a TV program, so it was not, technically speaking, a violation of the restrictions. He was mainly just stating the U.S. position. Occasionally something new would be said because the situation was developing so fast, but on the other hand, if he didn't do it, the Iraqi and Yemeni ambassadors would be out there putting their positions forward."

Pickering himself would not comment on reported tensions between New York and Washington, but he did expand on the uses of the press during the war. He said one of the best ways to get the U.S. message to other U.N. delegations was via the media. "We were pretty thin on the ground, and CNN is a wonderful amplifying mechanism. I also thought it important that *I*, rather than the British, French, Iraqis, or others, explain what it was that *we* in the United States wanted."

A U.S. ambassador serving in the Middle East during the Gulf conflict was emphatic in his support for Pickering's performance at the United Nations during the crisis. "It is wrong to suggest that Tom Pickering acted improperly or in some disloyal way in his up-front handling of the press at the U.N. during the Gulf War. I believe he was very effective, and I, for one, am glad he kept on doing it."

Background

> **Background**—*Attribution is to State Department or Administration officials, as determined by the official. The officials may be paraphrased or quoted directly.*[6]

This is the most common format for talking to journalists, because it allows officials to describe facts and policy more fully than they can on the record.

"President Johnson loved this kind of stuff," said Oberdorfer. "I was in a briefing once where he used five different kinds of attribution in one session: on the record, background, deep background, off the record, and *really* off the record!"

Since a relatively few senior officials do the lion's share of on-the-record work, most diplomats will encounter the press on background. A typical example is the political or economic officer overseas who briefs a visiting newspaper correspondent. In Washington, too, much of the briefing is done on background. Indeed, one regional bureau public affairs officer told me he did *everything* on background. "I never go on the record, ever. But I find I can tell almost any story on background. You should engage, help them tell their story, and help them understand."

Former spokesman Richard Boucher advocates mixing the ground rules as necessary at formal briefings. "The best way to handle briefings," he said, "is not exclusively on background but rather to do things on the record up front and then go to background . . . to show the parameters of our thinking, to let the reporters know what has been discussed and why, perhaps to let them know our ideas about what's coming up next, and to give them the view of foreign governments—which we cannot discuss on the record (it is for those governments to talk about on the record), yet the reporters need to know about it and we need to consider it."

When agreeing on attribution for background, the diplomat should consider his tone. He can usually make his wishes just as plain and firm in a polite voice as he can in a peremptory one. One skilled public affairs officer, who maintains excellent ongoing relations with the press and tries hard to be as forthcoming as possible when backgrounding, said he nevertheless took great care in the beginning when establishing ground rules. "What I will say is, 'This is on background. You may say "a State Department official." ' Then I will ask the reporter, 'Do you agree?' If I don't hear him respond affirmatively that he agrees to those ground rules, I will repeat the question. Sometimes a new reporter, or a reporter from out of town, might say, 'My editor says I can't do that,' in which case I simply say, 'Well, I'm sorry, these are my ground rules and you either do it my way or we don't do it.' "

A good reporter will understand the stakes; his main concern will be to get as much information as possible, not sour his source for a marginal gain on the phrasing of background attribution. There may still be some negotiating from time to time. Oberdorfer, for example, felt that officials sometimes overplay their hand in telling reporters what attribution to use. "They might say, 'You can say a senior administration official.' I don't like that. Now, obviously, you can't say 'a senior official high in the European bureau'—that's the same as naming someone.[7] But when people say don't use 'a White House official' or 'a State Department official,' I don't like it. Sometimes, though, I might honor a personal request to say 'an administration official' as opposed to 'a State Department official,' and sometimes I'll do it on my own, because I know the consequences of what I write."

Overseas, instead of State Department or administration officials, the background reference usually becomes "Western diplomats," or "diplomatic sources." Former under secretary of state David Newsom, in his book *Diplomacy and the American Democracy*, explained the need for these conventions. "The American press and public often question the insistence on anonymity by U.S. officials when providing information. The official may insist that [the] story may be attributed to 'a Western diplomatic official' or 'a government source.' This is done to protect an embassy in such circumstances. It is also part of a diplomatic convention that dilutes the official nature of a statement if the actual source is not given. The pressure is less, in such cases, to reply if it is not clearly 'an official statement.' " [8]

In this regard, use of "U.S. diplomats" does not suffice. On the one hand, the diplomats avoid giving their names and titles, but on the other, they still put the post on the record, even if informally. Officials should insist on more generalized sourcing, such as "Western diplomats," if there is a need to minimize the risk that the host government will feel compelled to react officially.

Yet another reason for brand-x sourcing overseas is that the diplomat has no idea how the information he imparts will be used and played back, once it is briefed. It could be juxtaposed with other sources' information that is less accurate, or is at odds with U.S. information, or that otherwise tends to distort the original material. Or the diplomat's briefing could simply be misunderstood and misrepresented.

If the diplomat has reason to think what is briefed will be sensitive for the host government, he or she should also consider checking whether the reporter is visiting *other* Western diplomats in town. This is certainly true in many Middle Eastern countries, where the security services keep careful track of the comings and goings of reporters. "If the local intelligence service knows that the reporter has seen only one Western diplomat, and that is you, and if the reporter says 'a Western diplomat,' then you're blown to no good end," said April Glaspie, former ambassador to Iraq and an experienced Middle East briefer.

In addition to diluting the official nature of a briefing, an important function of briefing on background is that it allows the diplomat greater protection for his or her sources. "What many reporters don't understand is that we have an obligation under the law to protect classified information," Ambassador Pickering said. "It's similar to the problem reporters have of protecting sources. How we get and protect information is subject to certain rules. You may not be *able* to make a wholesale effort to downgrade something, because you need to go back to the originating agency or source. Usually, though, people will talk on background, so that the reporter will not be misled and we can protect the source of the information."

Not infrequently, to the dismay of embassies in the field, officials in Washington will talk more freely about an embassy's sources than the post does, and burn them. When this happens, it can produce considerable friction between Washington and the field.

One experienced State Department official took diplomatic maneuverings over Iraq at the United Nations in 1991-92 as an example of how effective press backgrounding can advance policy goals. After Iraqi president Saddam Hussein unleashed his armed forces on rebellious Kurdish and Shia populations in the north and south, triggering large refugee outflows to Turkey and Iran, U.N. Security Council Resolution 688 *demanded* that Iraq cease repression of its civilian population and termed such actions a threat to international peace and security. Its predecessor, UNSC Resolution 687 establishing the conditions for a cease-fire, had been much tougher: sometimes dubbed "the mother of all resolutions," it expressly cited Chapter VII enforcement provisions of the U.N. Charter and *decided* that Iraq would surrender its weapons of mass destruction, facilitate the return of all Kuwaiti property, account for missing Kuwaiti citizens, and pay compensation for war damages. It also guaranteed the inviolability of the Iraq-Kuwait border, as delineated by a U.N. boundary commission.

Although Resolution 688 was not explicitly grounded in Chapter VII, the language it used about a "threat to international peace and security" was deliberately chosen to meet the requirements for Chapter VII action. The hard political fact was that some countries—however odious or wrong they might have considered the particular actions of the Iraqi regime—simply did not want to set a strong precedent for Security Council interference in cases of internal repression. Therefore, the Chapter VII authority in Resolution 688 was left implicit.

Although some people questioned whether Resolution 688 was sufficient to protect civilians in Iraq and demanded that the United States get a stronger Security Council mandate, the State Department official called this "a mischievous position," explaining, "You *can't* get a stronger mandate at the U.N. You've got to take what you've got and assert it, or abandon the idea and let these people be killed." Getting a better resolution was "an ideal, but it was completely impractical and dangerous, because it undercut the assertion you're making right now. The press spokesman can't deal with that in a direct way. You can't say the Chinese are the bad guys, that they're going to veto a stronger 687-type resolution. You can't finger India or the others. All you will do is damage your relations with them. But you *can* do it on background."

Deep Background

> **Deep Background**—*No attribution is permitted and no direct quotes. The reporter may use the information to help present the story or to gain deeper understanding of the subject, but the wisdom is his, not his source's.*[9]

This is a briefing format that will meet with much more resistance from reporters than simple background. As *New York Times* columnist William Safire has written, "*Deep background* and *not for attribution* mean, 'This is your idea, not mine'; good reporters try for an upgrade into background." [10]

A Department of State Press Office memo circulated in 1980 said, "Obviously, this ground rule permits you somewhat greater scope for frankness, but it also asks the newsman to assume a greater personal burden of responsibility for what he writes since there is no visible source for the facts. In turn, the officer assumes an even greater burden of moral responsibility not to mislead or misinform the reporter." [11]

When briefings are on deep background, it means diplomats give reporters the information; but if the reporters use it, it must well up in the story as if it were a product of their own knowledge. Although they could not pin the information on U.S. officials, they could lead in with, "It has been learned that. . . . " Oberdorfer told me, however, that this was the "old way" of handling deep background, especially in the late 1950s and 1960s. "But the other way is to just use it," he said. "For example, 'On January 14 the State Department informed the White House that such and such was taking place,' or just say 'reporters were told.' That doesn't attribute it to anyone. When things are very sensitive, officials want to get as far away from being the source as they can. Frankly, I don't see a lot of difference between 'an administration official' and 'reporters were told.' There are a zillion administration officials."

One department official who has dealt frequently with the press gave as an example of the use of "deep background" discussions with reporters on Arab and Palestinian reaction to the Israeli deportation of Islamic activists of the Hamas group in early 1993.

> You may not want to tell reporters on the record, or even as a State Department official, what different governments said. But you can go on deep background and say, "Look, there is not a government in the region that is not threatened to some extent by groups like this, by the cousins of Hamas in the region." So I would say to the reporter, "How much sympathy do you think they have?" And you could point out that the governments are in one mode with their public positions and in another with their private positions. You can give context that way on stuff you don't want quoted—for example, if you don't want to see a story that says "a State Department official says Egypt doesn't like Hamas."

Because of the tremendous amount of confusion that exists among reporters and officials alike over ground rules, some diplomats stipulate not only the form of the attribution, but which parts of the briefing may be quoted.

One senior U.S. diplomat with extensive briefing experience told me he *always* started out on deep background and negotiated specific exceptions with the reporter. "I do it on a very strict basis, no attribution. I will conduct the interview on that basis," he said. "I would say that, if you find a quote that is particularly useful, and I would anticipate that there would be one or two, then we can go back over our notes and jointly determine how it should be attributed. In addition to setting ground rules, I tell them that if my name appears in any way in the article, they will not be welcome again."

The "deep background" convention originated with Ernest Lindley, a reporter for the *New York Herald Tribune* and *Newsweek*, and later an assistant to Secretary of State Dean Rusk. It was therefore first known as "the Lindley Rule." William Safire quotes Lindley as telling him in 1968, "The Lindley Rule was laid down early in the Truman Administration to enable high-ranking officials to discuss important matters—especially those involving international and military affairs—without being quoted or referred to in any way. It was, and is, a rule of no attribution—thus differing from the usual 'background rule' permitting attribution to 'official sources' or 'U.S. officials,' etc." [12]

Diplomats and reporters alike should take particular care with the phrase "not for attribution" because there appears to be a considerable divergence of views among even very experienced practitioners about the exact meaning of this formula. Safire notes that "*not for attribution, in its strict interpretation, means not for attribution to anybody or anything.*" [13] I found this also was the understanding most diplomats had of the term.

But a number of reporters—both Washington and foreign correspondents—understood "not for attribution" to be equivalent to "background." Indeed, it was seen by some as a nonspecific formula allowing the reporter latitude to use whatever form of background sourcing he deemed appropriate. In other words, these reporters took "not for attribution" to mean not for attribution *on the record*, whereas diplomats generally understood it to mean not for attribution *at all*.

In this situation, clarifying intent is obviously vital: there can be a world of difference between "no attribution" and "not for attribution." Even with veteran correspondents, the most prudent course for any official setting ground rules is to employ the term "deep background," noting explicitly that it means *no attribution at all*.

Off the Record

> **Off the Record**—*The information may not be used in any form whatsoever and is meant only for the education of the reporter.* [14]

This is the most confusing, and misused, category of all. But "off the record" has a very precise meaning, and because it is so restrictive, its use should be rare. It does *not* mean "don't quote me." It means do not use the information I give you in any way, except for your own planning purposes. If the secretary of state is planning an overseas trip, an official in the Bureau of Public Affairs might tell reporters off the record that the trip is planned for a certain date and that specific issues might be on the agenda. That way, the reporter can make preparations to cover it, even if he can't write a story about it.

In this vein, Richard Boucher said he had once been asked by someone in the State Department why he had told reporters, and not State Department officers, about an upcoming trip by the secretary. "The fact is," he said, "I trust our reporters more, if I give them information they need for their planning purposes, to keep it confidential. But if I spread it in the building, it will increase the number of people who know what's going on, and the more people that know about it, unfortunately, the faster it leaks. Then it will be in the press when we don't want it in the press."

Boucher gave another example of an off-the-record briefing: "Suppose we were going to put a call in to [Russian president Boris] Yeltsin. The call has not occurred yet. To prevent a wrong story, we would tell the reporter off the record that we're going to put a call in, but we don't know if it will come off or not. This is not something we would want to see in print, but it would be for the reporter's information only and to prevent a wrong story getting out."

The 1980 Press Office memo cited earlier aptly says, "Nothing substantive should be discussed 'off the record' for the good and sufficient reason that nothing substantive ever stays off the record." The point is, it is unfair to provide a news nugget to reporters and then ask them not to use it. This puts them in the position of having to choose between responsibility to source and responsibility to story.

Several reporters observed to me that it was better to say nothing at all. "Don't assume anything you say is off the record," said one veteran correspondent. "Journalists talk to each other. Somehow, at some point, it is likely to filter into the news columns, however indirectly." According to Oberdorfer, "Any official worth his salt knows if you tell a person something it's not going to be a total secret—at least it's in the reporter's head. If you tell more than one reporter something that is so sensitive that by no means should it ever be in print, you're just kidding yourself, whatever the ground rules are."

The following story from William Clark Jr., a former ambassador to India who strongly favors briefing on the record as much as possible, illustrates some of the pitfalls of going "off the record."

When Clark was consul in Sapporo, Japan, in the mid-1960s, the number two man in the embassy came up from Tokyo to the consulate, and Clark arranged a press briefing for him. At the beginning of the briefing, the U.S. diplomat made clear he was speaking "off the record," and proceeded to answer questions quite circumspectly. At the end, an irate Japanese reporter came up and said, "You got us here under false pretenses. You told us it was going to be off the record, and that means you're going to tell us something. But you didn't tell us anything that's not in the public domain!"

The reporter had a right to be angry. Although the diplomat did not violate the proscription against providing anything substantive off the record, he did violate common sense. He cannot call a group of reporters to a briefing and then tell them what they already know, whatever the ground rules. If he tells them absolutely nothing new when he has gone "off the record"—and thereby heightened expectations for a juicy briefing—he adds insult to injury. If he tells them nothing "off the record," but what he actually meant to do was tell them nothing on background, he adds unprofessionalism to insult and injury.

It is possible the Japanese journalists themselves did not know the difference between off the record and background. But they surely knew they should have been given more than they got. A journalist's time, no less than a diplomat's, is valuable, and officials have an obligation not to waste it. If the diplomat in Sapporo wanted to be circumspect, he should have done the briefing on the record. That way, the result at least would have met with lower expectations. If he was not authorized by the ambassador to speak on the record nor prepared to say anything on background, he should not have done the briefing in the first place. Whatever the case, he clearly should *not* have been "off the record."

Substance over Form

Briefing styles vary widely: from envoys like William Clark, who do virtually everything on the record, to those who do it all on a deep background basis, negotiating specific exceptions with reporters. Both poles, and all variations in between, are paths in quest of the same thing: a burn-free briefing.

"There is widespread misunderstanding in and out of the profession about what these things mean," said *Time* correspondent Bruce Van Voorst, commenting on ground rules. "It's important to know what the rules are from the beginning when you talk to somebody—especially when you, the diplomat, are talking to a stranger or a correspondent you don't know. You can't say halfway into the conversation, 'By the way, that was on background.'"

I asked several experienced reporters what kind of briefing they would prefer: completely on the record or completely deep background.

The answer was consistent: Reporters are much less concerned with the ground rules for attribution than they are with the quality of the information conveyed.

So the diplomat should set the ground rules clearly and then, whatever they are, be sure he or she has something to say.

Chapter 8

Preparations
The Five P's

> When the highest type of men hear Tao,
> They diligently practice it.
> When the average type of men hear Tao,
> They half believe in it.
> When the lowest type of men hear Tao,
> They laugh heartily at it.
>
> —Lao-tzu

Secretary of State James Baker III paid scrupulous attention to materials prepared for his congressional testimony. The word in the bureaucracy was that he had a rule of thumb dubbed "The Five P's": Poor Preparation Equals Piss-Poor Performance. Bureaucratic apocrypha or not, the Five P's are a darn good rule, one any diplomat would do well to adopt in preparing for a meeting with a reporter.

Whether preparing for a briefing in the embassy or a gauntlet of local journalists after a meeting with the foreign minister, prudent diplomats will take a few minutes before any contact to anticipate questions and consider answers. They will think about the story the reporters are likely to go away with and what its headline will be. Time and again in interviews, experienced diplomatic practitioners returned to the importance of planning ahead and having a message.

"This is not a hard thing to do," said Assistant Secretary for Inter-American Affairs Alexander Watson, "but people tend to forget to do it. You come out of the minister's office, you're asked what you talked about, and you can get flustered."

Similarly, Phyllis Oakley, spokeswoman for Secretary of State George Shultz, said, "The principal thing that makes people good is that they have a clear idea of what they want to accomplish. They have a purpose, and they believe in a policy they want to promote. This is the clue to dealing with the press. You answer some of their questions, but you're also there to get a message out."

Having a message means being prepared. To prepare properly, diplomats must have a clear sense of what they want to achieve in a meeting.

To be sure, articulation of U.S. policy should be one objective. As government officials, diplomats have an ethical responsibility to present as persuasively as possible the views of the administration they serve. Whether they agree with those views or not is beside the point. The situation is not unlike that of a lawyer. "The question might be raised," one ambassador told me, "how a lawyer can advocate the innocence of a person he knows to be guilty. You must think of it as a legitimate part of a legitimate process. You are the agent of that person, regardless of your views."

The heart of the diplomatic profession is advocacy. But if it is to be coherent, the explanation of a policy must start with the policy's formulation, not follow as a public relations afterthought. Simple message programming is not enough. Officials must also make a serious effort to inform. Journalists will not be satisfied with a flat statement of policy, or with having the official guidance read to them. They will be looking not only for facts, but for a sense of purpose. They will want to know not only what the objectives are, but what the choices were and why they were made the way they were.

Set Pieces, Walk-Pasts, and Embassy Briefings

The high end of the spectrum of press contacts is when a diplomat has the opportunity to appear regularly and in a significant way as a spokesman for U.S. foreign policy, as Thomas Pickering did while serving as U.S. ambassador to the United Nations during the Gulf War. His walks back and forth across the road from the U.S. mission to the U.N. headquarters building became a daily press stakeout. I asked Pickering what sort of mental checklist he would run down in preparing for a meeting or a press appearance. He addressed two different situations: the set-piece appearance and the walk-past.

> [For a set-piece appearance] I would ask myself, What's going on that will provide the reporters with a newspeg, and that will give me an opportunity, as well as a challenge? My style is to prepare fairly thoroughly and use the resources of the people I have. A favorite technique is to get them to ask me the hard questions. I make a point of not asking for the answers—I want the toughest questions in any format. Then we would review the session and I'd get their input. I'd ask what they thought the reaction would be, whether there would be any backlash to what I had said, whether there were any additional facts I needed to have, and so forth.
>
> [On a walk-past] I always thought to myself, What is it that the American

people want to know about what we are trying to do? I'd either focus directly on our objectives, or indirectly try to give a sense of our objectives. Generally, I find it's much better to underpromise and overdeliver. For example, I would say, "This is the flow of events and stay tuned" rather than "Tomorrow we will pass a resolution 10 to 3."

It's important to think through what it is that an audience may know about a question. I would try to find a way to capsulize what I wanted to say, and to state it clearly.

My instinct is always to go back to first principles. What is the policy? How have we explained it? How have we dealt with the issue at hand? What can we say now? If you're doing your job, it's rare that the press comes up with an issue that can't be dealt with.

Many of these same principles can be applied in routine media contacts like embassy briefings. The format and purpose of an embassy briefing will differ somewhat, however, because overseas the information flow is two-way, more often than it is at home. Embassy briefers therefore should have an additional objective: to consider not only what they should convey, but what useful information they might be able to obtain. "Sometimes," Ambassador April Glaspie observed, "we may not be able to see the minister. Or if we do, it may not be diplomatic for us to ask the question. But journalists can."

When Phillip Habib was ambassador to South Korea, he had an iron-clad rule that he always wanted to be the first to see American journalists who came to town. He wanted to tell reporters what to look for, and then meet them again before they left to see what they found out. Recalled Stanley Zuckerman, his press attaché, "Habib wanted to be the first because he wanted to give them questions to ask others," not the other way around, with them asking him other people's questions. "He liked and respected journalists and they understood this," Zuckerman added. "He also understood that they could turn an issue upside down."

When Don Oberdorfer was *Washington Post* correspondent in Tokyo for three years in the 1970s, he went to Korea about twenty-five times while Habib was ambassador there. Oberdorfer, who had known Habib in Saigon when Habib was political counselor for Ambassador Henry Cabot Lodge, recalled:

The first time I went [to Seoul], I called him up and went to see him. Habib said, "Look, I'd like you to do something. I'd appreciate it if, whenever you're here, before you go back to Tokyo, you just stop in and visit." Well, I respected Habib and I did it. I'd sit there, and he'd say, "What do you think about the situation?" And we'd talk, and he'd rarely tell me anything I didn't know. He was very cautious like that.

One Friday Habib said, "When are you going back to Tokyo?" I said, "I'm going tomorrow." He said, "Well, don't." I said, "Why?" and he said, "Well, goddammit, I'm not going to spell it out for you, just don't!" Habib was very profane like that sometimes. He said, "I'm just telling you, don't. Take my advice." So I took his advice and canceled my flight. The next day, the president fired the director of the KCIA [the Korean intelligence service]. Now the head of the KCIA was the second most powerful man in the country. It was a very big story and I was the only correspondent there.

I always felt it was part of Phil Habib's way of paying me back, his way of showing his appreciation that we kept those lines open.

Attending to Opportunity

Claude Salhani is one of the premier photographers of the war in Lebanon, providing pictures since the outbreak of civil strife in 1975 to the Beirut daily *An Nahar*, the French photo agencies Sygma and Sipa Press, United Press International, and Reuters. A Beirut native, Salhani speaks Arabic, French, Italian, Spanish, and English. He is experienced and attuned to the many dangers of operating in the city. In 1983 he accompanied some U.S. Marines on foot patrols through an area they called "Hooterville," the predominantly Shia neighborhoods east of the Marine Corps encampment at Beirut Airport.

"The marines went out, and kids would wave at them and smile and shout," Salhani said; and when the patrol went back for debriefing, he stood against the back wall, listening. The officers asked the men what they saw, and they reported that everything was fine. "People were real nice. They were waving and everything."

After the briefing, Salhani went up to the marine officers and said, "I know it's none of my business, but you guys really ought to get some Arabic speakers out there. Just because those people are waving doesn't mean they're being friendly. The men didn't understand what they were saying. They may have looked friendly, but they didn't sound friendly." Behind those smiles and waves, the photographer told the officers, the residents of Hooterville were actually cursing the marines. "They were saying, 'By the [private parts] of your sister, you bastard, I'm going to stab you in the back some day.' This is not exactly a valentine card."

The point is, journalists can be valuable sources of information, not only for marines but for diplomats, not only overseas but in Washington. "I can't tell you how many times reporters have come in and given me information and views that I wouldn't otherwise have gotten," remarked then assistant secretary for Near East affairs Edward Djerejian. "This helps foreign policy makers a great deal. But it is something that is dimly—and I stress the word 'dimly'—perceived here."

On breaking stories journalists often sweep up information that the embassy lacks. In addition, there are frequently situations where they have more access than diplomats—for example, contacts with the Palestine Liberation Organization. In 1977, when April Glaspie was a political officer in Egypt, the Palestinian parliament-in-exile, the Palestine

National Council (PNC), held a meeting in Cairo. It was the first PNC session since 1974, that is, since before the start of the war in Lebanon, and discussions at the conference were expected to be an important indicator of how Palestinian attitudes toward the peace process were developing. Because of a ban on contacts with the PLO, however, U.S. diplomats could neither attend the meeting as observers nor talk directly to PLO officials. "It was terribly important for us to know what the PLO was thinking," Glaspie said, "and the American embassy was able to file three cables a day on that conference. Why? Because the U.S. reporters elected someone—on their own, not at our prompting—to come brief us three times a day. Then we'd meet at the end of the day and discuss what it all meant. We really could help each other."

Another occasion she recalled was the 1985-86 Syrian clampdown on the forces of PLO leader Yasir Arafat in Tripoli, Lebanon. The fighting was intense, and various PLO factions invited journalists to visit Tripoli to view the situation for themselves. Glaspie was in Damascus, and television reporters coming out of Lebanon shared their video. She said, "I saw what was going on, and I could help them interpret what they showed me, for example, by telling them what was written in Arabic on the side of a tank."

Similarly, Edmund Hull, then political counselor at Embassy Tunis, had extensive contact with journalists while working with U.S. Ambassador to Algeria Christopher Ross to cover—at one remove—a 1988 PNC meeting in Algiers. "The PLO was struggling to come to terms with our terms for discussions," Hull said. "There was a lot of contact with reporters and it was used to educate journalists that what was at stake was not the simple question of the PLO accepting Resolution 242 and automatically having a dialogue commence. The PLO was likely to say things that could be read in different ways. The idea was to avoid suggesting they had met conditions, but not ignore the real progress that was being made." When the PLO did finally meet U.S. terms for dialogue, Ambassador to Tunisia Robert Pelletreau conducted the discussions with PLO officials in Tunis, and Hull continued background sessions with the reporters who visited the Tunisian capital.

Before meeting a reporter, Hull said, he would try to determine what the journalist wanted to talk about, for example, the PLO or Tunisian politics, so that "if the journalist asked, I would have a good sense of the U.S. policy position. I would have the recent guidance and know what the State Department had been saying. But reporters mostly did not want just the official line. They wanted a reading of the significance of something they would have heard and would ask if there was anything new there. They would want to compare what they'd heard from other sources. So I would listen, and give them an honest opinion.

For example, I might point out that so and so is in the DFLP[1] and is not a mainstream person. Or I might note that another person is a self-promoter and doesn't always reflect accurately what the institution is thinking."

In addition, Hull would be keyed to what *he* wanted to find out from the reporter. "Perhaps I wanted to check out something a British diplomat had told me. Or I might be trying to get a feel for the in-fighting or dynamics in the PLO, what Abu Mazin was pushing as opposed to Abu Iyad." [2]

VOA correspondent Douglas Roberts noted two different approaches by reporters to embassy briefings:

> In one, you go in on a specific subject, and you have a set of questions you want to follow up on—for example, what's the situation with the PLO? What's the government of Tunisia doing on one issue or another?
>
> Then there is the more general briefing, where you have just gone from Cairo to Sudan and you're looking to find out what the story in the country is. You try out various ideas and comments and you look for elaboration from the diplomat. Maybe you're even looking for direction and this is an opportunity for the diplomat. If you're in Kuwait, and you're thinking of doing a story on the emir's 140th wife, and the diplomat gives you quotes on how a recent prodemocracy meeting was the most representative gathering since the foundation of the state, then you've got a better story and you're off in a different direction.

The briefing, then, is laden with opportunity: opportunity to provide the reporter with facts and context; opportunity to enunciate and explain U.S. policy; opportunity to get the firsthand observations of an active and skilled observer; and opportunity to suggest lines of inquiry that might not have occurred to the reporter.

Getting Organized

Even if newly arrived in country, reporters usually will have a few specific story ideas when they come to the embassy briefing. If they have been in the country for some time, the correspondents may have gaps to fill and analysis to cross-check. In either case, the embassy public affairs officer, when setting up meetings, should try to get a sense of what the journalists are working on and collect for potential briefers any items already filed.

Just as the reporters come prepared to the meeting, so too should the diplomats—by having clearly in mind what kind of story they would like to have come out of the briefing. This is particularly important in a group session, where officials may get buffeted by questions from different directions. In this situation, they need to understand both what the message is and what it is not. The briefers are there to convey a point of view, not just to answer questions.

"When I walk down the hall to that briefing room," former spokesman Richard Boucher said, "I try to tell myself what it is I want to say. If you're clear about what you want to say, you'll find five different ways to do it."

In a background briefing for an individual reporter, there may or may not be a specific policy message to convey, but it's always best to have a few clear-cut ideas to get across, keyed to the story the reporter will be working on. When preparing for a meeting with the reporter of a major news organization, the diplomat should set aside a few minutes before the session to think about what he or she wants to say. The main items to review are background, key points to make, and quotes. A thumbnail outline may be useful as a general road map for the meeting.

The diplomat should first consider whether the basic background needed is at hand, such as texts of relevant policy statements, figures on population, or recent voting results. If not, it should be gathered. Most posts have considerable unclassified background information and analysis a reporter would find useful.[3] The more background the official can hand the journalist up front, the better both sides can use their limited time in the meeting.

If the reporter is new to the area or the issues, it is useful to offer a brief presentation at the outset, and then take questions. Unless the reporter is coming in on a very narrow issue, he or she will very often appreciate this. This not only gives both sides a common baseline, but provides the journalist with a quick snapshot of how the diplomat sizes up the situation. No matter how brilliant the nonresident journalist, the diplomat in country should have an edge over the circuit rider in understanding the interplay of various issues. "An intelligent man can make up the lack of everything," Metternich observed, "except experience."

Having reviewed U.S. policy and general background, the diplomat should then consider how to benefit from the reporter's presence. (Several diplomats commented on this. Ambassador Samuel Lewis said of his media contacts in Israel, "I tried to be as responsive as possible, but I made it a rule that the name of the game is exchange of information and my goal—I would tell people this in conversation—is to learn more than you do. As long as it works that way, everything will be fine." Similarly, another ambassador remarked, "We are usually pretty busy. I won't waste my time if the journalist is not professional, that is, if there is nothing there for me, if it is only one-way. There has to be some promise there.")

Most experienced correspondents know a briefing works best when it is a two-way street. Often, in fact, they will be looking for ways to help, both to encourage some sense of reciprocal obligation on the diplomat's part and to provide an incentive for future meetings.

A mental checklist should be made. Perhaps the correspondent toured a border area that the diplomat has not visited for months and wants to ask about. Perhaps the diplomat knows the journalist has an appointment with a leading politician and can help with background and questions—with a view to a readout later. Perhaps the envoy just wants to remember to anchor the discussion in a central theme. To illustrate: Peace talks between government and rebels have their ups and downs, but the important thing is that they're still talking and some progress has been made, for example, in delivery of relief supplies.

Finally, it is always a good idea to try to think of a good quote for the reporter to use. For a newspaper or wire service journalist, this might be grist for the "so what" paragraph, usually the third or fourth paragraph that explains the meaning of an event:

> ANYHOW TOWN—Government forces and secessionist rebels today battled with tanks, rockets, and machine guns for control of this strategic southern town.
>
> The fighting raged into the night, but as dusk fell government forces appeared to have consolidated their hold on fortified positions on the outskirts of the city.
>
> Western diplomats said it was the rebels' most serious challenge to government forces since the insurrection started three years ago. If the rebels succeed in capturing the key railroad junction at Anyhow Town, the diplomats said, it would give them effective control of 70 percent of the country's copper exports and greatly strengthen their hand for U.N.-sponsored peace talks scheduled to open next month in Geneva.

The conventions of newswriting are such that correspondents normally must attribute, not assert, information and analysis. The diplomat therefore has sourcing value to a journalist. The use of the words "observers" or "analysts," in journalistic code, is frequently understood to mean that the reporter himself is making the observation. However keen the correspondent's insights or dubious the diplomat's, editors tend to prefer attribution to "Western diplomats" over "Western observers" in the unwritten hierarchy of attribution solidity. If a cynical editor sees "observers" or "analysts" too often, he or she may entertain the notion that the reporter has not done enough legwork and is simply providing his own unscrubbed analysis.

Thus, even if reporters think they know better than the diplomats what's happening and why, these officials can still be of value if the journalists can put their thoughts into the diplomats' mouths by getting agreement, or at least drawing no objection, to their own analysis. A diplomat should therefore listen carefully when a correspondent offers his or her thoughts, because if the official nods agreement, or does not disagree, the analysis could conceivably appear in a story under the rubric of "diplomatic sources."

Since the journalist faces the tough task of translating a complex foreign reality into an American cultural reference, it also helps to think of as many "bridging" concepts as possible. This might be a simple matter, such as saying that Country X is the size of New Jersey or that its capital city has the same population as Buffalo. It might mean saying the governor runs his political organization like a Chicago ward boss, or that the country produces enough chromium every year to supply U.S. needs for a decade. Or it might be a more complicated matter, like explaining how the old Kuwaiti custom of setting aside a *diwaniya* room to greet guests grew out of the earlier practice of merchants and *dhow* captains talking tides and pearl prices, and that the *diwaniyas* evolved into hundreds of mini-town halls that provide a unique forum in Kuwait for political discussion and evaluation of government performance.

The point is not to manipulate, but to be prepared. It does not help reporters if their briefers are piles of jello. Journalists can scent uncertainty, and it stimulates the predatory instinct. If the diplomats do not have clear ideas of what they want to convey, chances are they won't convey anything clearly. It is far better to have a sense of purpose and direction, even against the wind, than no mental moorings. But the message should be used by the briefers as a compass, not a jackhammer: they should have a few ideas in mind and look for logical moments to get them across.

Diplomats should also be mindful of their own limitations. The U.S. embassy is not the only game in town. Reporters will measure what they hear at the embassy against their own observations, the words of other diplomats and of local politicians, and common sense. If there are holes, they are likely to find them. Therefore, it is unwise to suppose either that one is smarter than reporters or that one can put something over on them.

"I always assumed that the reporter was smarter than I was," said Edmund Hull. "And when I was with Judy Miller of the *New York Times*, or someone of her caliber, I *knew* I was with someone a hell of a lot smarter than I was. If you fool yourself into thinking that you're intellectually superior and that you can control the reporter, you're letting yourself in for a fall."

One correspondent warned against attempts to manipulate or mislead by relating how he and another reporter once learned in detail about the circumstances of a coup in a small Third World country from a relative of one of the officers involved in it. The public affairs officer at the embassy knew what the two had heard, he said, but did not like the ambassador and did not warn him before the two went in to see the envoy about the issue.

"U.S. policy was built around the other guy," the reporter said, "and the ambassador starts telling us these outrageous lies. Now you have to picture the situation. [The other reporter] and I are sitting on a couch in the office. The ambassador is sitting opposite us. The PAO is standing behind the ambassador—in other words, out of the line of sight of the ambassador, but in our line of sight. Every time the ambassador told a lie, the PAO would shake his head and grimace—because he knew what we knew.

"You can't tell lies to people. It may work once, it may work twice, but you will be found out. Everyone will know, and as a result, your ability to control the flow of information will be compromised."

Reporters come to meetings prepared; so do prudent diplomats. Reporters will appreciate access and respect competence. Whether or not they like various envoys as individuals, they will want them as sources.

Diplomats should always have something to say, and forgo no opportunity to say it. But it is important to remember The Five P's. There is no substitute for thorough preparation, and knowing one's message is the first and most important step in any contact with the press.

"Grasp the subject," Cato the Elder said. "The words will follow."

Chapter 9

The Reporter
"Forester" or "Strip Miner"?

> *Beware the one you benefited.*
> —ARABIC PROVERB

After considering the news organization, the competitive situation, and the filing constraints reporters are likely to be under, next to consider are the reporters themselves. Are they U.S. journalists, familiar with ground rules, or local reporters from a country with a very different press tradition? Are they stringers, paid only if a story is accepted for publication, or regular staffers? Are they correspondents based in the area, with an interest in seeing you again? Or are they parachuting in for a single story and unlikely to return?

Locals and Khawajas

In Arabic, the term *khawaja* means "Mr." It is a form of address reserved especially for use with Christians and Westerners, with or without the name of the person addressed.

Too often, when we think of the press and foreign policy, we tend to dwell too much on the *khawajas*, and the *khawaja* news organizations, and not enough on the locals. But however important the care and feeding of the *khawajas*, cultivating good relations with the local press is also a top priority for embassies, especially in societies where the press is free to reflect. To do this effectively, mission leadership must clearly enunciate its press policy, ensure that key officers engage with the local press, and include local journalists in representational events.

This becomes more important every year, as information technology becomes more pervasive and more invasive, as more countries aspire to open societies, and as more of them spawn fledgling free presses. As a matter of course, a lot of inexperienced local journalists will be coming onstream. Some will not understand or play by ground rules as an American foreign correspondent will. Some will be politicized. Some will not be very competent, which heightens the risk of mistakes, especially when an interview is conducted in English with a non-English speaker. "It's always important to learn about the press in the country you're assigned to," former ambassador to Israel Samuel Lewis said. "Who are the local newspapers? Who are the editors? Whom do they represent? You should really devote yourself to cultivating them, along with the politicians."

Like a number of other diplomats, Lewis stressed that press contacts should not be the exclusive preserve of any one section of the embassy. "The political section should also be doing this, not just USIA," he said. "Some USIA officers are not as interested in the politics as they are the cultural aspects of a country. If they're not as interested, it is hard for them to be as effective in appreciating and soliciting the insights of the reporters."

By the same token, Assistant Secretary Alexander Watson underlined the importance of not boxing USIA officers into narrow job descriptions, citing especially the political reporting potential of the PAO. "He is out there every day doing contact work with the best-informed people in the society. He should be a voluminous political reporter. In Peru, our PAO was one of the best people we had. He zapped out notes [for inclusion in political reporting cables]. He talked to the press as the political section talked to the politicians, and this gave us a dramatically more comprehensive view."

A World of Stringers

Much of the foreign news we read is provided by stringers, that is, nonstaff journalists who file to news organizations. Usually, stringers are paid on the basis of items used, plus reasonable related expenses.[1]

When I was UPI bureau chief in Beirut in the late 1970s, a major aspect of my job was maintaining and managing our stringer network in Lebanon and the region. We worked out of the offices of the respected daily *An Nahar*, and its resident correspondents in south Lebanon filed written dispatches via taxi since there were no phones working. I made deals with several of them to send us copy at the same time. Everybody was happy—we got accurate news more quickly than any other wire service, the correspondents (doubling as UPI stringers) made extra money, and the cab drivers who couriered the handwritten Arabic reports were paid extra for the same trip.

In fact, I had more information about south Lebanon than I could use, a situation that the political counselor at the U.S. embassy, Paul Molineaux, was quick to discern. He later told me he regularly used items gleaned in conversation with me but that never made the UPI wire, such as reports of minor Israeli incursions across the border into various Lebanese villages, an occurrence that became so routine it was not worth filing for the UPI wire on a daily basis unless it resulted in a major clash. But the embassy craved detail.

The level of professionalism among stringers varies enormously. Two of the most well-known journalists in Beirut when I worked there were Palestinian-Lebanese locals Ihsan Hijazi and Tewfik Mishlawi, who together published a useful digest of Arab news and press comment called the *Middle East Reporter*. Their subscribers included nearly every embassy and news bureau in town, and they doubled as stringers for the *New York Times* and *Wall Street Journal*, respectively. Their copy was as good as or better than that of any full-time staff correspondent for the major news organizations in town.

Unfortunately, not all stringers are that competent. They run the gamut from moonlighting host country reporters to experienced reporter-spouses of people transferred to the area, to expatriate students, to adventurers and ideologues. Local nationals tend to have special expertise and stay put. Expatriates often float from one country to another, following the action (and the money), especially to war zones. It is not uncommon to find many of the same people covering the war in Lebanon one year and Central America the next.

The far-flung local stringers of wire services are numerous and a particularly uneven lot. In a high-profile country like Syria, which will be regularly visited by most news outfits but where few or none maintain a bureau, the local stringer often works for several noncompeting news organizations at once. In the late 1970s in Damascus, one local stringer worked for AP, the *New York Times, Time* magazine, Radio Monte Carlo, and CBS while another handled UPI, the *Washington Post, Newsweek,* VOA, NBC, and UPITN (the video agency that later evolved into Worldwide Television News).[2] Such stringers will not be issued a press pass unless they agree to work with the intelligence service. If I went from Beirut to Damascus, I had no doubt that one of my stringer's jobs was to keep an eye on me for the Syrian government. If she were not willing to do it, she would not have had the job. There is little recourse; if you fire the stringer, the replacement will be no different. What I liked about our stringer was that she liked nothing better than beating the AP stringer on a story.

In a police state, however, stringing can be a touchy business, even for those who cooperate with the intelligence services. On one occasion during my tour in Beirut, an outgoing *Washington Post* correspondent filed a long analysis on Syria that the government evidently found distasteful. The story appeared, inexplicably, in the *International Herald*

Tribune under a DAMASCUS (UPI) dateline. Since our stringer worked with both UPI and the *Washington Post,* the Syrian government simply unplugged her telex, putting her out of business. They suggested we use the AP stringer in the future. I said I would rather do without, and for the rest of my tour in Beirut we covered Syria from Damascus Radio, the Syrian News Agency, and periodic visits.

I let go a local stringer in Amman, Jordan, for another reason: he had fairly good connections and provided adequate minimal coverage, but he also worked for our competitors, AP and the German news agency, DPA. This fellow would write a story, cut a telex tape, and send the same file to all three news agencies. He ran the tape to us last, because we paid him least. Then he would bill all three of us for the same news items and, I have no doubt, the same expenses.

When stringers are paid only for items used, which is usually the case, the less professional ones may be tempted to exaggerate what they file. I had a problem with a stringer in southeast Lebanon who used to pose his militia buddies for photos as though they were shooting over stone walls. I had to reject several of these posed pictures and threaten to cut him off entirely before he got the message. On the other hand, if the stringer gets paid the same amount no matter what he files, he has little incentive to make an extra effort. There is no easy solution to the dilemma, and the supervisory correspondent must pay close attention to prevent abuses.

Despite the headaches, stringers are important for the wire services and other news organizations. Staff correspondents cannot be everywhere at once, particularly if, as in our case, they must cover a region as extensive as the entire eastern Arab world. The utility of stringers is to provide basic coverage, a dateline, and early warning if something major starts to brew. When a big story actually breaks, a regular staffer flies in.

Veteran USIA officer Stanley Shrager, who was teaching a course on the media at the National War College when we talked in October 1992, pointed out that dual-hatted stringers—such as the correspondent in the Philippines who reported for both the *Manila Times* and the *New York Times*—are likely to be increasingly common.

As new countries and new governments proliferate, you are going to get more and more stringers being used by news organizations in places like Tajikistan and Croatia, where news organizations may want coverage but don't want to maintain a bureau or full-time correspondent. This means diplomats will probably be talking to representatives of local news organizations who represent other organizations.

It was easier in the old days, because you'd be talking to either the reporter for the *New York Times* or the reporter for the *Manila Times*, and these were two different audiences. Now the same reporter may be representing both. So you've got to keep that in mind, in terms of the audiences and the level of sophistication required.

Brookings scholar Stephen Hess, who was working on a major study of foreign correspondents at the time I spoke to him in early 1993, said more and more of the world is being covered by stringers: "Hong Kong is a good example of a very important place that is covered almost entirely by stringers." He added, "Very few people, really, tell us about the world. There are only twenty-two people in the foreign press corps of the *Wall Street Journal,* and that's a good one. *USA Today* has a foreign editor, but no foreign correspondents. They send people out for short periods. It's just total parachute journalism."

Long-Term Relationship or One-Night Stand

When a reporter for a major Western news organization comes to town and asks for a briefing, the first thing you have to ask yourself is whether this is a long-term relationship or a one-night stand. "People tell lies to each other on one-night stands," noted one correspondent.

If a journalist is based in the country and has a vested interest in seeing you again, he will probably treat the contact with care and work to build an ongoing productive relationship. "I don't expect much of a story the first time I go in to see someone at an embassy," said Doyle McManus of the *Los Angeles Times.* "It's important to establish a relationship."

The resident correspondent can be a rich vein to mine, both for information and independent analysis. When I was the political section chief in Kuwait, tracking the prodemocracy movement in the year before the Iraqi invasion, I made a point of staying in close contact with a wire service correspondent who was the only Western journalist resident in Kuwait. We both got around a lot, but in different ways, so our information tended to be complementary.

Although many prodemocracy activists in Kuwait are now also pro-United States, in those prewar days most of them had no desire to be identified with the U.S. embassy. For our part, we were extremely interested in following closely all aspects of Kuwait's vigorous internal debate, but not becoming actors in it. We managed to follow opposition activities through a variety of contacts and also had lines out to a broad swath of Kuwaiti society—universities, women, the Shia minority, government officials, intellectuals, ruling families, journalists, youth, businessmen, and the military.

The wire service correspondent was sought after by the opposition because he could publicize their activities via reportage that was played back to the region on the BBC and VOA Arabic services. Anti-government leaders therefore regularly fed him their statements and manifestos and notified him of upcoming meetings and events of interest.

The reporter's calls and visits to my office often tipped the embassy to details of opposition meetings and demonstrations. We would compare notes, and I would try to give him as much context as possible, including my best reading of the significance of what we had both pieced together. His reporting, and the Arabic news playbacks, eventually proved to be more than the government could endure, and a few months before the Iraqi invasion he was expelled.

At the opposite pole to the resident correspondent is the unknown reporter who comes to town on a one-time swing through the region—perhaps a freelancer trying to build a portfolio, or a hometown reporter who has turned his vacation into an exotic overseas feature series for his paper. The diplomat should be extremely careful of such visitors, especially if they have limited experience operating abroad and are likely to leave and never come back. With no malice intended, the reporter might apply city hall rules, and quote you by name and title, just as he would any official in the mayor's office. The briefer should spell out the ground rules very carefully and elicit a positive statement that the reporter accepts them—*before* starting to talk. Even so, the briefer should assume a 40 percent chance he will be quoted by name or in some other way that will readily identify him.

Between the poles of resident scribe and fly-by-nighter is a sizable universe of visiting correspondents for major news organizations. Most of the journalists who make the rounds of countries off the beaten tourist path are reputable, regionally based representatives of major organizations, who will want to come back again. In such cases, the relationship is almost institutional, with each side hoping the other will leave a good word with his successor.

Stan Meisler is a well-known Africa hand, having spent ten years there with the Peace Corps and the *Los Angeles Times.* When such a reporter comes to town it can be immensely useful for the post. "The memory of an embassy is two years at the most," Meisler said. "I'd walk in and find myself briefing the political officer. For example, in the Nigerian civil war in 1968 embassy people didn't really have a feel for what happened in 1962 that actually caused the war."

Even if there are more parachutists than Meislers covering the world these days, it is still usually in the diplomat's interest to brief. While there may be less analytical expertise to tap in a parachutist, the diplomat can still glean information on fast-breaking items, get the reporter's observations, and furnish him the facts and background he needs to put what he has seen in accurate context.

Most reporters try to have a story or two in mind before arriving in country, but sometimes they don't have much time to prepare. "When reporters fly in now, they know little except what they've read in the *International Herald Tribune* on the way in, or what their offices told them over the telephone, or what has been on the AP wires," said former *CBS News* correspondent Marvin Kalb. "They need help. They are going to turn, number one, to their colleagues, who may or may not help them and, number two, to the embassy, which should help them. They need as much briefing as possible in order to get context and understanding. There is no obligation to tell them anything secret, but how wonderful it would be if when they write their stories they had the benefit of your general wisdom and knowledge of the area."

What Does This Person Bring to the Issue?

After sorting through the broad categories of U.S. or local, stringer or staff, and long-term interest versus one-night stand, the briefer must make the final and most subtle judgments: on the reporter's experience, reputation, and trustworthiness.[3] While the latter point cannot be finally determined except in the meeting itself, a little preliminary spadework by the PAO can help on the first two.

Reporters and diplomats acquire reputations with each other for skill, style, and integrity—or the lack of it. Experienced reporters are well aware that diplomats will carefully weigh both the reporter's stake in returning and his or her personal reputation. As *Time* correspondent Bruce Van Voorst put it, "The important thing is to know the reporters and to judge them—just as the reporters judge the officer."

Ed Cody, an experienced *Washington Post* foreign correspondent, felt, "It's a question of attitude. Some diplomats simply think it's the right thing for a reporter to come along and ask questions. A diplomat like that will, to the best of his ability, and within the restraints under which he must operate, try to answer the questions as best he can. With other diplomats, you feel at once that there is an adversarial relationship, and the meeting is a sparring match right from the start."

In similar fashion, a senior career Foreign Service officer told me he divides U.S. journalists into two categories—foresters and strip miners. "Some harvest and plant, and give as good as they get—or at least don't stab you in the back. They're always thinking down the road and they put a fair amount of investment in the issue or country. Others are more of the rob, rape, and pillage school—the Woodward and Bernstein strip mine approach. They maintain that the public has a near absolute right to know and reporters have a near sacred obligation to expose." This same official observed, however, that the strip miner tends to be an anomaly overseas, since most correspondents are based in a region for several years and have an interest in return visits to embassies in their territories.

How to judge? Another senior official, who has held policy positions and ambassadorships in several major geographic areas, shared his mental checklist with me:

> I ask myself, first, will this person show professional respect for the rules on attribution?
>
> Second, is this person experienced and intelligent enough to write a story so that it will not be clear to any idiot who it is that made the statements? After all, a quote can be placed in such a way as to identify the source.
>
> Third, what does this person bring to the issue? Some of the issues we deal with are not only foreign, but obscure in the extreme. Does the reporter have the facts? Does he have the context in which to put what I say? If not, I'd better supply it.

If a diplomat does not know a reporter at all, and has not heard about him from other diplomats, the PAO can usually help. Unfortunately, some journalists tend to regard PAOs primarily as useless obstacles en route to more informed sources, whether in Washington or at an embassy overseas. This is shortsighted. It ignores not only the fact that the PAO usually has excellent local contacts and keen insight on the local scene, which can be weighed against what others have to say, but also that the PAO tends the tabernacle of reputations. The first thing any diplomat will do if he or she does not know a journalist asking for an interview is consult the PAO. Now it is entirely possible that the PAO has never met the reporter. But if the journalist is active in the area, chances are the PAO has heard of him or can check with other PAOs, Washington, other diplomats, and journalist friends. Most important, the PAO will form his or her own impressions from talking to the correspondent.

"Experience is the most important thing," said Phil Arnold, who served as Ambassador Pickering's PAO at the United Nations during the Gulf War. "Is it a young kid working for UPI or is it John Goshko [of the *Washington Post*] or Elaine Sciolino [of the *New York Times*]?" Goshko and Sciolino he would talk to as colleagues, Arnold said. But if the reporter isn't particularly experienced, or is working to a compressed format or deadline (for example, a CNN reporter preparing a brief spot report), Arnold would be factual, brief, and try to provide a tag line, or a epithy summary quote.

George Sherman has seen the public affairs job from both sides in Washington—first as diplomatic correspondent for the *Washington*

Star, and then in the Near East bureau as Henry Kissinger's handpicked PAO during the shuttle diplomacy era. His advice for reporters and diplomats alike: Don't deal in stereotypes. "As a journalist, I judged my sources by the reliability of what they told me. Journalists can use as an informed source any government official who tells them anything. A source can talk about something he knows nothing about, and just because he is a government official, the journalist will run it."

Just as journalists should distinguish among government officials, government officials should learn to distinguish among journalists, not lump them all together as a package. "Some [reporters] are responsible, and some are not," he said. "One part of your job as PAO is to advise on whom to stay away from."

If a reporter calls and says he's Joe Y from newspaper X, and the diplomat has never heard of him, the first thing the diplomat should do is find out whether the journalist is who he says he is. Sherman advises: "Stall, get a number, and say you'll call back." (It helps if the official has a secretary, who is trained to check as a matter of course before putting any calls through.) After checking with the PAO on the reporter's bona fides, *be sure to call back.* If a promise is made to call and this is not done, it needlessly annoys the journalist and adds to reporters' jaundice toward officialdom.

While most correspondents will have few illusions about getting a big scoop talking to a diplomat, they do not want to be met with frozen reserve, either. If the diplomat cannot talk, because he either does not know the subject, is not authorized to speak, or if he can't talk for some other reason, he should say honestly that he simply cannot discuss the matter. If possible, though, he should give the reporter a line on someone who can help. There are few subjects that cannot be talked about at all by anyone.

The Basic Unit of Trust Is the Individual

Nothing is more important to establish, or easier to lose, than trust. Trust determines content. The absence of trust will block access and freeze the information flow to a reporter. Even so, nothing is better calculated to make reporters squirm than telling them they are "trusted" by officials. This smacks of being too cozy with one's sources. The mean for both sides should be fair play in an adversarial situation, trust tempered by healthy skepticism, and common decency without coziness.

The clearest situation is when you already know the reporter well from previous dealings and have a strong sense from those dealings of his or her experience and professionalism. One State Department public affairs officer told me that the high-level access enjoyed by *New York*

Times correspondent Thomas Friedman during the tenure of Secretary of State James Baker was not merely a function of the newspaper he worked for but of the fact that "he rarely got things wrong." The officer said, "He had access because he could be counted on to get things right and understand what he was being told."

A number of officers contrasted this sense of confidence with the unsettling feeling one gets from "quote-shoppers"—that is, reporters who have a story agenda firmly in mind and are just looking for officials to fill in what they want to hear.

"I have found that, with one or two exceptions, most of the folks you deal with are pretty good about using quotes in a responsible way and dealing with the information responsibly," said Lawrence Pope, who was acting coordinator for counter-terrorism when we spoke. "Motivation is the problem. The reporter may be quote-shopping. He may call ten people until he gets the one person who says what he wants and gives him the quote that fits the story line he has in mind. He won't misquote you, but he'll ignore nine people and quote the one he wants."

Those who do this might register a temporary gain by getting play for their stories, and some of their stories might be very good. But they also can become so bewitched by their own ideas that they blind themselves to the meaning of events that do not fit their preconceptions. The reporter who does this persistently will acquire a reputation very quickly and is likely to find himself working in a world of guarded briefers. Perhaps, it might be countered, he would rather be feared than trusted by officials. Perhaps this would even be seen as a badge of professional achievement. Perhaps. But, seen from the other side of the fence, it is not honest inquiry but someone working his own agenda.

"The basic unit of trust is the individual reporter," said CNN Vice President Stuart Loory, who has been a journalism professor, Moscow correspondent for CNN and for the *New York Herald Tribune,* White House correspondent of the *Los Angeles Times,* CNN Washington bureau chief, and managing editor of the *Chicago Sun-Times.* "I used to tell my students at Ohio State how important it is to look at bylines. They're not there to massage the ego of reporters, but as a truth-in-packaging label."

Establishing trust cuts both ways. If a relationship of trust has been established, an official will be able to call a reporter in a crisis and give him a readout with credibility. If he believes something is untrue, he can say so to the reporter with authority. In the same way, a correspondent must protect his own credibility. "There are two things that will kill you as a reporter," said Tom Friedman. "One, a reputation for loose lips, and two, [a reputation as] somebody who makes up quotes."

Diplomats need to remember that, trust or no trust, reporters have their own professional requirements. They need to file stories. "The relationship must be based on news, not handouts," Friedman said. "For this to happen, the official needs to give the reporter what he needs to do his job. He has to establish credibility."

Honest-to-God Confidence

Both reporters and diplomats made the point that respect and trust, once earned, are long-term commodities. "Whether you have friends when you need them depends to a large extent on whether you made friends when you didn't need them," said Doyle McManus.

A diplomat working on a case involving the kidnapping of an American journalist in the Middle East found that contacts made years before in Beirut with two senior figures in the journalist's news organization paid off unexpectedly. One of these contacted the diplomat during the kidnapping and confided that he planned to recommend that the organization send representatives to Libya to seek the kidnapped reporter's release. He asked for the diplomat's views on whether this was a good idea and was told that such a move probably would have raised the value of the hostage in the kidnappers' eyes and very likely complicated, not facilitated, prospects for his release. After the diplomat advised against it, the trip did not materialize. "They had honest-to-God confidence in what we said," the envoy noted, adding that in most cases the news organization would probably go ahead and do whatever it thought best, and they might tell you, or worse, they might not. "It was the relationship we had which helped us out in that situation."

A reporter recalled a mission chief in Latin America whom he characterized as "a lousy ambassador, full of bluster, somebody who conducted a lifetime of bad briefings." According to the correspondent, when it was discovered that this ambassador had had a peripheral role in the Iran-contra scandal, "reporters were only too happy to investigate. They gave him very little protection because he hadn't been any help at all to them when they needed him."

By contrast, another reporter told a story about how he squelched a negative story on an ambassador-designate whom the correspondent had known well when both were stationed overseas. "When I needed him, he was there," the journalist said. "I went out of my way on this one." According to the correspondent, congressional staff opponents of this envoy's nomination to a sensitive post picked up an allegation that he had mishandled a management issue while ambassador at another mission. "They were trying to destroy his nomination," the reporter said. "The allegation was unfounded. Others would have just put down what he said and what the other people said. I talked to him, and he explained the situation. I know the guy, I trust the guy, so I talked to my editors. I told them we're not going to run this story. And we didn't."

"A Word That Goes Down Hard with Journalists"

Shortly after he retired from the *Washington Post,* Don Oberdorfer commented that he felt he was "toward the end of a generation that is more likely to have"—and he hesitated—"I hate to use the word 'patriotic,' but stronger feelings about the overall results of things." He then recalled chatting on the telephone with an official who has held a number of senior foreign policy positions. The official told Oberdorfer he had always found him a person he could trust.

"I grimaced," Oberdorfer said. "That's a word that goes down hard with journalists." The official asked if the diplomatic correspondent remembered the 1983 Rangoon incident. Oberdorfer said he remembered the event—a bomb in Burma, planted by the North Koreans, that narrowly missed killing the president of South Korea and did kill several of his cabinet members. But he did not remember what the official told him at the time. "You collect so many factoids in your head over the years that after a while you forget them," Oberdorfer said.

The official then recounted the story: Oberdorfer had called, saying the *Washington Post* had information that the Burmese had requested the assistance of the CIA in investigating the bombing and that the CIA was sending a team. Was that true? The official said he didn't know what to do; the story was basically correct. The Burmese had asked for assistance, and a team had been authorized (although it never actually got there). The official did not know Oberdorfer very well at the time, but decided to just take a chance. He explained the situation and said that if the story were printed, that would end it, and the cooperation would not take place because it would be too embarrassing and the Burmese would call it off.

Oberdorfer asked, "What did I do?" The official replied, "You didn't print it."

In recalling the exchange, Oberdorfer observed that there could be a good argument over what behavior is appropriate for the reporter in this case. He did not remember his train of thought, he said, or even the incident, but one thing that probably weighed on him at the time was that a number of the people killed were friends of his, people he had known well from his days covering Asia. Furthermore, he said, "I probably asked myself what conceivable public interest would be served by publishing the story. My guess is that the next generation of reporters would be more inclined to run it."

I asked Oberdorfer what kind of editorial deliberation process he goes through when he has to make such a decision—does it all happen in his head, or in consultation with an editor? He replied that it depended on how heavy the issue was. On some occasions, he had felt the issue was too big to decide without consulting, but "in this case, it was probably me." Most of the time, he said, he would make the decision himself or have a strong say in how the information was used.

Final Assessment

It is extremely important to know with whom one is dealing, whether the reporter is local or U.S., stringer or staff, parachutist or resident.

The *khawaja* press's reporting may get the most attention in Washington, but contacts with local reporters and stringers are bound to grow in frequency and importance and deserve close attention in the field. For this significant aspect of the diplomat's job, there is simply no alternative to thorough study of the local press culture. On stringers, the key thing to remember is that nearly all get paid for stories or items *used*. That means they will be inclined to angle their stories as sharply as possible.

With U.S. correspondents, the foremost considerations are the level of professional experience and whether the reporter has an interest in coming back or not. The PAO can advise on a correspondent's track record and should be consulted closely on all major contacts. The safest course is to be cautious initially, even with well-known, regionally based correspondents, until the diplomat has a personal feel for the reporters' expertise and what they do with information given.

Whether the correspondent is a well-informed and professional resident reporter or a parachutist who has landed with scant preparation, the bias of the mission should always be to brief. That does not mean the diplomat is not entitled to be careful or to exercise discretion, an essential element of which is making a judgment about the journalist. It's a little like putting coins in a vending machine. A quarter fits in a certain slot and gives a certain value. A dime goes in a different slot and gives a different value. If you misjudge and put the wrong coin in the wrong slot, either nothing happens or you lose your money. With reporters, the first thing to figure out is whether you have a quarter, a nickel, or a dime. Then you'll know where to put your money.

Chapter 10

Field of Play

> You can't always get what you want
> But if you try some time
> You just might find
> You get what you need.
> —MICK JAGGER AND KEITH RICHARDS

"The reporter is trying to elicit information you don't want to give," says Assistant Secretary of State Alexander Watson. "It's like baseball. The pitcher tries to make you swing where the ball isn't. If he succeeds, it doesn't mean he's evil. It means he's good."

The interplay between diplomats and journalists is both cooperative and adversarial. Sometimes their agendas coincide, sometimes they collide, most often they coexist warily. How much to brief? Not surprisingly, most reporters feel that the diplomat should unload fully. Ed Cody of the *Washington Post* said, "I would share just about everything. There would be some areas [excluded], perhaps, particularly sensitive discussions that are ongoing, or where you don't want to burn your relationship with a particular official and have your own sources of information dry up."

Bernard Kalb, host of CNN's *Reliable Sources* program on the media and a former State Department spokesman, said, "The basic rule in talking to the media is to tell them everything you can without violating security. When you're not able to tell the public what the reason is for what's being done, you're mucking around with American values, and when you do, you will fail. And you should fail."

However, when asked specifically to put themselves in the position of an ambassador about to receive a *Washington Post* or *New York Times* reporter the ambassador did not know, a number of experienced reporters again cautioned about the diplomat's need to know something about the reporter.

"I would be very careful," said one correspondent, who cautioned diplomats to use their own judgment about what to convey and to evaluate whether the reporter has the professional acumen to deal with the information and to "get it out right." He added, "If you're afraid of getting into an information transaction with a reporter, stick to analysis."

The hardest thing for the diplomat can be knowing where to draw the line between being helpful and being indiscreet. This is a subtle, difficult, and important task that ultimately turns on personal judgment.

Even so, every game has its rules.

The Bohlen Rules

Former ambassador to the Soviet Union Charles "Chip" Bohlen, one of the most illustrious U.S. diplomats of the post-World War II period, devised seven rules for dealing with the press. They were shared with me by another distinguished diplomat, Ambassador Paul Nitze of the Paul H. Nitze School of Advanced International Studies at the Johns Hopkins University. Nitze recited the seven "Bohlen Rules" from memory:

1. *Always take the press seriously.* They can really hurt you or help you. And they are important to the issues you care about. Corollary: Always return telephone calls from the press and try to answer their questions frankly.

2. *Never tell the press an untruth.* If you do, it can come back to bite you, with serious consequences.

3. *That said, you don't need to tell the press everything.* They may make fun of you or try to get you to make statements you don't want to make, but they will understand a reply of "no comment."

4. *Never discuss an "iffy" proposition.* Don't get drawn into answering "if such and such happens, what then?" You don't need to, and if you do, you'll rarely get it right. Just say it's a hypothetical question and you don't propose to deal with it.

5. *Never deal with a question that is in the process of being decided in the executive branch.* If you do, you'll probably get it wrong; "no comment" is generally a better reply.

6. *Never denigrate a fellow worker in the executive branch.* If you do, you may find that he can pee on you with greater skill than you can pee on him.

7. *If you don't know the answer to a question, don't be embarrassed to say so.*

"I've always found that the press has been very kind to me," Nitze said. "I think it is in part because I've always tried to follow these seven rules from Chip Bohlen. If I ever got in a jam, I'd just say, 'Sorry, that's a violation of rule number three or rule number six.' And I've never found a media person yet who thought those seven rules were unreasonable."

One gloss on this sound advice might be to add that when the response is "no comment," merely uttering the phrase in response to a yes or no question, or a request to confirm something, is unlikely to be sufficient. This is because "no comment" in these circumstances might be construed by reporters as oblique confirmation. If the question cannot be answered, "no comment" should mean giving the reporter some sense of *why* the diplomat cannot comment (for example, noting, as Nitze did, that it violates rule number three or six) and, if there is any room for ambiguity, stating explicitly that no signal should be inferred.

Former under secretary of state David Newsom offered three addenda to the Bohlen guidelines:

1. *Do not run down your country's policy.* Some Foreign Service officers, especially in countries involved in bitter regional disputes (such as the Middle East), may express their sympathy for the host country position and, to curry local favor, criticize Washington's policy. A Foreign Service officer should accept the fact that Washington's policy is the result of a political process of which the officer may know only a part. Whatever the officer may be saying in classified cables to the department, in meetings with the media that officer should attempt to uphold and explain the policy.

2. *Never forget you are an official.* No such thing exists as a publicly expressed personal opinion to be distinguished from one's "official hat." The media and foreign officials will seldom make that distinction.

3. *Never tell one reporter what you are not prepared to tell another.* Exceptions exist to this rule in the kinds of relationships, for example, that secretaries of state developed with James Reston of the *New York Times*. For the average official, playing favorites can only lead to unpleasant relationships with those who are left out. This was one of Phil Habib's cardinal rules; although he rarely told the media anything startling, he was highly respected because they knew he played fair with all.

Finally, bearing in mind that mistakes inevitably will happen, diplomats would do well to review the following summary of advice *Washington Post* media critic Howard Kurtz gave his fellow journalists on prompt and fulsome reporting of their own mistakes:

1. *If there's bad news, break it yourself.* By getting out in front you not only set the initial tone, but ensure your explanations are included in follow-up pieces.

2. *If you admit to a negative, you get credit for a positive.* Eating crow removes the taint of coverup and shifts the spotlight from the initial blunder to your efforts to deal with it.

3. *Don't dribble out the details.* The best way to turn a one-day story into a two-week saga is to go the "modified-limited-hangout" route (letting out only *some* of the facts). Put all embarrassing facts on the table or others will do it for you.[1]

Foreign correspondents and Washington reporters are skilled observers, attentive to nuance and significant detail. To do their jobs well, they will have developed a good nose for news that enables them to quickly scent both uncertainty and the odor of double-talk. They will have multiple sources for cross-checking information. The only reliable approach for the diplomat is to be as well prepared and straightforward as possible.

A good reporter will know where the edge of the envelope is and, since that is where the story lies, that is where he or she will explore. "I'll say here is what I've heard, and ask them to help me sort it out," said Tom Friedman of the *New York Times*, who summed up the reporter's perspective as follows:

> I'm going to write the story whether you tell me something or not. I can do it with or without your point of view in my head. But don't entertain the idea that because you don't talk to me, I'm not going to write it.
>
> The story will come out. People can say it is all wrong. They can bitch, they can be embarrassed. My attitude is, I have my own point of view, I will hear your point of view, and I will reflect it in a fair way if you bother to take the time to talk. It may be in a "but" clause, or it may be an "on the other hand" clause, but I will try to reflect it fairly.

Reporters need information to write their stories; they will appreciate brevity and a good quote. Most will approach an embassy briefing or a Washington background session in a straightforward manner. Nonetheless, the diplomat should learn to spot a few basic techniques of the reporter's craft—the use of silence, the loaded offhand remark, the premise thrown out casually for inadvertent confirmation, and the leveraging of fragmentary information for further disclosure. Some reporters might play to a briefer's ego by suggesting the official is in the dark on an issue, thus tempting a prideful and fact-filled rebuttal. Others might try to coax the information tap open wider by projecting sympathy for the briefer's position vis-à-vis bureaucratic rivals.

There's nothing particularly untoward about this. These are all tools a reporter might use in pursuit of a story. Navigating these shoals, as William Macomber observed in *The Angel's Game*, requires that the diplomat "be frank, helpful, and accurate—but never careless and never indiscreet. In his dealings with both the press and other diplomats, he must also remember always that indiscretions come about in part, as well as in whole—that a fragmentary indiscretion can be as damaging as a whole [one] in the hands of an adroit recipient whose business it is to collect and piece together many parts from many sources, thus coming to understand the whole."[2]

Angles of Approach

Common sense, a chance remark, a hunch, a tip—there are many ways a reporter can get the first whiff of a story. This soon translates into a series of contacts or phone calls, and the hunt begins. The following is a sampler of what can happen along the way.

Firing Point-Blank

The most common approach, and very often the most effective one, is the point-blank question. Directness disarms. The quick, bold, straight shot gives an official minimum time to think and appeals to the natural impulse (even diplomats suffer from this) to candor: Is the secretary going to Country X? What do you think of the decision to bomb the warlord's headquarters? What's the sticking point for Country Y in the negotiations? Did you threaten to stop aid to Country Z or not? There is no difficulty in giving a good, direct answer to a good, direct question. If it is the business of the diplomat asked, he or she should know the right answer.

The main risk is that some officials plunge ahead on impulse without first asking themselves, in that split second after the question is posed, whether they are in fact qualified, by virtue of their authority, instructions, and command of the facts, to answer. Confusion does not arise when people who know what they're talking about answer media questions. Confusion arises when people who don't know what they're talking about answer media questions.

Although reporters have an obligation to distinguish as carefully as they can among potential sources and not make more of what an official says than it deserves, they will not know in every instance which potential briefer has what information. It is therefore incumbent upon the official to shoulder responsibility about whether and how to respond.

Leveraging

Another basic technique in story development is to take a fragment, or an educated guess, and build on it. One new arrival to Washington observed that reporters are like paleontologists: "No matter how small the fossil fragment in their possession, they're convinced they can reconstruct an entire dinosaur from it." [3]

The art of leveraging is bluff and synecdoche: making the piece of available information appear to stand for as much of the whole as possible in the eyes of potential sources. If the official thinks the journalist is in command of a larger body of fact than he actually is, it opens the door to more spillage. This is particularly true if the source is under the impression that he is only *commenting on* what someone else has already revealed, not *divulging* it himself. Success for the reporter depends on both substantive knowledge and skillful deployment of facts. The briefer, in turn, must mind his premises.

"If I understand the policy well enough," one correspondent said, "I can often intuit things. I'll take a scrap here and a scrap there and I'll try to put it all together. Then I'll call someone—say, a Pentagon source— and I'll say, 'Well, you know I spoke to people at the State Department' and they'll say, 'Well, damn, but you know, point number five is not quite like that—it's like this.' I can't tell you how many times I've broken stories in this way."

The Backhand

A variation on this is when reporters project the impression that they command a body of material and then seek backhanded confirmation from a source under the guise of confirming minor details—when in fact the reporters actually are nailing down the main elements. This, too, centers on the loaded premise.

One official related how a newsmagazine correspondent once called him in the early 1980s after a newspaper had reported that Saudi Arabia was expelling Mormons. The correspondent said she had the story and was going to run it, but "just wanted a few details." While the diplomat was used to briefing reporters, he was also aware that in this instance the individuals involved wanted no publicity. He therefore declined to answer the reporter's questions. [4] "She was outraged, said she was going to run the story anyway and told me I was the most uncooperative officer she'd ever spoken to," the official said. "Well, they didn't run the story. It never appeared. They probably had it from [the newspaper report] and wanted separate confirmation, but couldn't get it." The diplomat shrugged. "We do the same thing. It's legitimate for them to try to get confirmation in a backhanded way like that."

The Red Herring

One public affairs officer said he had been burned several times by what he called the "red herring trick." This happens when diplomats are drawn into responding to what may or may not be an accurate piece of information. "The reporter would raise a red herring by saying for example that he had spoken to someone else, who said A-B-C, and try to get you to react to that instead of talking from your own perspective."

Certain foreign reporters in particular, he said, had pulled the red herring trick on him more than once. "They'd call up and pretend to commiserate about something the government [of Country X] had done. They'd say, 'Boy, the United States really has a right to be angry—they're such jerks, don't you think so?' And you say, 'Yes, I guess so,' and the next day you see a story saying that a U.S. official says the government [of Country X] is a bunch of jerks."

Former assistant secretary for African Affairs Herman Cohen noted there are occasionally times when a diplomat has to say "I really have nothing to say" or "I can't comment on that." Other times, the diplomat may simply wish to point out that the premise of the question is wrong. The reporter might say, "All Somalis reject the U.N. Don't you think the United States will be stuck in Somalia indefinitely?" Cohen might then respond, "Well, I disagree with the premise of your question. The Aideed faction does reject the U.N., but not all Somalis do."

Or the question might be, "If you send troops to Somalia, why don't you send them to Yugoslavia?" The answer here might be, "The premise of your question is that we're not being consistent. There is nothing that says we need to be consistent. There are different ways to achieve one's objectives in different places, based on local conditions."

Diplomats must examine the facts and the underlying logic in a question and then ask themselves whether they accept those facts and premises as presented. If not, the starting point for an answer is not the question, but the premise. If they are not in a position to make that initial judgment, they are presumably not in a position to answer the question. In that case, the answer is some variation of "no comment" or, better, a referral to someone who can answer more fully. Alternatively, they may simply wish to rephrase the question in terms that they can accept and respond to.

Suppose, for example, that a reporter quotes an unidentified foreign official as saying his government plans to export missile technology to a developing country despite the objections of the United

States and other countries. The proper course is not to react to the allegation, but to note that the country involved is a signatory of the Missile Technology Control Regime and has always scrupulously adhered to its MTCR commitments. The reporter might then follow up by asking what the U.S. government will do if it *is* confirmed. At that point, of course, the diplomat would immediately recognize a looming violation of Bohlen rule number four and decline to answer a hypothetical question.

Silence

One of the simplest information-collecting devices is the effective use of silence. The best reporters are not necessarily big talkers, but they *are* necessarily skilled listeners. U.S. diplomats, like many other Americans, are often naturally inclined to openness. Furthermore, when a pause or moment of silence develops in a conversation, it is natural to become uncomfortable and feel an urge to fill it. The wise reporter will wait for the diplomat to do this.

As a result, one of the most important skills a briefer can learn is not to run on. This can be difficult. "I found a tendency on the part of some Foreign Service officers to say too much once they were into a meeting," said USIA officer Stan Shrager, an experienced PAO. "You should just answer the questions. Don't volunteer information that can lead to new questions. It is just as important to know when to end an answer as to know what to say."

(One public affairs officer said his solution to the silence tactic is to just stare back. "If they don't proceed, you say, 'Well, if there's nothing else, thank you for coming by.' ")

Ego Plays and the Sin of the Courtier

Good correspondents will be respectful of the diplomat's expertise and intently interested in what he or she has to say. To have a well-known reporter from a major news organization hanging on one's every word is a very flattering, even heady, experience for many officials. It makes them feel important. The corollary of this is that the officials may not want to lose the respect and esteem of the reporter. This makes them vulnerable.

"They'll play on your confidence and your ego, on your not wanting to be taken for a fool and not knowing something," said former deputy spokesman Phyllis Oakley.[5] "Some people may feel embarrassed and not want to let on they don't know. It takes someone with confidence to say, 'Look, I just can't talk about this with you any more.' "

Along with these ego plays, there are a number of potential pitfalls related to both Bohlen rule number six (never denigrate a fellow worker in the executive branch) and the Newsom caution against running down your country's policy.

One gambit might be called "crocodile sympathy." This approach, in which the reporter projects himself as a sympathetic friend and ally in the bureaucratic wars, tends to come into play with two types of stories: conflict in Washington among various agencies and alleged wrongdoing of some kind on the part of an administration. Said one senior FSO, "I'm not willing to have a reporter say to me, 'I know you're a good guy, but tell me what those other bad people who oppose you are saying and doing.' I'm not willing to play that game."

Besides seconding injunctions against discussing personalities or washing bureaucratic dirty linen in public, one ambassador cautioned against trying to demonstrate one's own importance by indiscretion. He called this the "sin of the courtier." There is a dangerous temptation for career people when talking to reporters "to present whatever they are presenting in a self-serving way," said the ambassador. "For example, someone might say 'I found a shambles here and I fixed it up.' "

He also advised: "There is internal debate until a decision is made and then you abdicate your personal opinion. That is the nature of bureaucracy, and in a democracy it is expected that bureaucrats will be loyal to the views of their political superiors. You shouldn't wing it. If a policy or individual is controversial, a purpose of the reporter may be to contribute to that controversy. If that's the purpose, you should find a way to be dull and dim-witted. I have no respect for people who run down their superiors in order to register their private views."

Intimidation and Sloth

Bluster and intimidation are not common, but they do occur—on both sides. One official described a newspaper reporter who confronted the ambassador to a Middle Eastern country with information about alleged intelligence operations, saying "either you tell me more about it or I'll write it the way I've got it." The ambassador reportedly asked him to leave the office. On another occasion, a correspondent threatened an official that he would write a story about the State Department's choking off news on an issue if he didn't get more information. The officer said he informed the journalist that would reduce what access he had to zero.

In a third instance, a reporter was angry at not being included in a background briefing. He obtained a copy of the briefing and told a public affairs officer he didn't feel bound by the rules. The officer responded that it was a cheap shot to take someone else's story, and if the reporter did so he would never get anything from him again. "The important thing," the PAO said, "is to respond in a way that makes clear the threat won't work."

Another officer described a briefing by Assistant Secretary for Near East Affairs Edward Djerejian on the Middle East peace process. The reporter was after an insider account of how Secretary of State James Baker had negotiated with Syrian President Hafez Assad and, specifically, how he had brought Assad into line on the peace process. This was sensitive for two reasons. It involved an ongoing negotiating process. It also involved a Middle East leader known for ruthlessness, whose country was a state sponsor of terrorism.

Djerejian was reluctant to reveal details of these sensitive meetings, lest Assad lose confidence in the American role. At the same time, he wanted to be honest. He told the reporter that at one point, when the conversation was not moving very well, Secretary Baker jumped to his feet, threw open a heavy velvet curtain covering one of the windows, and said, "Let's let some light in on this." The Syrian president was astonished. No one had ever done anything like that to change the mood of one of his meetings. It was a rather dramatic moment, and Assad had burst out laughing.

"Now, this was a good strong example of the secretary in action," the officer said.

> It showed he was not toadying to this dictator, that he was playing a leadership role, that he had caught the Syrian president off guard, and that he used the incident to say let's move things forward. I thought the anecdote would be useful, but the reporter reacted by complaining, "Oh, that's nothing new. I'm not getting what I need out of this interview." This was not only rude, but a conscious technique, a maneuver on the part of the reporter to get Ed to feel that he ought to say more. I held my breath, because I knew what the journalist was doing. Ed, who was trying to be as straight and open as possible, took a breath, was silent for a moment, and then said, "Well, that's the best I can do." He didn't go for it, and that's why he's effective. A less experienced officer might have fallen for it.

Needless to say, journalists don't like being pushed around, either. One newspaper reporter described how a U.S. ambassador tried to bully him when he queried the envoy about alleged irregularities in the local government's use of U.S. aid money to procure certain military supplies. He said the ambassador flew off the handle, accusing him of not knowing what he was talking about, and of coming in and "flying low." "He tried all these tactics instead of dealing with the situation," the reporter said. "What he should have done is say, 'Listen, I understand your question, but I can't answer it, the matter is under investigation.' " He added,

"If you don't want to answer the question, there is a way to do it and a way not to do it. I really resented his attempt to steamroller me."

Another situation that can affect diplomats, but over which they have virtually no control, is intellectual sloth on the part of reporters. It is easier to deal with what correspondents do than with what they don't do. If a journalist steps over the line in an aggressive effort to get a story, it may be unpleasant to deal with, but the briefer at least has a chance to grapple with the situation and keep a potentially wrong story out of print. On the other hand, if a journalist simply panders to preconceptions—either his own or his editors'—and writes a story without scrubbing down the facts and the analysis, there is little that can be done. (It should be noted that stories skewed in this way complicate the lives not only of government officials but of other journalists who *are* making an honest reporting effort and then have to deal with callbacks from editors on a bogus piece written by someone else.)

An officer who served in the embassy in Seoul said this was a particular problem during the 1987 elections in Korea.

> The world press descended from all over and there was not a great deal of expertise on Korea. Journalists who came had a preconceived idea of what the story would be, often formed from TV images of rioting and students in the street. We had to do a lot of work to chip away at this, to indicate that the symbiotic relationship between demonstrators and TV crews was not the only thing, or even the most important thing, going on. But people are under orders from their editors to write about those TV images. Even if we got through to the reporter, we found we often didn't have the job done because his editor would be likely to reject the story.
>
> One wire reporter would just check the police blotter every day. Well, this was a very inaccurate and self-serving source of information, but he would just get the police version of the numbers. He usually did not even go out to cover the story, he just kept churning out the same story and getting away with it. People in his home bureau thought it was terrific. Even if we had some hope of affecting the *New York Times* and *Washington Post*, this is the story that was repeated in newspaper after newspaper. It was a case of a particular individual working for a particular wire service, taking a shortcut and reporting inaccurately. That individual decision, and that style of doing the job, had a tremendous effect.

The Greatest Pitfall

Whatever the pitfalls of engagement, and there are some, the greatest pitfall is to fail to engage. "Always see people," advised Tom Friedman. "Even if you see them and tell them nothing, at least they have a sense of access. They're not being snubbed."

Those who make it to the top of the diplomatic profession will spend a significant amount of their time briefing the press. Although individual methods and approaches differ, the importance of these press contacts was stressed by every senior diplomat I spoke to. As Bush administration spokesman Richard Boucher pointed out, "There's nearly always something to say, and usually no harm in saying it."

Good reporters will realize the constraints diplomats are under and understand that officials occasionally will need to keep some things back—provided those officials are forthcoming in other areas.

Diplomats should trust in their judgment and the Bohlen Rules. They should treat reporters as equals, with courtesy and respect. They should remember that they are not the only ones with professional concerns and bear in mind the competitive pressures and organizational dynamics journalists face. Diplomats should try to return phone calls promptly. They should keep in mind that journalists are not infallible, and mistakes can happen, but the odds are better when correspondents are well briefed. If the reporters are doing their job well, they will probe for information, very likely more than the diplomats would like. The journalists will not be thinking in terms of the national interest—that's the diplomats' job; the reporters have deadlines to meet.

On the other hand, diplomats do have a right to expect ground rules to be respected and any information provided to be handled in a fair and responsible way. Fred Friendly put the rule for reporters well in a 1958 memo to staff during his tenure as managing editor of the *Washington Post:* "Conduct yourself so that you can look your source in the eye the next day." [6]

Don Oberdorfer advised officials to take reporters seriously, to be as open as possible, and to be discriminating. He said there was an enormous difference between officials who view reporters seriously and those who do not. Arms control negotiator Paul Nitze was a paragon, in Oberdorfer's view. "He treated you as an intelligent person and basically said whatever he could, unless there was some big controversy going on and he felt he couldn't. But he would tell you everything he knew with exceptions," instead of telling the minimum with exceptions.

Added Oberdorfer, "You've got to be discriminating. There are reporters who take officials seriously and there are those who do not." The latter are "basically heedless of the consequences of what they write." It is not enough, he said, for officials to be open and to take reporters seriously—they must also know with whom they are talking.

Assistant Secretary Herman Cohen put it another way: "You need to size up journalists pretty well. They're like plumbers or doctors. You can't say they are all honest or dishonest. You need to know the background of the individual reporter. Eighty-five percent or so are pretty square, and about 15 percent are going to fool around. I may be a bit naive, but I found that if you treat them nice, they treat you nice."

Chapter 11

Read It and Weep

> *"Is it true that the Ambassador lives on nightingale sandwiches?" he asked. "The* Daily Express *says so."*
> —LAWRENCE DURRELL

A favorite story among journalists and diplomats to describe the unpredictability of events in the Middle East is the tale of the frog and the scorpion. The scorpion wants to cross a river and asks the frog to carry him to the other side. "But I'm afraid you'll sting me," replies the frog. "Why would I sting you?" the scorpion says. "If I did that, we'd both die." The frog sees the logic in this, and agrees to give the scorpion a ride. Halfway across the river, the scorpion stings the frog. "Why did you do that?" the frog cries with his dying breath. "Now we'll both die." Replies the scorpion: "That's just the way it goes in the Middle East." [1]

There's no such thing as a risk-free briefing. In every backgrounder there is an element of the frog and the scorpion. That's just the way it goes. Neither journalists nor diplomats are perfect, and misunderstandings occur. Some reporters are more experienced than others, and all have editors behind them with authority to edit what they file.

Although minor contretemps are common, with both U.S. and other journalists, deliberate treachery on one side or the other is not. If a diplomat briefs regularly, he will probably feel singed at some point. It's usually not the end of the world, and the benefits of contact with the media generally outweigh whatever risk there is at the margin. The only defense is to be as discriminating as possible in learning the local press culture, judging the reporter, setting ground rules, and choosing what to say.

Most people, understandably, do not like to talk about mishaps or misunderstandings. I am therefore particularly grateful to those who shared their experiences with me. It would not have been difficult to make this a chapter of woe, compiling a catalogue of alleged abuses by diplomats and journalists alike. The object, however, is not to pass judgment or titillate, but to examine some of the ways misunderstandings can occur so that others are better placed to avoid them in the future.

There is an Arabic adage that every steed is permitted a stumble, and every sage a lapse. Nobody is perfect, and even the best reporters and diplomats occasionally slip up under pressure. In fact, most of the criticisms I heard involved people on both sides who were well-established and experienced professionals. The only thing this proves is that those who enter the lists are bound to collect a scar or two along the way. But it is better to stumble and get up again than to avoid the fray altogether.

Egypt: Bolting Ranks

Hermann Eilts spent thirty-two years in the Foreign Service, the last six of them from 1973 to 1979 as ambassador to Egypt, during the period when Secretary of State Henry Kissinger was engaged in his Middle East shuttle diplomacy. Eilts's public affairs officer in Cairo for much of this time, William Rugh, commented that Eilts did not trust the press but was an excellent briefer if he could be persuaded to sit down and talk. The *Washington Post*'s Don Oberdorfer seconded this, recalling that in Cairo Eilts once gave him "about the best briefing" he'd ever had.

I visited Eilts in November 1992 at Boston University, where he was then chairman of the political science department. He admitted up front that he was not particularly trustful of the press. Like others, he noted that the climate for dealing with reporters seemed to change after the Vietnam War, but he also cited a number of personal experiences that had shaped his views.

Early in his career, Eilts said, a reporter for a leading daily visited him at his office in the Bureau of Near East and South Asian Affairs (NEA) in Washington. "This guy was a sneak," the ambassador said. "He was the kind of person who would try to read papers and stuff on your desk." Eilts had briefed the reporter, he said, but "what I told him was taken completely out of context. I was furious. I wrote a letter to the NEA public affairs office, which sent it to [the newspaper]. I accused the reporter of journalistic thuggery, and in fact I got an apology." But the incident had made such an indelible impression that it was one of the first things the ambassador cited when asked forty years later about his dealings with the press.

Another thing that made Eilts gun-shy was working for Henry Kissinger. While Kissinger himself was famous for his assiduous courtship of journalists, the secretary could be notoriously thin-skinned about others under him doing so. "Kissinger was very concerned that no one speak to the press except him," Eilts said. "Very shortly after I arrived, I spoke to a reporter; Kissinger didn't like it at all, and he jumped on me very quickly."

A third negative experience was a backgrounder the ambassador did for five or six correspondents permanently based in Cairo. "I gave them quite a detailed talk at my home. A little while later, the Foreign Ministry called me at home. Evidently one of the reporters had gone out and written a story citing me by name. This was very sensitive stuff at the time. We didn't know if the peace process would move forward or not. In any case, the Egyptian censor stopped the story and reported it to the Foreign Ministry. They complained to Washington, and I got another rapped knuckle."

Eilts concluded, "I wasn't that trustful of the press, I must admit— and it was because of things like that fellow who ran out and wanted to send the story despite clear ground rules. That kind of thing makes you suspicious."

Israel: Pressure Cooker

If U.S. diplomats awarded a prize for the world's leading local media hot seat, Israel would probably win, hands down. The press scene there is a unique mix: highly competitive, politically charged, chock-full of good information and disinformation, and with high impact on a bilateral relationship of great importance to both countries.

"The situation was so politically sensitive," said former ambassador Samuel Lewis, who served in Israel from 1977 to 1985, "that to a large extent I was my own press attaché." Lewis, who had extensive contacts with both the Israeli and Western media, noted that Israel is a small, tense place with a great many people who read and debate politics twenty-four hours a day. The media situation is enormously competitive, and Israeli journalists tend to stretch and twist ground rules more than their American counterparts.

An official in the State Department's Near East bureau gave a Washington-end example of how ground rules can be treated fast and loose in the Israeli press: "A bureau officer might give a background briefing on the peace process. The stories will be printed quoting 'a U.S. official,' but then Israeli journalists will tell all the movers and shakers in the Israeli government that it was Officer X." The effect, of course, is to negate substantially a major purpose of doing the briefing on background: that is, to dilute the official character of the statements. When I checked with one of the officials involved in such backgrounding, he confirmed that after the last two he had given, officials from the Israeli embassy were on the telephone within hours asking that he elaborate on certain points he had made.

Because the Israeli press is a dynamic and essential component of the political scene, there is a degree of political engagement that dictates different rules of the road from those in the United States. Lewis recalled one veteran journalist with an inside pipeline to the prime minister's office who wrote a daily column for a leading Israeli newspaper purporting to reflect the prime minister's thinking. "During periods of strain in U.S.-Israeli relations, his columns would often be highly distorted in terms of what they reflected about our policy. At first, I just thought this reporter was kind of lazy, and that he just wasn't checking things out. I would invite him over to the house, and bitch about his sloppiness, and he would be very apologetic and say how busy he was. It took me too long to figure out that what he was putting out was just the version that the prime minister's office wanted out. It was not sloppy at all."

Lewis said, "There are a bunch of papers fighting each other to get the scoop," as in the United States a generation ago. "The result is that even Israeli journalists trained at the Columbia Journalism School almost never double-check. The pressure is to print, not get a second source, much less check with the individual concerned—for example, at the U.S. embassy if it concerns U.S.-Israeli relations."

One journalist actually told him: "Right, we should check, but if it's not true we'd lose the scoop!"

"What can you do?" Lewis said. "This is the philosophy."

Given the hazards, some diplomats posted to Israel prefer not to get involved at all. Said one, "The whole ethic of trying to get it right isn't there. If you see a vicious article attacking your integrity, you know the reporter is acting as a foil for some politician." He cited the case of a journalist who published a story that was untrue and then could not understand why the diplomat involved refused to have anything to do with him again. The reporter complained that the diplomat should realize that a certain Israeli politician had given him the story. "There was no feeling that he shouldn't have published it," the official said. "They attach themselves to whoever will give them the most headlines. They allow themselves to be used. They're vying for front-page space, and it has nothing to do with journalistic ethics, or right or wrong. One actually said to me, 'So I get it wrong today, maybe I'll get it right tomorrow.' "

Notwithstanding the undoubted risks, Lewis was a strong advocate of engagement. "Many FSOs are very wary and need to be encouraged," he said. "I encouraged my officers to stay in touch with the press. There were no great gaffes."

It is not uncommon for relatively junior officers to have a variety of press contacts in Israel, but even junior diplomats must learn to tread carefully. One political officer told me he had lunched with a reporter and, taking care to use the phrase "I understand from Israelis that . . . ," probed for the reporter's views about reported differences between then-Chief of Staff Rafael Eitan and Minister of Defense Ezer Weizman.

> So we had lunch, I paid for it, and the reporter then apparently called up Ezer Weizman and said, "Ezer, do you want to know what the Americans are saying about you?" Weizman was really angry. He called up the ambassador and said, "What the —— are you people saying?" This was a very sensitive period in U.S.-Israeli relations, and the ambassador was not pleased.
>
> Now, the fact is, I had not said anything, but this reporter used my question about the dynamics of the national security structure and turned it into a wedge he could use himself, either to improve his own relations with Weizman, who would be a more important contact, or to develop or concoct a story on U.S.-Israeli relations. He used what I thought was a delicate and safe approach and twisted it to his own ends.
>
> I never wanted to have anything to do with that reporter ever again. I had no confidence that I could hold any conversation with him without being burned.

Mexico: Trust Betrayed

A U.S. consular official in Mexico suffered a potentially dangerous burn in the late 1980s at the hands of a reporter for a newspaper in southern California with whom he thought he had developed a relationship of trust. The diplomat said corruption by the Mexican Federal Judicial Police, including alleged involvement in car theft from the United States, was a concern during his tenure. Among other things, he said, a senior Mexican police official had had a new Porsche stolen for him from a showroom in California. Eventually it was tracked down and returned, but with $4,000 worth of damage done, and only after the official had used it for a two-week vacation. At one point, frustrated California Highway Patrol officers referred a reporter for a southern California newspaper to the U.S. official for information on the alleged criminal activity.

"Now, these are nasty people," the diplomat said. "They are the guys that are suspected of killing DEA agent [Enrique] 'Kiki' Camarena.[2] I told the reporter up front that what I would be telling him would be completely off the record and only to point him in the direction of things he could check out."

Notwithstanding this clear injunction, the reporter used the material in a story and attributed it to U.S. government officials in Mexico dealing with stolen cars.

"I called up the reporter and said, 'What is this? I told you it was off

the record.' He said, 'Well, I didn't use your name, only "U.S. officials." '
I said, 'You might as well have used my name. There aren't more than a
handful of us dealing with the issue, and I'm the closest one to [the areas
discussed in the story].' "

The diplomat said he felt betrayed. "I had dealt with this reporter
before," he recalled, "and the only reason I agreed to talk with him
at all was that I felt I had a relationship of trust. This happened at
the end of my tour, but had I stayed longer, he would have been off my
list."

Friendly Reminder

Friendships between journalists and diplomats are natural. The
two very often have similar interests, benefit from talking to each
other, and genuinely enjoy each other's company. Nevertheless, friendships mixed with professional relationships can be tricky. Another
Middle East proverb says, "Be careful of your enemy once and of
your friend a thousand times." The worst kind of hurt is sometimes
not intended.

A reporter with experience both in Washington and as a foreign correspondent overseas told me the following story about inadvertently
breaking a confidence. It illustrates the perils of speaking off the record,
even to friends.

"I was once told something by a friend, completely off the record,"
the reporter said. "I was told I couldn't use it unless someone else told
me first, or unless he changed his mind."

Then a leading newspaper reported the information, and it was read
over the phone to the reporter by his editors as it had appeared in that
paper. "What I didn't realize was that [the other newspaper] didn't have
all the details. When my story was published, it was buried on the inside
pages, and practically no one noticed it—except the secretary of state,
who evidently saw it in his press clips, and ordered lie detector tests in
connection with the leak. I don't know what happened after that, because the diplomat never spoke to me again."

The reporter added that this made him more cautious about ground
rules, and more determined that people be able to trust him. "It
is hard to draw a line between professional sources and friends. I would
never have been told what I was told if we were not friends, and that
is why it was so devastating for me. Not only did I betray a professional
source, I betrayed a friend." That is the danger of developing friendships, he observed. "People tell you things. So now I draw a line between
people who are sources and people who are friends. If they are friends, I
don't ask."

London: "He gained a minnow, but sacrificed a ten-pound bass"

A member of the senior Foreign Service with two decades of experience in Europe and the Middle East described a contretemps with a British reporter during a London tour. "I had been in the country from about six months to a year," he said, "and a journalist I regarded as a friend, and had a great deal of respect for, burned me for what I considered a small gain."

The diplomat said he heard from a contact at the Foreign and Commonwealth Office (FCO) that two British envoys had gone to Libya. He mentioned this in conversation with the journalist, who remarked that he had not heard it. The diplomat said, "Oh, well then, that should be off the record." While the trip was not secret, and FBIS (the Foreign Broadcast Information Service) had reported on it, the FCO had not announced it and the British media had not picked up the item. The official was therefore worried about embarrassing the FCO and damaging his own relationship with them.

The journalist got very formal, however, and pointed out that the diplomat had not indicated beforehand that it was off the record. "It wasn't a big deal," the American official recalled. "He could have followed up with the FCO, who never would have thought much about it since it was in the media later. But the reporter could see I was concerned, and he used the material anyway."

The reporter was technically in the right, of course. But what annoyed and puzzled the diplomat was the journalist's handling of his request for confidentiality. "I never could really figure out why he did it. He gained a minnow, but sacrificed a ten-pound bass. I was going to be there for several years. He lost a chance to tap into me for a lot of background and information."

This incident also illustrates the hazards of informal settings and contacts. At a social gathering, a casual conversation can turn almost imperceptibly into a substantive discussion. In such a situation, it is easy to fall into the trap of saying something and then trying to put it on background after the fact. In many cases reporters will agree, rather than annoy a valuable source; but as the story above shows, this is not always the case.

The Philippines: No Such Thing as Off the Job

When USIA officer Stan Shrager was the PAO in Manila in 1989-91, the United States was engaged in high-profile negotiations with the Filipinos over the future of U.S. bases in the country. The U.S. negotiating team, headed by Richard Armitage, would fly in for a week at a time for the talks. "We were pretty secretive about the date for security reasons, because the New People's Army was assassinating Americans," Shrager said. As a practical matter, he added, it was very tough to keep a lid on a date known to many officials on both sides. "I always felt we were doing pretty well if we kept it secret until at least a week beforehand, so as not to give them time to organize anything."

The PAO noted that he gave big receptions at his home from time to time, and sometimes U.S. officers would say things they thought were off the record, just cocktail chatter, only to find the remarks in the newspaper the next day. "Anything you said could be in the papers," Shrager said. "So before one of these receptions, I would announce it at a country team meeting and warn people that there would be reporters present and to be careful what they said."

At one such occasion, a junior U.S. Information Service officer was chatting to a reporter who asked whether the next round would be starting on a certain date.[3] Not thinking the reporter would ever write it up, he said, "Yeah, sure, the talks are going to start on the 25th."

"Well," Shrager said, "this was a big scoop for the Filipino, and it was in the paper big time the next day." The lesson, of course, is that there is no such thing as "off the job."

A corollary, also underscored by David Newsom (see chapter 10), is that there is no such thing as "personal opinion." U.S. diplomats cannot take refuge in "personal" statements when talking to reporters. The journalists are interested in the diplomats because they are diplomats, not because they are nice guys.

After all, diplomats don't ignore such remarks in their own official contacts, either. If a host government leader leans over to the ambassador in a meeting, says he wants to speak personally, and asks notetakers on both sides to stop writing, no one in the room puts out of his or her mind what comes next. On the contrary, when the diplomats return to the embassy, they reconstruct the gist of what was said and speculate about why it was done. Perhaps the host government is sending a trial balloon or unofficial signal. Therefore, if officials don't treat such "personal" statements as such themselves, it is not realistic to expect thoughtful reporters to do any differently.

On Treacherous Ground

The most difficult landscape for contact between reporters and officials is when U.S. policy or actions are in flux, under criticism, or otherwise sensitive. This inevitably puts officials, who have a responsibility to uphold stated policy regardless of personal views, and reporters, who have a responsibility to question it, into an adversarial position. When the two sides meet on such potentially treacherous ground, it is particularly important that each be as straightforward as possible.

If a diplomat gives a reporter only part of the story, and thereby leaves him with an incorrect impression, then the reporter, when he or she inevitably finds out about it later, will fairly conclude the diplomat has not been straightforward. If the reporter took the official at his word and feels deliberately misled as a result, he should get back to the official in person (or, failing that, to the PAO) and get an accounting. Any correspondent has a right to be concerned about the integrity of what he or she reports, since it reflects on the reputation of both journalist and news organization.

Sometimes, too, reporters will collect various pieces of a story and then go to the embassy to try to fill in gaps. But if the correspondents don't tip their hand to their story line, and later plug pieces of information gleaned at the embassy into a context very different from the one discussed, the diplomats may feel the reporters are not playing fair. This is particularly true when the story concerns U.S. actions or U.S. policy. If the game is going to end up in the diplomats' court, reporters should make a reasonable effort to at least give U.S. officials a swing at the ball.

Setting ground rules clearly is especially important for the official if there is any sensitivity to the discussions. The reporter should take care not to underplay intent in an effort to loosen up a source, for example by stressing that the session is to be "internalized" for background only—when the correspondent fully intends to draw on the material and attribute it to Western diplomats.

One misunderstanding I am aware of arose when a U.S. official gave a "not for attribution" briefing to a reporter about a certain Asian issue. The material appeared soon after in a front-page story attributed to "Western diplomats" and "a senior diplomat here" and included other internal references that made clear to any informed U.S. government reader just who had done the briefing. It also led to considerable criticism of the diplomat within the U.S. government and stiffened resistance to ongoing efforts by this official and others to implement an important policy shift.

The crux of the misunderstanding from the diplomat's point of view was his very clear recollection that the information would be for background only and that, if drawn on at some later date, it was not to be attributed in any way.

The crux of the misunderstanding from the reporter's point of view was that the diplomat could think he was "that far off the potential for creating news when he talked to me" or that the reporter would not have the benefit in print of what the official was saying. The journalist noted as well that the diplomat may have been unaware that the correspondent had spoken to a range of other sources, including some who had talked to the American official about the same matters and reflected the same themes. "Sometimes," he said, "you find that things are being widely discussed in a small circle."

Not least important, it turned out that the two sides had a divergent understanding of the meaning of "not for attribution." To the diplomat, this meant *no attribution at all* (and this is the way other officials I spoke to understood it as well). The reporter took it to mean *no attribution on the record,* that is, normal background attribution (and I found a number of other journalists who shared that interpretation, too).[4]

Misunderstandings can occur because of inexperience on one side or another, or imprecision about ground rules, or any number of other reasons. The cardinal rule for any official was enunciated by one veteran reporter: "If you don't want to read about it, don't say it." The cardinal rule for any reporter should be: Think about the consequences of what you write, and if in doubt about proper handling, get back to the official and confirm the understanding. The surest recipe for avoiding problems is for both sides to be as straight in their dealings as possible and to agree on the exact form of attribution at the beginning of the meeting.

A potential hazard for diplomats is keeping material conveyed reasonably consonant with ground rules. This is particularly true for deep background, when the diplomat is asking the reporter to take personal responsibility for content. If the official lets down his guard and moves beyond context and background to provide the grist for a timely spot story, he may find that the cover of ground rules, including "not for attribution" or "deep background," starts to wear thin. In this situation, what the official is doing, in effect, is giving the reporter a good story and then asking him not to use it.

When a journalist has information for a story that will be widely and closely read, the piece cannot be all smoke and mirrors if it is to have any credibility. One course—the unprofessional one—is to simply conclude the diplomat is being too fussy and unilaterally upgrade the sourcing. More likely, the reporter will redouble efforts to get the same material from a different source or sources.

Failing this, the journalist would have an obligation to get back to the diplomat to negotiate an upgrade from deep background to background for some parts of the story. It usually happens that the two sides can agree on a formula that preserves the interests of each. Needless to say, however, when reporters and officials meet on treacherous terrain, if there is any ambiguity about ground rules, such as using "not for attribution" when each understands the term differently, unfortunate results can ensue.

Limited Recourse

When burned, the diplomat should not panic, but consider who is at fault. If the misstep is the official's, it is useful to keep one's perspective. Has real damage been done, or is it merely a case of embarrassment?

"It's very rare that something will appear in print that actually harms the U.S. government," said a USIA officer who has served both as a PAO overseas and as a public affairs officer on detail to the State Department. "Ninety-nine times out of a hundred, any negative effect is simply that someone is mad that you allowed yourself to be quoted. It's usually not the information itself that is harmful; with most things that happen, people don't even bother or notice."

If the reporter is at fault, *always* get back to him or her. "If you established the ground rules and the reporter agreed to them, and you feel the reporter broke the rules," advised Thomas Pickering, "it's incumbent upon you to get word to the reporter, say you are displeased, and hear what he has to say."

The most drastic option is to cut the journalist off entirely, but this is often neither practical nor desirable. A better course is to show less trust for less trustworthiness shown. "If it turns out he was confused," Pickering said, "or this is an important reporter and I have to see him again, I would do so, but I would be very careful. If I had not been using a tape recorder before, I would start. This can have a dampening effect."

If a correspondent burns a diplomat in Country X, he or she likely will find the embassy next door in Country Y less hospitable. In other words, the reporter may get one trip to the well, but the breach of confidence increases the risk that the next stop will be a dry hole. It's not so much what happens as it is what does not happen. One ambassador recalled that after a misunderstanding with one correspondent, "I didn't see that reporter again for two years, and then I was extremely careful and bland."

This is true not only overseas but in Washington. A reporter who gets a reputation for taking cheap shots or breaking rules will find access increasingly tight. "If you've got fifty phone calls to return," one public affairs officer explained, "and you only have time to return ten or twelve, then you have favorites."

Similarly, if a reporter calls up to request a briefing, the public affairs officers can handle the call several ways. They can contact the most knowledgeable official and say, "So-and-so is going to call you, I know him, he's responsible, and I think you should talk to him." Or they can say, "So-and-so is going to call you. I think you should talk to him. He's okay most of the time, but you should be aware that he badly misquoted the assistant secretary once last year, so be careful." Or they can say,

"So-and-so called today. He's doing a story on our relations with Country X. You know what happened the last time Jones talked to him. He swore he'd never speak to him again. If you want to do it, you should be careful and I should sit in."

Most diplomats, whatever their annoyance with a particular story, harbor no lasting grudges and sometimes will not even mention their concerns or dissatisfaction to reporters. But, as noted above, such incidents can affect access. Thus, while a diplomat may not wish to alienate an influential journalist, it is best for all sides if the official or PAO gets back in touch, requests an accounting, and clears the air right away. Journalists are just as concerned about their reputations as diplomats are, and a good correspondent would much rather sort things out than have his or her reputation harmed or access impaired.

Chapter 12

In the Embassy

A little neglect may breed great mischief...
for want of a nail the shoe was lost;
for want of a shoe the horse was lost;
for want of a horse the rider was lost.
—BENJAMIN FRANKLIN

In 1986, a year of elections and revolution in the Philippines, Manila was a media jungle. President Ferdinand Marcos, opposition leader Corazon Aquino, and other local political figures were performing for television. U.S. senators, members of Congress, and various White House officials were frequently in town, all talking to the press. In this supercharged atmosphere, the U.S. embassy, led by Ambassador Stephen Bosworth, became an important broker of information.

"The embassy became our point of reference for sanity checks," one correspondent said. "If a senator made a charge, we would check with the embassy to see if it had any legitimacy, and then we'd say whether the charge was legitimate or knock it down. This is the difference between a headline and paragraph 10. That's a worthwhile position for the embassy to be in, I would think.

"It worked because Bosworth was respected by the press. He had relationships with people, and he worked at it. So did his PAO, who had a direct line to him. When we would call, we'd get something back through the PAO."

Setting press policy is a central element of mission management. It requires internal and external coordination and, in the embassy overseas, should feature simple, standard procedures. Contacts with the local press should be geared to a specific country plan, with established goals and an assessment of the means available to achieve them.

There may be considerable variation in press policy from one post to another, according to local circumstances and the inclination of the chief of mission. The key is that the policy, whether written or oral or a combination of both, make clear how press contacts are to be coordinated, who can speak on the record, who can speak on background, and who can speak by themselves on background with a reporter and without a USIS officer present.[1]

Policy Coordination

To the ambassador falls the primary job of coordinating with Washington on policy matters and making sure the staff is properly briefed. In any fast-breaking situation, much work will be done on the telephone, on both open and secure lines (and if it is an open line the assumption should be that officials of the host country, and possibly others, are listening in).

Israel is a good example of where this kind of coordination between embassy and Washington can be particularly important. When Sam Lewis served as ambassador in Tel Aviv from 1977 to 1985, he noted that the Israeli press was hypersensitive to any statement in Washington on the Middle East and to reporting by major news organizations like the *New York Times,* whose stories were often perceived as reflecting official U.S. government views.

"I put a fair amount of time and energy into phone calls—interpreting, clarifying, straightening out, and directing," Lewis recalled. "It was very important for me to have a fast relay on key stories appearing in the U.S. press or wire services. In that regard, the Wireless File and other less formal communications channels from the department and USIA were very important in getting us what was actually printed and said.[2] If I had the facts, I could at least argue. I worked very closely with my press attaché and asked him to do a lot of calling and clarifying as well."

Lewis, whose tenure in Israel overlapped with the prime ministership of Menachem Begin, said he made it a habit to talk to Washington late each afternoon by secure phone. "I was after what would be the next day's explosion, so that when the prime minister called I could deflect it immediately and cool the situation down—before it got reinforced by press stories leaked by the prime minister's office. Immediacy is the key. You've got to get a sense of what the bombs will be, get the facts, and be able to rebut."

He also noted the importance of listening to the 7:00 A.M. Kol Israel radio newscast to find out what the day's news would be. "In this broadcast we would learn what the Israelis thought was the latest perfidy from the White House press spokesman. I listened because the prime minister listened. More than once, I would be called about 7:15 A.M. by the prime minister asking what in the world was the intent of the statement that had been issued by the White House or State Department. If I listened, I would at least know what he was talking about. Then I could call Washington, get something, call him back, and calm him down. This was one of my regular functions in the Begin era."

Post Coordination

In addition to this kind of high-level external fireproofing, posts must coordinate press policy internally. It is impossible to overstate how important it is that embassy officers tell each other what they are saying and doing. If the political officer or the deputy chief of mission goes beyond agreed guidance in briefing a reporter and does not inform the PAO, the results can be decidedly awkward. According to a number of PAOs, this happens quite frequently, to the detriment of their credibility and effectiveness as the embassy spokesperson and primary point of contact for journalists.

In the early 1980s Secretary of State George Shultz was visiting an embassy in Central America. The secretary's party put it about with reporters that they should stick around for the toasts after an official luncheon. The secretary praised the ambassador in his toast, noted that he had just been promoted, and added that he had the full confidence of President Reagan—hardly earth-shattering news. A newspaper correspondent covering the event wondered what the administration was trying to accomplish. Then he recalled that the ambassador had been the target of local right-wing assassination plots. He also remembered that the right-wingers felt the envoy was going beyond the president's views in pressing for a crackdown on the activities of those believed responsible for human rights abuses.

The correspondent said he asked the PAO about the significance of the toasts, and specifically whether there had been any more assassination plots. The PAO reportedly looked startled and said no, that it was just a well-deserved honor. The correspondent then went off and found another senior embassy official, who said yes to the same question and provided details.

From the reporter's point of view, the PAO had misled him. "The PAO should realize that there are other people," the journalist said. "Furthermore, this is something the administration *wanted* out. People shouldn't be fooled. You need to deal with the PAO. You need to be polite. But someone like that can lose the confidence of the entire press corps and not know it."

When such differences occur, a reporter will quite properly exploit them. It is therefore important that there be full understanding, from the ambassador on down, about what can be said on policy issues. In this particular case, it can be argued that if the PAO had been unsure of what to say, he answered too hastily and should have shifted gears, promising to get back to the reporter after checking into the matter.

But it also often happens in situations such as this that the PAO is following post guidance while someone else is going beyond it. This can be very harmful to the credibility of the press officer, and therefore harmful to the embassy. "The PAO frequently feels kept on a leash, while the political section and DCM [deputy chief of mission] are not," one experienced public affairs officer said. "If someone does go beyond the guidance, he ought to call up the PAO and say so, otherwise the journalist can see that the PAO is out of the loop and won't want to deal with him."

Another coordination issue is rivalry over sources, including journalists. In this regard, one veteran USIA officer commented that some diplomats—who, like reporters, need good information to do their jobs well—tend to be jealous of their sources. This can lead to counterproductive rivalry among embassy officers over journalistic contacts. "Journalists get treated almost like lovers," he said. There is usually no harm in more than one person having regular contact, for example, with a well-informed local newspaper editor. The harm usually comes from hoarding contacts or information rather than from multiple contacts and the sharing of useful material with interested colleagues. The issue should not be who gets the goodies, but what gets reported back to Washington.

Embassies are organisms. The ambassador is the head, but various other parts deal with political, economic, commercial, consular, administrative, aid, military assistance, drug, and myriad other issues, depending on the size and location of the post. Whatever the issue, it is important that it be properly coordinated not only with Washington but within the mission, from ambassador to DCM to section heads to public affairs officers to junior officers to secretaries. Certainly the ambassador must set the overall tone; but other senior officers must also carry the message, junior officers need to learn by sitting in on briefings, and secretaries have to play an important role as initial point of contact.

"Our embassies are full of people who deal with critical issues," said Donna Oglesby, a veteran PAO and senior USIA officer. In addition to Foreign Service officers, she noted, there are "Drug Enforcement Agency folks dealing with narcotics, commercial officers doing trade issues, AID doing aid, the military working arms sales, and others. In fact, the military often have their own public affairs policy. Embassy demographics are such that the ambassador must cast his press management net broadly. The Agriculture guy, for example, can create problems if he's too loose-lipped. You have to think about these things in terms that go beyond just the political or economic section. Standard operating procedures are important."

The day-to-day mechanism for coordination is the regular country team meeting of the ambassador and his section heads. At many posts, the session is built around an initial presentation by the press officer of key items in the local press that day. At the meeting, officers report on their activities, exchange information, and request whatever guidance they may need. Section chiefs then go back to their offices and brief their staffs on key points and convey any instructions from the ambassador. The information flow should be both top-down and bottom-up.

On the bottom-up side, Ambassador April Glaspie recalled that at one point in 1989 she heard first from the Turkish ambassador in Baghdad about the presence in Iraq of Farzad Bazoft, a controversial Iranian-born correspondent for the *London Observer*.[3] As it turned out, however, Bazoft had spoken not only to the Turkish commercial officer but to members of the U.S. mission, although none of them thought it significant enough at the time to mention to the ambassador. "At staff meetings," Glaspie said, "even in a small embassy, it is important to discuss press issues because sometimes the left hand doesn't know what the right hand is doing."

On the top-down side, several senior diplomats made the point that knowledge is an essential element of discretion. "I spent a lot of time briefing the staff about what, in U.S. policy terms, I was doing in my contacts so they could use this in their contacts," Ambassador Lewis said of his eight-year tour in Israel.

Similarly, former ambassador to India William Clark Jr. commented, "You need to be sure that those in the embassy who are likely to speak to the press, whether at a party or elsewhere, are in the loop about what's going on," at least to the extent that they can respond prudently if questioned at a party. "Even if they are not informed of everything," Clark said, they need to know enough to realize "this is something the ambassador and the secretary have on their minds, and they had better check and not give an off-the-cuff answer."

Press policy at any mission normally will stipulate that the ambassador and PAO are the only ones to speak on the record. But it should also be clearly understood who speaks on background and under what circumstances: for example, the PAO always confirms the arrangements, prebriefs the reporter on ground rules, and then sits in when appropriate.

The first issue any embassy must consider in an interview request is who does the briefing. The ambassador is usually requested, but if demand is heavy he or she won't be able to do it all. Former ambassador to Egypt Hermann Eilts commented that working with the press is like working with an embassy country team: you tend to work with those who have the knowledge, the information, and the contacts. Eilts said he usually found himself dealing on a private basis not with the entire foreign press corps, or even all the U.S. press corps in town, but with specific individuals. He cited two reasons for this: "(a) You develop a relationship over time that they honor with whatever restrictions there are, and (b) they are sometimes useful to you. They're plugged in. [But] this is not true of every U.S. reporter, and you need to be careful, because you don't want to project the image that you're discriminating. They all want private interviews, which are time-consuming. The greatest problem an ambassador has is time, and this lends itself to dealing with a few people."

One ambassador with considerable experience briefing overseas and in Washington said he saw no point in always having the ambassador do the background briefing. "It's perfectly acceptable if the political counselor does it, for example. The ambassador doesn't know anything he doesn't know, or at least, anything that he wants to tell the press about. Other people should be encouraged to do the briefings as long as they follow the guidelines. If several U.S. journalists ask for a meeting, I'll do it, but I don't see the point if the journalist just wants to punch a ticket by interviewing the ambassador."

While this is true, and many reporters routinely will seek out the expertise of various section heads, the ambassador will remain the top drawing card and ordinarily will lead the mission's briefing effort. "One thing I've learned is to always go to the ambassador," says Doyle McManus. First, the ambassador "understands the process" and "knows how to do it." Second, "no one in a mission is in a better position to speak with authority and not worry about it."

Another issue is who sets up the meeting and who sits in. The officer who does the ambassador's press relations is a key person in any mission. Normally, this is the PAO or, in larger posts, another U.S. Information Service officer who concentrates exclusively on press and information activities. (The PAO's responsibilities are quite broad: he or she will supervise not only the press and information function, but also all educational and cultural affairs, including USIS libraries, the Fulbright scholarship program, and international exchanges.)

Just as some diplomats suggested thinking of USIS officers more often when it comes to political reporting, so too a number of senior diplomats recommended thinking broadly on press and information issues and not always confining press relations exclusively to USIS officers. Former under secretary David Newsom said he'd seen "political officers who had a better sense of the kind of public affairs climate the ambassador faces in Washington and the field."

Ambassador Thomas Pickering listed what he looks for in a press officer: "someone who is alert to the changing scene, who knows and can spot when troublesome issues come up, who knows what we've done in the past and how to get to the ambassador and DCM to formulate how to deal with those issues in the future."

Practice in setting up and conducting embassy meetings with reporters varies considerably. At some posts, it is not unusual for ambassadors to meet alone with reporters they trust and know well. The most common practice is probably for the PAO to sit in on all interviews with the ambassador, and on other backgrounders at his discretion. Ambassador Mike Mansfield in Tokyo reportedly not only made it standard practice for a USIS officer to sit in on *all* embassy press interviews; he also wanted them *all* recorded.

The Role of the PAO

Some correspondents object to the PAO's presence, considering that the PAO at best adds nothing to the conversation and at worst can be a wet blanket. When ambassadors are heavily dependent on their PAOs and bring them in, "it's bad," one correspondent told me. "I don't like three-way conversations. I don't mind if the PAO sets it up, but PAOs tend to be skittish and whiny."

But ambassadors may want their PAOs in on such meetings for practical reasons that have nothing to do with being a watchdog, since most ambassadors have a pretty good idea what to say to a reporter without coaching. The ambassador often wants the PAO to attend the briefing so the PAO will know what transpired and thus be able to reflect that knowledge in subsequent contacts and briefings, in providing guidance to other embassy officers, and in handling any follow-up that may be necessary with the reporter.

Even when an officer and a reporter who is requesting a briefing already know each other, all sides benefit if the PAO sees the reporter first.

The reporter benefits, first, because the PAO can ensure that the reporter sees the right briefers. If the topic is human rights, for example, either a political or a consular officer may be tracking the issue, depending on the post. If it is trade difficulties with a neighboring country, the most knowledgeable briefer may be in either the economic or commercial section. If it is security assistance, the best address may be either the political section, the political-military section, or a military officer attached to the embassy.

The PAOs are often more attuned than others in the embassy to the needs of the press, and many will go out of their way to be helpful.

Correspondent Ed Cody recalled one PAO he felt was particularly skillful in steering reporters in a straight way:

> He wouldn't actually give away the store. I would get a whiff of something. I'd go to [him] and say, "Do you know what this is about?" He would say, "Oh, gee, I can't talk about that"—but he would refer me to someone in the local military. I would go to the military and say, "[The officer] suggested I talk to you." They think, "Well, if [the embassy officer] sent him over, I guess it's okay to talk," and they would talk. Then, I would come back to him with what I learned from the military. He would say, "Damn, you'd better talk to the military group." Then, I'd talk to the U.S. military group and confront them with 80 percent of the story, and they'd have to deal with it. The PAO never told me anything himself, but he steered me in the right direction each time.

The PAO is also a potential advocate for the reporter in embassy councils. Even veteran foreign correspondents sometimes seemed unaware of this. Many are the meetings I have attended in which a PAO has doggedly intervened to persuade a skeptical ambassador to make room on a clogged calendar for a visiting reporter or group of reporters. Reporters who go straight to the ambassador's secretary may cut out an ally in the bureaucracy and reduce their chances of getting the answer they want.

"The advantage of being on the outside as a USIS person," explained one PAO, "is that you can barge in and say, 'Look, you need to say this.' There is a certain amount of protection from my agency if I need to be aggressive about it. Media concerns don't enter into the mindset of the State Department in the same way, so we can understand and complement each other. In a way, you're like the little guy in the Oliphant cartoon—close enough to understand, but still be critical."

The briefing officer benefits if arrangements are made through the PAO because the PAO will not only lay out ground rules, but also scope out what stories the reporter is most interested in pursuing. This allows the diplomat to gather any relevant information and prepare a more productive session for both sides. The PAO might also happen to know whether another reporter in town wants the same briefing. This allows the post the option of deciding, provided the reporters concerned have no objection, to consolidate briefings.

Finally, the PAO benefits because it preserves his or her role as gatekeeper. If reporters routinely get direct access to the ambassador or other embassy officers without the PAO's facilitation, it can create problems not only for the USIS chief, who loses the authority that comes with the ability to secure such access, but also for the mission as a whole. Most ambassadors simply don't have time to be their own press attachés.

The PAO must serve as the ambassador's press adviser and the eyes and ears for press contacts in the mission. It is therefore vital that he or she be fully informed of all such contacts, whether local press or visitors. Keeping a single point of contact prevents the ambassador from being blindsided and allows the post to track coherently the professionalism and ability of the various journalists who seek embassy contact. Furthermore, if the PAO is cut out or otherwise undermined, he or she may not have the access or credibility to carry out the ambassador's wishes. Thus, even if separate arrangements are made from time to time, the PAO should always be informed as soon as possible.

Since USIS is not staffed to sit in on every media contact of every officer in every embassy, deciding who sits in is usually at the discretion of the officer concerned and the PAO. If a political officer meets with an American journalist who has visited an area denied to the embassy, for example, it is as much to gain as to give information. In this case, the political officer might conduct the meeting one-on-one, and simply keep USIS informed of the contact.

One of the most important benefits of working with reporters is access to this kind of information and independent feedback. In addition, as one senior FSO pointed out, there is sometimes too much bias in official reporting in favor of the local powers that be. Contact with the press can be a useful tonic for any tendency to underplay human rights abuses or repression or civil rights violations, or to overlook such things in policy terms.

Junior Officers, Taping, and Other Considerations

An issue senior diplomats should keep in mind is the need to expose younger officers to briefings, a point noted by Thomas Pickering. "You need to build confidence and create opportunities for people," he said. "Otherwise, they can get to senior positions and be very jittery about dealing with the press." Pickering recalled that "it was very valuable for me to sit in with my boss, [Ambassador] Ron Spiers, and watch him dealing with reporters."

Most reporters would have no objection. "I don't mind if a junior officer sits in," commented *Time*'s Bruce Van Voorst. "As a matter of fact, it's good for the reporter to meet younger officers to keep up with the turnover."

Another issue is use of a tape recorder, whether by the correspondent or the embassy officer. Again, this is a judgment call. Some embassies will tape both on-the-record *and* background interviews as a matter of policy. Other posts, however, might determine that taping is sometimes out of place. An officer might conclude it would put a chill on the meeting with the American journalist who had just visited an area denied to the embassy if the officer whipped out a tape recorder as the reporter recounted her experiences. Reporters may also hesitate to introduce the formality of a tape recorder. *Boston Globe* correspondent Mary Curtius said she found, as a correspondent overseas, that use of a tape recorder was "incredibly off-putting to diplomats," although it was fairly standard procedure covering the State Department.

Don Oberdorfer recalled only a few interviews when the situation was so sensitive that he did not wish to introduce the recorder, although he normally relied on it, even on background, and could not remember anyone ever objecting to its use. "The idea is to get it right," he said, "which is presumably in the interest of the official."

Pickering said he started using tape in El Salvador when there was a significant possibility of difficulties arising from the resulting stories. "Normally, the reporters came with their own tape recorder and this would be settled in advance. The PAO might say that the ambassador likes to keep a record, that we will be taping, and the reporter should feel free to as well. I prefer to have it that way, and I'm pretty relaxed about taping as long as the reporter follows the ground rules. In fact, if you tape the ground rules, you have additional protection with the department or others about what you say." [4]

Group backgrounders are another occasion when taping is appropriate. "We would tape if General [John] Vessey was coming out of Vietnam and did a background briefing for a group of reporters on the POW-MIA issue," one PAO told me. "But we wouldn't routinely tape one-on-ones."

Times to consider taping include:

- When the reporter is taping;
- When the issue under discussion is particularly sensitive;
- When there is a chance of confusion, for example, if the reporter does not speak English well (non-English-speaking journalists sometimes *like* to have a tape available, so they can revisit material a second or third time);
- When there is other reason to believe there might be a problem, for example, if the PAO advises that the reporter has a reputation for burning sources or not getting things right.

Reporters normally won't object to being taped if they can tape, too. "A PAO in Seoul once told me I could *not* tape a backgrounder with the ambassador—only he could," recalled Doyle McManus. "So I started the backgrounder by complaining about that to the ambassador, whom I had known for several years, deliberately embarrassing the poor PAO. Needless to say, the ambassador said of course I could use a tape, too."

Having a Plan

The importance of preparation for any individual meeting with a reporter (The Five P's) has already been noted. In addition, all officers who might have dealings with host country media should be familiar with the PAO's annual "country plan" outlining the themes and subjects for the post's public diplomacy program. This plan is coordinated annually with the different sections of the embassy, approved by the ambassador, and sent to USIA in Washington for review and approval.

Besides giving a general review of bilateral relations, the PAO's plan "describes the barriers, problems, and opportunities affecting the communications process in the country. Such items as censorship, literacy, freedom of the press, internal political processes and divisions, public attitudes toward the United States, cultural differences, and societal anomalies are set forth." [5] The plan then lists specific public diplomacy objectives and the most cost-effective ways of reaching target audiences. Former USIA officer Hans Tuch notes that in a European nation such as Germany, a short-term objective might be explaining U.S. arms control policy or persuading the younger generation of Germans that the ties between the United States and Germany will preserve both democracy and peace.[6]

Preparation of the USIS country plan should not be an idle bureaucratic exercise that simply produces another paper for the PAO's files. It should focus the embassy's public affairs effort and tie in smoothly with the mission's overall goals and objectives. The input from all sections should be real, and so should the follow-up. This point requires special emphasis, because a common attitude among Foreign Service officers is that the media are something for USIS to handle. This is wrong. From the ambassador on down, there should be a clear awareness of key issues in public affairs, how they affect the post, and how post leadership wants to deal with them.

Alexander Watson gave an example of how active public affairs work served U.S. narcotics control efforts in Peru during his tenure there. He said the post put on a full-scale media campaign to explain its efforts and views, using prepared materials, interviews, films, and briefings. A particularly effective theme, developed and presented by the embassy in Lima, was that narcotics production is bad for the environment.

Watson said Greenpeace and other environmental groups perceived crop eradication efforts as a policy that could "turn the Amazon into a Sahara"—despite careful selection of herbicides for impact only on target plants and formulation so that they would bind in the soil, have no lasting effect, and not leach out. "The counterargument we developed was that these drug producer groups are stripping the hills bare, dumping kerosene, acetone, and other stuff in the streams. This became a major argument to the world through the media."

In addition, the post took journalists and Peruvian and Western environmentalists out to the drug-producing areas to see for themselves what was happening. This was dubbed the "Oh, shit" trip, because invariably people would look out the window of the helicopter at coca plants stretching as far as the eye could see, and say, "Oh, shit, I didn't know it was as bad as this."

Anticipate, Cultivate

In any mission, the elements of good media relations are commonsense. Besides effective coordination with Washington, good internal communications, and well understood standard procedures, all officers who come in contact with journalists should make an effort to study the local media culture.

At most missions, USIS will have done a media analysis of some sort. This is a subject on which the PAO will frequently brief visiting journalists, to help them sort through the welter of information and disinformation they face. It is particularly important to do in a place where the local media may be corrupt, that is, where some newspapers are known to be paid agents of one kind of political influence or another. This was the case in Lebanon when I was there in the 1970s—the daily *An Nahar* was independent and quite reliable, but most other newspapers reflected the political views of different parties and countries in the region.

Anticipate

The best way to deal with an issue is to be in front of it, not react after the fact. Internally, this means thinking of the media implications of any issue *from the start*, to avoid floundering without a coordinated answer when a reporter poses a perfectly predictable question. Admittedly, this is not always easy to remember in a breaking situation. The main thing post leadership should keep in mind is to include the PAO or other media relations officer in all important meetings and make it that person's duty to anticipate and advise on the media implications of the crisis.

An experienced PAO recalled one occasion, after a coup in an Asian country, when the State Department issued a strong statement deploring the interruption of constitutional government. The ambassador set up a ten o'clock meeting with the coup commander and a twelve o'clock meeting with the civilian prime minister. Upon hearing this, the PAO immediately realized that the footage of the 10:00 A.M. meeting would make the local midday news, but the footage of the noon session would not get on until the evening newscast. Thus, the image of the ambassador with the coup commander would be in the public domain for six hours before the visuals with the civilian prime minister appeared. The PAO pointed this out to the ambassador, but by that time the appointments had already been made and he had to go through with them. The PAO scrambled all afternoon to turn the story around and had some success with items filed to the United States. He was not so lucky with the in-country play.

Thus, post leadership should make a habit of at least trying to check with the PAO or media officer before making *any* media appointment, even in a breaking situation. It's not that the ambassador, the DCM, and other senior embassy officers are unaware of how the media works. The problem is that they will be focusing priority attention on how to take the issue to the local government and on coordinating with Washington. It is the job of the press officer or PAO to be thinking full-time about the media implications.

Cultivate

Diplomats should make a point of seeing reporters *when they don't need to.* This greatly enhances the chances that the reporters will be there, and will listen, when the diplomats *do* need them. Phone calls should be returned as promptly as practical, if not by the ambassador then by a designee. If the ambassador simply cannot accommodate an interview request, and this may frequently be the case, then the bias of the mission, barring good reason not to, should be for someone else to brief or meet.

One thing diplomats should keep in mind is that the personal circumstances of reporters are often very different from their own. Foreign correspondents have no administrative section to help them find housing or get a telephone, to run interference with the local bureaucracy, to make repairs to their house, or to register their children in school. A spouse may often be left alone for extended periods while the reporter travels outside the country.

Correspondents have no commissary and live off the local economy. However adaptable journalists may be—and foreign correspondents are usually pretty resilient—even the most determined expatriate will appreciate a taste of home from time to time. I remember well when I was a reporter how much I enjoyed visiting the homes of diplomats, or attending embassy functions, and tasting things like hot dogs, steaks, American beer, bacon, and peanut butter. Similarly, if a correspondent is visiting town, he or she will appreciate a dinner invitation rather than having to eat alone in a hotel.

Even when contact with the reporter is limited, there is still scope for consideration. In the 1970s a U.S. reporter obtained an exclusive interview with King Hussein of Jordan. The interview did not start until late at night, and the reporter stayed up into the wee hours of the morning writing and filing his story. Early the next business day—not long after midnight Washington time and only a few hours after the reporter had finally gone to bed—an embassy officer called asking for a copy of the story. The reporter groggily explained he had just gone to sleep and asked if it could wait a few hours, but the officer insisted on coming immediately. The ambassador probably had said he wanted a copy during a morning staff meeting.

Normally, the reporter not only would have provided a copy as a courtesy but, if asked, might even have let the official listen to the entire tape of the conversation. But because of his annoyance at what he saw as lack of consideration on the part of the embassy, he made no offer of the tape and provided only copies of stories actually filed—copies that presumably were already available in Washington.

In other words, the embassy rushed to get information at an hour when no one in Washington would be around to read it. By needlessly alienating a well-disposed journalist, it missed out on potentially useful taped material that had not been filed. By waiting a few hours longer, the post could easily have had more information—and in plenty of time to compile and send a cable to be read in Washington the same day.

I mention it because I was that journalist, and I still have that tape.

Standard Procedures

Media work at an embassy overseas is not something for USIS officers alone. To be successful, it requires the active involvement of all sections of the post. Post management should make coordination of media policy and establishment of simple standard procedures a high priority. In addition, the mission should have clear-cut goals for its in-country public diplomacy, supported by careful analysis of the means available to achieve them.

For those in contact with journalists, it is important to study the local media culture and anticipate the media implications of any issue *from the outset*. The bigger the issue, the more important this will be. Finally, contacts with the media should be ongoing. To have the ear of the reporters when it needs them, the embassy must be available to the reporters when it doesn't need them. It's like saving for a rainy day.

Chapter 13

Washington
Eunuch Games

> ODYSSEUS: *Unwisdom marks thy words and actions both.*
> NEOPTOLEMUS: *If just, 'tis better than unjust and wise.*
> —SOPHOCLES

"The Department of State behaves like a microcosm of Washington," said one experienced ambassador, "and the public sees the Beltway as a palace wall behind which eunuchs cavort, playing eunuch games that no one else understands."

Washington presents a very different operating environment from that experienced overseas. A substantial metamorphosis occurs in the role of diplomats, in their press contacts, and in their relationships with other U.S. officials when they move back behind the palace wall. It is the difference between being a news source and a news subject.

An FSO who spent twenty-one years in Europe, the Middle East, and Washington explained: "Overseas, the reporter and the diplomat can exchange information on a constructive basis. Oftentimes, the reporter needs background and perspective on how what he has seen fits into things. You help him pick up the thread. Back in Washington, there is less cooperation. They have less to give you. Basically, they're coming in for a feed. So it tends to be more confrontational and not so much of a two-way street. The diplomat realizes he could have his name in the paper. He needs to be sure the ground rules are clear. It's a different kind of cooperation."

In addition to a different role vis-à-vis reporters, returning officials will find themselves in a different role vis-à-vis other U.S. officials. Overseas, the emphasis is on implementation, and there is usually an established policy framework to guide the actions of all U.S. government employees. In Washington, at the wellhead, the State Department is one of a number of bureaucratic participants in a competitive, politicized, and occasionally turbulent policy process.

141

Decision Making under Siege

The diplomat also returns to a decision-making process under siege by technology. In many fast-breaking situations, television will supplement or partially displace slower official channels as a tool of high-level communication and a source of information. There is thus not only less secrecy but less time to react.

At the same time, the proliferation and immediacy of images have shifted issues increasingly out of the abstract into concrete visual impressions. This adds enormously to the pressures and complications of decision making by officials who must be sensitive to public opinion. It is one thing to plausibly conclude that the United States should not allow itself to become involved in a ground war in the Balkans; it is another to make that argument in the teeth of daily televised images of horrific slaughter in Bosnia. In effect, television has put more emotion into the foreign policy calculus.

Reflecting in March 1993 on violence in Bosnia and the former Yugoslavia, former secretary Eagleburger said,

> There was a time when we would have dealt much more cautiously, not only with Bosnia but with the collapse of Yugoslavia in general. Our administration tried to do this, but the fact is that we were driven—and the new administration is being driven—by TV. If CNN had covered Nagorno-Karabakh as carefully, we'd be wrapped around the axle on that one too.[1]
>
> This, and [the legacy of] Vietnam, means that foreign policy is made in a much more defensive manner today. It's not just reactive, but defensive: What can we do not to be attacked? So we tend to make policy seriatim, and you can make serious mistakes.
>
> There is a terrible tendency in the U.S. mind to think any problem is solvable. But some are not, or they would take such a massive involvement that it's just not workable.

The Deterioration of Trust

In addition to changing roles and working in a policy process on fast-forward, the returning diplomat should be aware of changes occurring year in and year out in the relationship between reporters and officials in Washington. In recent years the government has grown bigger and harder to cover. Less and less seems to be said on the record, which means more and more is said by anonymous sources, many of whom have their own agendas. At the same time, the press has become relatively more powerful, at least in its ability to shape the public agenda.

As detailed in the third chapter of this book and referred to above by Lawrence Eagleburger, many officials and reporters believe there has been a significant breakdown in trust between reporters and government officials since the Vietnam War. In the view of a number of thoughtful officials—and some journalists—more and more reporters appear to be caught up in "gotcha" journalism, feeding what one official termed Washington's "culture of scandals." Upon retirement from the *Washington Post* in April 1993, Don Oberdorfer contrasted the atmosphere in Washington with the overly trusting and uncritical ways of the press when he first came to the capital in 1958:

> Thirty-five years later, many reporters have gone to the other extreme, assuming that nearly every official statement is a lie or half-truth until proven otherwise. There is a pervasive sense of being manipulated by official spokesmen, a sense that is intensified by the widened physical distance between reporters and officials.
>
> No doubt, greater skepticism was sorely needed in the earlier era, when reporters tended to be unquestioning consumers and purveyors of official information. But today's climate is also unhealthy. Without at least a modicum of trust on both sides, it is difficult to see how reporters and officials can relate effectively.[2]

For some officials the perceived lack of trust has signaled a narrowing of the terms of engagement. "I'm no longer willing to schmooze on the phone when a reporter calls up," said one. "Five years ago I would have. I don't trust them any more. Why should I? What's in it for me? Journalist X has never burned me, but I don't accept any more the premise that she is my colleague, and it's because of what I have seen in my experience in Washington in the last six years."[3]

Another FSO, who has been a deputy assistant secretary and held other key jobs in Washington, declared that he wished he had had a better understanding at the beginning of his career of the difference in the press's mission at home and abroad. He too cited the deterioration of trust that he had seen in Washington over the course of a career spanning two and a half decades:

> It's getting worse and worse. There is cooperation between the two sides abroad, but then they come back and try to screw each other here. The antagonism has gotten more acute. There has been a breakdown in confidence in government. It's probably a combination of things over the years, from the Bay of Pigs to the Gulf of Tonkin to Watergate. The attitude is that the government's secrets are the problem, that bureaucrats are the problem. What we need to do is recognize and find ways to have an appropriate adversarial but not dysfunctional relationship with the media.

Terms of Engagement

In his 1986 Harvard study of the media and federal policy making, Martin Linsky examined the growth in the influence of the press, noting that both policy makers and the public depend more and more on the press for information on how government is working.

"In order to make policy well," he said, "officials increasingly have to take into consideration the press and public relations aspects of their programs and decisions." He added, "Having more policy makers who are skilled at managing the media will make for better government." [4]

Linsky anticipated—and dismissed as "wrongheaded and short-sighted"—the criticism that this means training government officials to manipulate or control the news. "It is a bit disingenuous but not surprising for reporters to be critical of an effort to give officials better resources for dealing with them and their colleagues. And whatever the criticism, policy makers cannot be expected to develop thoughtful and strategic press relations unless they learn how." [5]

His recipe for how to do this contains many of the same elements I heard again and again from various diplomats and reporters:

• Officials must understand the role of the press, the conventions of the press, and the changing relationship between policy makers and reporters.

• Instead of underestimating their ability to influence press coverage and leaving public communications considerations to the last minute, officials should be activist, establishing goals in their press relations and assessing the means to achieve them. In other words, they should get in front of the news.

• Officials should develop professional relationships with reporters—not as friends, not as partners in policy making, but as colleagues in public affairs with different interests. [6]

How should this be accomplished in the area of foreign policy, especially given the deterioration of trust cited by Secretary Eagleburger, Don Oberdorfer, and others? How does a diplomat—or a journalist—cultivate "professional relationships" in a hothouse Washington environment of high pressure, rushed decisions, small circles, excluded experts, rising press influence, and hordes of would-be players and leakers who seek to influence virtually every aspect of policy?

The first thing for a diplomat to understand is how the Department of State organizes itself to meet the press, and how he or she fits into that hierarchy.

The Scale of Accountability

There is a scale of accountability in media work, and diplomats returning to Washington should understand their place on it. The secretary of state is at the top, assisted by his spokesman, and it goes down through various seventh-floor under secretaries, to sixth-floor assistant secretaries and deputy assistant secretaries, to office directors, desk officers, and staff in the various regional and functional bureaus.

Accountability for policy generally increases as one goes up the chain while accountability for facts and detail generally increases as one goes down. The secretary will have the big picture, but not the details. The desk officer may not have all of the policy pieces, but he will have texts of U.S. policy statements as well as facts on population, election results, and ethnic makeup. "One needs to make a clear distinction between what policy officials can do, that is, deputy assistant secretary and assistant secretary on up, and what we can do," said one office director. "They can choose on their own to put a policy spin on a story. The rest of us should not. While we can tell the reporter what the policy is, we really are not free to say more than the spokesman. The function we have is to give depth and understanding of what's behind the policy, of what the context is."

The department's public face is the spokesman. To do this job effectively, he or she must have access to all levels of the department and clear guidance, from above and below, that seeks to answer reporters' questions rather than avoid them.

Edward Djerejian, who served as a deputy spokesman at both the State Department and the White House, recalled the guidelines Secretary of State George Shultz gave him when he began the job: "Your credibility as deputy spokesman is my credibility. It is the president's credibility. Therefore, you will know everything that is going on so you're never put in a position of misinforming the press or the public. For that to happen, you will have to have full access."

Djerejian added, "You have to work at access. It is not automatic. You've got to gain the confidence and trust of your colleagues as spokesman, and you must convey a sense of real competence, that you know what you're talking about, so that people will take you seriously. You must sensitize them to the reality—and some don't appreciate this fully—that their credibility is on the line, and that if they do withhold information or mislead the spokesperson, it may come back to haunt them."

The Shultz precepts are the right precepts. The spokesman must have access to the principals, whether it is the secretary or the president or the national security adviser or the chief of staff. "When it works like that, and it should always work like that, things will be fine," Djerejian said. "You have to be dealt a full deck of cards. It can't work any other way."

The Spokesman and the Daily Briefing

The noon briefing is the department spokesman's daily platform.[7] It is designed to satisfy virtually no one, since the bureaucracy always wants the spokesman to say less than he or she should and the journalists want the spokesman to say more. What makes the process work is the quality of information. In a bureaucratic culture naturally resistant to disclosure, the spokesman's job is to shake the bureaucratic tree every day and break loose as much fruitful information on foreign policy decisions as possible, whether on the record at the briefing or in follow-up background sessions. "We don't have to give the whole story," said former spokesman Richard Boucher, "but we can give reporters elements of the story."

Foreign policy is frequently a matter of bargaining. In this process, the United States sometimes gets what it wants, and sometimes it doesn't. There is often no harm in explaining on the record after a meeting what was achieved and what was not. "We tend to paper over differences with other countries, to speak in generalities, and to stay away from specifics," Boucher said. "Sometimes, this is justified—for example, if you have an ongoing negotiation—but not always. We tend to portray everything with regard to other countries as sweetness and light and harmony. This just sets us up for a fall when we don't get what we want."

The spokesman must take the broad view, and this can put him at odds with various regional bureaus. "The regional bureaus tend to say things only from their perspective," Boucher said. "If you say something about Somalia and the U.N., for example, it could box you in on Cambodia and the U.N."

Since the advent of television cameras at the noon briefings in the late 1970s, a common criticism among reporters has been the decline in the relative utility of the briefing as a source of information. In 1982 UPI's Jim Anderson declared the term "noon news briefing" a complete misnomer: "It does not take place at noon; it rarely produces news; and, in view of the lack of information, it is not brief."[8]

It is sometimes suggested that the briefing would be better if the secretary came down more often. Boucher disagreed. "We should bring the secretary down when he is actually in a position to say something," he said. "Many times he can't really go into issues for one reason or another and to bring him down in that situation would be mutually unsatisfactory. He wouldn't be able to go into the detail he would like, and reporters wouldn't get much out of it."

A common criticism among diplomats is that there is no real need for a daily briefing. It rushes decision making. They feel the department could reduce the pressure on policy makers, consider issues more carefully, and improve the decision-making process if it didn't go live every single day. Most public affairs officers disagree, however. "The other way of looking at it," said one, "is that it would keep people in the dark longer."

Intense journalistic rivalry is a factor that has fed reliance on individual reporter-official information transactions, and this has contributed to the devaluation of the noon briefing. "In pursuit of stories, reporters will often not raise questions at official briefings in order to keep attention away from the topic they are investigating independently," said former spokesman Robert McCloskey. "This is especially frustrating for official spokesmen who work hard to prevent leaks, partly out of self-interest (because they want to be the recognized authoritative voice) but, more important, also because they believe that the public interest is best served on the record, where policy can gain the respect that comes with clarity and consistency." [9]

The Real Manager: The Secretary of State

While the spokesman presents the department's public face on a day-to-day basis, the real manager of press relations is the secretary.

As Secretary Eagleburger noted, the effectiveness of many people in the career service is limited because they are afraid of the press, and unprepared to be straight and honest. "This kills you over time," he said. "We have a terrible tendency to be disingenuous or fluffy or fuzzy or not answer the question. You have to recognize you can't get away with it for a long time."

Although Eagleburger clearly advocated openness and candor with reporters, he did not favor indiscriminate talking by State Department officials at all levels. While acknowledging that lower-level officials often had factual information reporters would find useful, he pointed out that not all officials have the whole policy picture. "What most often happens is there is a leak of an uninformed comment," he said.

In addition, Eagleburger felt, the tendency of many career officers not to think constructively about press relations hampers their effectiveness. "Many react defensively, many react with the panic button," he said. If they are to be useful, "people in the establishment and the career service must greatly improve the way they think of press relations."

Finally, Eagleburger noted the issue of accountability, citing policy differences within the State Department on the former Yugoslavia as a classic case. Eagleburger and other senior U.S. policy makers felt a sober assessment of U.S. interests militated against getting drawn into ground involvement in the bloody civil warfare. Others, like former Yugoslav desk officer George Kenney, strongly believed that "only Western military intervention can solve this crisis." [10]

On 25 August 1992 Kenney resigned to protest what he saw as a failure in U.S. policy. He wrote, "We need to ask whether, by not acting to stop genocide against Muslims in Bosnia, the West will ever stand up for its values, whether we may poison our relations with the Islamic world. Americans need to ask profound questions about our responsibilities as a world power." [11] Observed Eagleburger, "It's not a matter of whether Kenney was right or wrong. He wasn't the guy who had to make the decisions." [12]

In any crisis, officials face two humps. The first is to resist the clamor for precipitate action on the front end, and the second is, having decided a course of action (or nonaction), to work as actively as possible at a senior level to explain the policy rationale.

Eagleburger said it was the job of the seventh floor to spot a problem coming up and then explain why the United States was doing something or not doing something. "In a case such as Yugoslavia, you just have to decide you're going to take it for a while as you sort out the policy," he said, adding a candid coda: "Of course, in our case, we took it, but we didn't sort out the policy."

Media relations fall into two general categories: day-to-day matters and longer-running, politically sensitive subjects like the former Yugoslavia and the so-called Iraqgate issue. "One of the things we didn't do with Yugoslavia or Iraqgate," Eagleburger said, "was have an active public relations effort to explain our position. We're not very good at that." On Yugoslavia, "We probably should have laid out the analysis fairly carefully, and then hung onto it." On Iraqgate, he cited the department's failure to respond more fully to press play that "totally corrupted the facts." [13]

On the level of strategic thinking about press issues, Eagleburger felt a seventh-floor mechanism was needed to "think these things through and to explain policy—not to propagandize, but to get ahead of criticism." He believed the State Department needed an institution that was identifying emerging issues and "laying out our case—when an Iraqgate starts to gel, you get the case out"—a suggestion he made a number of times during that episode. But the prevailing view was to take a low-key approach to the efforts of Rep. Henry Gonzalez, head of the House Banking Committee and the Bush administration's most persistent congressional critic on Iraqgate issues, assuming that if the department raised the issue, that would only "hype the whole thing." In retrospect, Eagleburger considered that decision a mistake that reveals "how the Department of State thinks about public relations and the public explication of policy questions."

Another press issue requiring a high-level strategic response is terrorism. While beyond the scope of this book, the important thing to note is that terrorism, media coverage, and government response are interactive. In a hostage taking, for example, government officials will seek to be active and firm, not panicked or overdramatic, which could raise the value of any hostages in the minds of those holding them. The media, meanwhile, will generally be trying to keep the public informed without playing into the terrorists' desire for publicity and their efforts to achieve political objectives by manipulating images, emotion, and public opinion.

In this situation, it is always difficult to calibrate the government response, which will inevitably have an effect on the way the event unfolds. Pressures can develop suddenly, and quick decisions often must be made on what can, and cannot, be said. Here again, responsiveness is key, and responsibility for policy and tone—if not the actual briefing— must rest with the seventh floor.[14]

"In a serious crisis," former under secretary David Newsom advised, "the department should establish as quickly as possible after the events a series of information briefings for the press. What is important is to establish a *pattern* of briefing," so that both the rules and the context are understood.

Setting the Tone: The Assistant Secretary

It is important to think of press implications at the beginning of policy formulation, not only at the end. "My litmus test," said Assistant Secretary Edward Djerejian, "is, do I want my name associated with this decision when it appears in the *Washington Post* and *New York Times?* Is it something I can coherently and assertively defend as being in the U.S. national interest?"

Assistant secretaries are at the interface between the working level and the policy level. On media policy, they set the tone for their bureaus: If the assistant secretary thinks of the press early and often, so will others in the bureau. If he or she gives the bureau's public affairs officer instant access and attention, so will others. If the assistant secretary insists on strong, informative press guidance, so will others. This is important, because regional bureau PAOs are the real front line, getting more press calls than any other bureaucratic target.

Not only do the assistant secretaries have final say on most day-to-day media matters, subject to seventh-floor review, but they are also, because of their expertise, a major force in shaping policy approaches in their areas, even if responsibility rests ultimately with the secretary of state. The assistant secretaries are the key gatekeepers deciding what information and actions must be passed up the chain, and these are the key interpreters for their bureaus of seventh-floor actions and how they relate to the bureaus' work.

The assistant secretaries also have the most important voice in determining how much attention foreign audiences get from U.S. policy makers. Since senior officials, and the department as a whole, tend to focus heavily on the U.S. press and domestic audience, important foreign audiences often get less attention than they deserve. Perhaps a cable summarizing key public diplomacy themes will be sent to embassies in the field. But it is just as important for senior officials to make time for a press conference at USIA's Foreign Press Center or to sit down with the Washington-based reporters of countries in the region (who have instant access to page one back home) for on-the-record interviews.

Even when senior officials want to make an effort to speak to their areas, they may find that many of their usual contacts in the U.S. press simply are not interested.

"Sometimes," said Herman Cohen, when he was assistant secretary for African affairs, "I want to talk to Africa or Europe and the U.S. press doesn't really help. So I will talk to Reuters or AP, which have external outlets overseas, or AFP or the BBC or Radio France or Radio-TV Portugal. All of these have much more of an appetite for the nitty-gritty of African affairs, as does VOA. If I want to get a message to Angola, the VOA Portuguese-language service is a good vehicle. On Somalia and the Horn of Africa, I might call the BBC. If it is Francophone Africa, Radio France. They never say no. Usually, they're calling me for interviews and I fend them off."

USIA's Worldnet television service also provides an effective, interactive forum for U.S. officials to engage with reporters overseas, but USIA officers sometimes feel it is like pulling teeth to get senior policy makers to appear. USIA is often seen as just another set of people making demands on the time of senior officials for whom the foreign press is a comparatively low priority.

The low priority attached to tending foreign audiences is matched by the marginalization of the U.S. Information Agency in Washington foreign affairs work. I have worked with many USIA officers, spoken to many in connection with this project, and participated in a detailed 1993 study of USIA by Georgetown University's Institute for the Study of Diplomacy.[15] Many express frustration with their Washington tours and can't wait to get back overseas, where they are an integral and important part of the embassy country team. In Washington, they are physically removed from the State Department and often feel underemployed. If foreign press activities are to be considered a central, not peripheral, part of the policy process, the agency charged with getting the message to audiences overseas should be brought into policy development early and often.

In the Ranks

Although the primary job of explaining U.S. policy will fall on the secretary, the spokesman, assistant secretaries, and other senior officials, there are a great many other State Department officials throughout the ranks who will come into daily contact with the press.

Generally speaking, in day-to-day contacts with reporters, the foreign affairs official should feel an obligation to be as helpful as possible. The official must bear in mind, however, that while the First Amendment gives broad support to the press's right to ask, that is not the same as an untrammeled right to know. Freedom of the press does not mean there will not be times when the government must withhold information. It does mean that those times will be comparatively few, that they must be well justified, and that officials should bear in mind the possibility that the information will eventually become public.

How do officials balance responsiveness with responsibility? Whatever their rank, as public servants diplomats must faithfully serve their country's interests and carry out its policies in accordance with the instructions of the president and secretary of state, who are accountable to Congress, the press, and the public. The element of accountability is a key point. When the president or the secretary makes a decision, he is accountable for it. By contrast, the low-level leaker who undermines that decision is accountable to no one.

If premature disclosure of negotiating tactics to a reporter could result in a failed accord or tangible lost benefit to the United States, then the official has a firm obligation not to reveal such information. Otherwise, he or she is betraying a trust. If discussion of the itinerary of the secretary of state or of a special envoy has been withheld for security reasons—so that terrorist groups will not know when or where his airplane might land—then the official must keep that back, too. Otherwise, he might put someone's life in danger.

If a reporter asks a question that involves intelligence sources or methods, it is unlikely the official will be able to answer, even if he thinks he knows the answer and would like to provide it:

• If the query is to a State Department officer, the official may not be authorized to treat the information at all. There is a very important rule in government, and it is especially important in intelligence matters, that one agency cannot declassify or disseminate another agency's material unless authorized by that agency.

- The officer asked may not have all the pieces, since intelligence is usually disseminated on a "need to know" basis. Thus, even if the diplomat tried to answer as honestly as possible, he or she could still inadvertently mislead if not privy to the whole picture. That is why answers to intelligence-related questions need careful coordination and clearance.
- The inadvertent disclosure of sources and methods can have very high costs that are not always immediately apparent. Not only can people's lives be put in danger, but large amounts of taxpayer money can be squandered and policy makers deprived of future access to important information—for example, if the product of an expensive reconnaissance satellite monitoring clandestine nuclear weapons research is carelessly compromised in a news story, the target country can take countermeasures to deceive or elude the satellite.

Most reporters who cover foreign affairs have a realistic perspective on these things. They know there will sometimes be limits on what officials can responsibly say. By and large, when they feel officials are trying to be as accessible and informative as possible, most journalists will try to be fair. What sends up red flags is the feeling of being shut out.

Martin Linsky makes a related and important point in *Impact*: "When an official has information that a reporter is seeking and the reporter knows that, the official's stake in withholding that information has changed." [16] In this situation, which crops up time and again in fielding foreign affairs issues, the policy maker's interest in providing the information increases.

Confronting an issue is almost always better than avoiding it when the press is already on the scent. This was Eagleburger's complaint about the department's reluctance to respond on the Iraqgate issue. It is often the difference between being whipsawed by revelations trickling out according to the agenda of self-interested leakers, and presenting a coherent view that maximizes chances the government will achieve its objectives. It can also happen that the *very effort to be open* will result in journalists tending to give officials the benefit of the doubt.

A related touchy area concerns questions about military operations. There is no more sensitive question an official can be asked than one concerning the possibility of impending military action. How does a diplomat respond if he knows U.S., British, and French planes are about to bomb Iraq and a reporter calls up and asks point-blank whether military action is contemplated? The official does not want to deny, mislead, or avoid the issue—or to stiff a journalist working a legitimate story. But he also does not want to put the operation at risk.

On 12 January 1993 Assistant Secretary Djerejian was in exactly this position. Iraq had declared it would stop cooperating with weapons inspectors of the U.N. Special Commission and refused to allow a U.N. surveillance helicopter to enter the country's airspace. It had deployed antiaircraft missiles in the northern and southern "no-fly" zones and its jet fighters had violated the southern no-fly zone repeatedly. On January 13, British, French, and U.S. planes bombed Iraqi missile and radar sites. I asked Djerejian how he handled calls from reporters on the eve of the air strike, asking about imminent military action.

"I would say the situation was very serious, and why. I would mention the [Iraqi] flights, the U.N. Special Commission, the missiles. I would say that we could see a pattern of pushing the envelope and defying U.N. resolutions that was very serious. I made clear that we would not permit violations and missile deployments and that there would be no further warnings. Now if a reporter asked me if we would take military action, I would say I won't answer a question like that because it is operational. But you don't mislead, and you inform by leaving the impression that the situation is very serious."

The role of the press, then, is to press. The role of diplomats is to inform as fully as they responsibly can, but without wreaking havoc on their duty not to violate security or otherwise put lives at risk; and without running down their superiors, or undercutting a policy they are pledged to uphold, or undermining the hard work of negotiators; and without compromising an embassy's sources, or jeopardizing intelligence sources and methods.

The Virtues of Openness

Before engaging in the eunuch games of Washington, returning diplomats should understand the differences between the role of a State Department official and that of an embassy officer. Just as they would study the media culture overseas, so too should they study the media culture in Washington.

Overseas, the diplomats were reporting, analyzing, and implementing; stateside they are dealing primarily with policy development, coordination, and formulation. Relationships with reporters will be different because, as department officials, they are now likely to be not merely news sources, but news subjects. Relationships with other officials, though often cooperative and collegial, will be affected by bureaucratic competition.

Press and public affairs work is already an important but time-consuming element of foreign policy work. This is because senior officials, who are politically experienced and accountable to the press, demand that media policy get high-priority attention. And, as Richard Boucher has noted, responsiveness generally increases the higher one goes in the bureaucracy.

What has not occurred is a general realization at all levels of foreign affairs work that public communications are an integral part of the policy process. Many diplomats still have the archaic notions that press work is an intrusion and that reporters' questions are an aggravation to be borne instead of an opportunity to explain and advance policy objectives. As a result, the public communications aspects of policy too often get short shrift, especially at the working level, where expertise is often greatest and effective early intervention is most likely to be able to head off future problems.

Therefore, returning diplomats should analyze their own positions on the public affairs scale of accountability. Clear public affairs goals and priorities can then be set. Whatever niches the diplomats occupy, they should consider press relations an integral part of the policy process. This means anticipating at the beginning how to explain the policy in the end. It means looking at each contact and piece of press guidance as opportunities both to inform and to explain and advance U.S. policy objectives.

The bias should be toward openness, but tempered by a clear understanding of such competing priorities as security considerations and the need not to compromise intelligence sources and methods. If diplomats work in geographic bureaus, they should think not only of feeding the alligators of the U.S. press, but also of reaching foreign audiences via USIA and posts in the field.

Sometimes, when U.S. policy is controversial or under attack, the game can get rough. In such cases, it is particularly important for officials to remember where accountability lies—at the top. Reporters want stories, and even the best will try to pull a lower-level official offside from time to time. But when diplomats are not the accountable officials, they should stay within the limits of their responsibilities—seeking to be as forthcoming as possible, but within their piece of the message. Officials should try to inform, but not participate in blame-games, discuss personalities, or stray across the line into areas they are not authorized or competent to discuss.

At all levels of the system, and in whatever circumstances, officers should bear in mind the practical virtues of openness. When the State Department is not forthcoming, it does not follow that stories about foreign policy will not be written. Quite the opposite. Being accessible and forthcoming can prevent inaccurate stories from being written.

"Some may imagine that by stifling the flow of information the administration may escape the publication of some unfavorable or unwanted news stories," wrote former UPI State Department correspondent Jim Anderson. "But there should be no mistake: the frequent failure of the press office to provide access to information does not curtail the stream of news stories about foreign policy. They continue to be written, but much of the information comes from the worst possible sources: unhappy partisans who leak or fabricate information, foreign embassies, congressional sources with their own axes to grind, and other agencies in the government (including the White House staff) which are busily trying to undercut the State Department." [17]

The usual reason for not disclosing material is neither malice nor criminal mischief nor even trying to hide mistakes, but the belief that such disclosure is premature. "One of the great mistakes we made in the Carter administration was the number of times we accepted this argument," Hodding Carter said. With both the Panama Canal and Salt II treaties, he noted, the press office pushed for public explanations, but the answer always came back that talking would jeopardize negotiations. Meanwhile, opponents of the treaties talked up a storm. "We didn't get out the facts," Carter said, "and consequently our thesis was badly misunderstood." [18]

The simple fact is, the more that senior officials like the secretary and his spokesman can put on the record, and the more that is authorized at a senior level in the way of meaningful background, the less that will be available to leakers pursuing narrow agendas. This not only opens up the foreign policy process but puts a crimp in leaking, one of Washington's preeminent eunuch games.

Chapter 14

Looking Ahead

The order is rapidly fadin'.
And the first one now will later be last
For the times they are a-changin'.
                                    —Bob Dylan

The substance of diplomacy—the effort to reconcile differences and achieve policy objectives through diplomatic interactions—changes little over time.

"To talk about new and old diplomacy," wrote French diplomat Jules Cambon, "is to make a distinction without a difference. It is the outward appearance, or, if you like, the makeup, of diplomacy which is gradually changing. The substance will remain—firstly because human nature never changes; secondly because there is only one way of settling international differences; and lastly because the most persuasive method at the disposal of a government is the word of an honest man." [1]

But even if the substance stays much the same, the outward appearance and makeup—that is, the arena of diplomacy and its tools—can, and do, change. The fast-evolving communications and technology revolutionizing nearly every aspect of international relations are also reshaping the way governments do business with one another.

In this whirlwind of change, it is plain that more information than ever will be available to publics in the twenty-first century and that this will profoundly affect the conduct of international affairs. Not only will information media and technology play a central role in the shaping of public policy, but the efficacy of diplomacy as a tool of policy will depend to a large extent on how well diplomats adapt to this reality. Public communications skills—already in the toolkit of the nation's best diplomats—must be added to the enduring, traditional core skills of reporting, analyzing, and negotiating.

Henceforth, diplomats will also be required to transmit the substance of their work across the media spectrum to different audiences. Effective internal communications will be an important adjunct of this. Computer literacy will be no less important than language proficiency, because diplomats must be able to understand, and use, the information technology that helps them do their jobs. It does no good to assemble a brilliant analysis, or acquire valuable information, only to have it arrive the day after the relevant decision has been made.[2] Beyond issues of mechanics and equipment, however, there is a more basic issue of psychology: the institutional self-image needs an update.

Updating the Image

Not a few diplomats see themselves as practitioners of quiet diplomacy. This is a world of discreet conversations with influential foreign government officials, discreetly reported. The currency of this world is the classified cable, drafted in secure embassy precincts, encrypted, and then transmitted for a select but appreciative audience of official readers in Washington. The diplomats who inhabit this world often assume a limited, professional view. Not for them political games; theirs is the straight path of pure diplomacy.

Journalists, who have occasional utility as sources of information, enter this world either as supplicants or as leprous supplicants. Overseas, USIS and its importuning PAOs handle their needs; in Washington, this is primarily the job of the State Department spokesman and public affairs officers in the various bureaus. Careful diplomats will have as their objective in preparing press guidance that the spokesman betray no more than is strictly necessary. When required to brief a reporter themselves, the diplomats' objective will be to get through the unpleasantness quickly, preferably with reputation intact and having provided as little for the reporter to twist to self-serving ends as possible. The State Department is *not* a news agency.

This, of course, is a caricature. Very few professional diplomats totally embrace such a benighted view. Indeed, nearly all those I spoke to not only recognize the influence and importance of the media but feel strongly about the need to explain foreign policy fully and responsibly to the U.S. public. I daresay, however, that many diplomats would find the basic outlines of the "limited view" familiar, and others might even concede that this vision, or something very like it, colors many department officials' dealings with the media. It is there, like a bureaucratic ego or superego, whether at the level of the conscious or the unconscious.

This back-of-the-mind sense of what proper diplomacy is, when combined with the natural fear and uncertainty that comes from venturing into unfamiliar waters, adds up to considerable reticence on the part of many officers in their dealings with the press. It is one thing to help develop and implement policy; it is quite another to explain it to the public via the media.

"The culture is, you write a memo or a cable, and that's it," observed Ambassador Robert Oakley, former special envoy to Somalia, ambassador to Pakistan, and coordinator for counterterrorism. "Your job is complete. If anything actually *happens* or not after that is a whole other question."

This is in no sense to disparage quiet diplomacy. As Cambon suggested, confidential negotiations are bound to remain a feature of relations between states. Whatever the importance of public communications and the media, when countries deal with each other solely in public statements, the area available for compromise and accommodation—and thus for peaceful resolution of disputes—is severely constricted. The issue is not the value of quiet diplomacy, but rather whether diplomats choose to limit their role to its confines.

This is simply not practical in an era when so much information is in the public domain, when the course of international affairs depends so greatly on the quality of that information, and when the diplomat is a vital link in the foreign affairs food chain. He or she is the government's expert on the spot, a *supplier* of information and analysis that becomes the grist for decisions. Diplomats are also potentially important *disseminators* of information, whether overseas or in Washington—explaining and promoting their government's policies, and providing journalists (as well as businessmen, academics, members of Congress, and other interested parties) with information and background that helps them do their jobs. Diplomats do not serve their country's interests if they take themselves out of the information chain just because they find contact with reporters unfamiliar, risky, or disagreeable.

In fact, the diplomats who are most successful and rise to the most senior positions usually have a highly developed, often self-taught sense of the importance of the media and the need for positive engagement with journalists. "Most of us have learned from the ground up, finding our way," says Thomas Pickering. "It can be hard, and a little steering early on would be useful."

The information-induced turbulence in the waters of international affairs cannot be wished away. An effective diplomat will learn how to navigate the chop even while keeping track of the larger currents underneath. He or she can begin, not by lamenting the intrusion of the press into policy or despairing over new pressures on policy making, but by analyzing the skills needed to cope, and then working to develop them.

If it is admitted that the effective diplomat must develop public communications skills, the issue then becomes not whether to engage with the media, but on what terms. This requires understanding the nature of the relationship, where the individual diplomat fits on the scale of official accountability, and some basic rules of engagement.

An Acceptable Risk

The nature of the relationship between reporters and diplomats is both cooperative and adversarial. The two are not partners, but cohabitants in the field of foreign affairs with differing interests. Diplomats and journalists have agendas that sometimes coincide, sometimes conflict, and most often coexist warily. As one correspondent put it, "We have to maintain relationships that are adversarial, cooperative, and autonomous, sometimes all at the same time."

Over the years, as the influence of the press has grown, there has been discussion from time to time among journalists about ways to make the press as an institution more accountable for the excesses that occur. The discussion never gets very far. As Don Oberdorfer observed,

> For all its good points, the press has absolutely no self-monitoring capability. There are very few institutional organizations or arrangements that would chastise people or discipline them if they're doing something ludicrous. About all the press has are general peer pressure of colleagues and praise or approbation when people do something good, and that's not much. There are people doing things, even at the *Washington Post,* that I don't agree with and I don't like, and the *Post* is probably the best. If I think some guy is off the beam with a particular set of sources, I couldn't, and I wouldn't, intervene unless it involves me. That's just not part of journalism.

Ombudsmen are helpful, Oberdorfer said, and media reporters are useful, but "the problem is, the media reporting on the media is a chancy operation." He found professional journals like the *Columbia Journalism Review* and the *American Journalism Review* also beneficial, but only as moral suasion; and he hoped there'd never be "anything greatly more powerful than that." [3]

Briefing the media will never be a precise or risk-free process. The only way to avoid all risk is not to engage, and not to engage is to serve incompletely. This is like the diplomat who sends in a cable with a hedged comment on the significance of what he or she reports, saying "on the one hand . . . on the other hand . . . only time will tell." It protects the individual from the possibility of being wrong, but it also deprives the government of the judgment of its expert on the spot, a judgment that expert is paid to make. In the same way, diplomats who consistently avoid or minimize media contact may protect themselves from possible harm. But they also fail to serve by not providing the public with useful information or by neglecting opportunities to explain or advance the government's policies, both of which they are paid to do.

Several senior officials cited lack of confidence and fear of the press, and especially fear of saying the wrong thing, as obstacles to effective communications. Alexander Watson remarked that too many diplomats are reluctant to recognize that they "*are* in fact an authority, or an authoritative spokesman," and fail to take the initiative unless they get a cable instructing them to do something. Watson, who served as deputy to U.S. ambassador to the United Nations Thomas Pickering during the 1990-91 Gulf War, noted that most people get their news from the electronic media, "like it or not. It's instantaneous, it's evanescent. You must go on those TV cameras immediately, there is no other time to do it."

In the view of Peter Tomsen, who served as special envoy to the Afghan resistance, "You've got to realize that the media are very important in shaping U.S. policy. Then, in interviews you've got to do what you think is best for the U.S. interest. There is some risk, but you have to take it."

To communicate effectively, diplomats need to understand the differences among the media, that is, how various news organizations do their jobs and what their organizational requirements are. The media are not a single species. They are a kingdom, with broad phyla (television and print), classes (broadcast, cable, newspapers, magazines, wires), orders, families, genera, species, and subspecies. While detailed knowledge of every news organization is not necessary, every official should know something of their basic features—for example, that television conveys experience and impression, but is limited in its ability to convey information; and that print media provide more detailed, linear information and analysis, but do not have the same mass audience and impact as television.

In 1993, when Doyle McManus was State Department correspondent for the *Los Angeles Times,* he addressed diplomats in training at the State Department's Foreign Service Institute.[4] He was asked whether "the media" had a set of formal ground rules, whether "the media" consulted together on what kinds of questions to ask at State Department briefings, and whether "the media" got together and decided to criticize policy on Bosnia, or President Clinton's approach to running the White House, or other matters.

"The media," McManus said, "are not a single organism, but a large and disorderly collection of separate organisms, something like beasts at a waterhole. They seem to be doing the same thing most of the time, but it's because they are responding to a set of similar urges and to the demands of an environment that is beyond their control. They certainly aren't capable of much coordinated thought or action, and they are alarmingly easy to stampede."

Diplomats tend to think of news organizations primarily in political terms. But the task of information gathering and the role of political watchdog are not the exclusive determinants of media behavior. News organizations are also businesses subject to commercial pressures. This means they will be responsive to market conditions and quick to adopt technology that improves their product or profitability. Diplomats who want to get their message out should be aware of how the changing media marketplace relates to their efforts to communicate across the media spectrum.

Some media organizations, for example, are "dumbing down" (shorter articles, more pictures) to meet the requirements of a changing market, while others are "smartening up" to secure their specialized niches in an increasingly segmented market. Some are opening more foreign bureaus, others are closing them. In the ferment of a changing news marketplace, some organizations are opting to maintain fewer experts of their own overseas, resorting increasingly to parachute coverage.

For correspondents thrust suddenly into the swirl of complex foreign events the embassy can—and should—provide useful context and analysis. In a shrinking world of television, flash crises, and shortened response times, the diplomat's briefing can inform not only domestic and foreign opinion but the policy-making climate in Washington.

Setting Media Policy

Media goals and objectives, as well as the means of achieving them, should be carefully considered and articulated—whether for the annual country plan overseas or for a series of briefings in support of a policy initiative in Washington—so that all staff members understand what the policy is, who is doing what, and what their individual pieces of the message are. Access to reporters should not mean a breakdown in discipline, or a proliferation of anonymous policy criticism. It should mean not losing any opportunity to gather information, to explain U.S. policy, or to inform the U.S. public about the implications of foreign events that can have an impact on their lives.

Just as there is differentiation among media organizations, so too is there differentiation among government officials. It is the job of the secretary of state and other senior officials to appear on television and carry the message of foreign affairs to a mass audience. It is also up to them to give much of the testimony that is required on Capitol Hill and even to conduct briefings on policy matters for key opinion leaders like the *Washington Post* and the *New York Times*. But those with more specialized information—whether the political officer abroad or the deputy assistant secretary in Washington—also contribute by filling in background and detail.

The interactions of government officials with the media should occur on different levels—the most senior, accountable officials set and carry the message to the general public through television, press contacts, and congressional testimony, while those with specialized knowledge flesh out detail for influential elites through background briefings.

In addition to carrying the largest burden of contact, the State Department leadership bears primary responsibility for strategic thinking about media issues. "Effective public communications" means thinking of public affairs at the beginning of policy formulation, as an integral part of the process, and not merely as a problem of presentation after the decisions are made. This boils down to a constant effort to anticipate issues and follow through with a reliable mechanism for transmitting information down to the bureaucracy and out to the press. It means staying in front of the news.

Effective anticipation is bolstered by good early-warning radar and bottom-up information flow from the ranks. What often happens, however, is that those doing the day-to-day policy work amidships feel unconnected to the captains of policy on the poop. On follow-through, too, desk officers are hampered—for example, in writing press guidance—if they do not work from a solid conceptual understanding of what the policy is and what its aims are. Thus, there is no more important element of leadership than projecting, and frequently repeating, as clearly as possible, what it is the leadership is trying to achieve.

As one ambassador put it, "For a bureaucrat to be useful to a journalist, he must know at a minimum what the mindset of the leadership is. If the political leadership doesn't communicate its mindset, or doesn't have one, the sensible bureaucrat will have no interest in pronouncing on what does not exist. It is not the job of bureaucrats to make policy, but to implement it. If the government is well managed, the problem takes care of itself. Guidance does flow from the top down, and people do have a sense of what is politically correct."

Breaking Out of the Circle

Many will object that, while it is fine to argue for constructive engagement with the media and for as much openness as possible, the grim reality is that the real-life terms of engagement between journalists and officials have steadily deteriorated since the Vietnam War. The media are more powerful, competitive pressures are fierce, government is bigger and harder to cover, there is less on the record, leaks often rule the public agenda, and, most important, there is simply a lot less trust on both sides.

All of this is true. It is also true that part, perhaps half, of the fault for this increasingly institutionalized distrust lies with reporters. Government officials can do little to correct this, and the only known antidote is simply to know with whom one is dealing and exercise individual judgment in each case.

What officials can do, however, is recognize how their own actions feed the downward twists of the Washington information helix:

• When policy makers restrict decisions to small circles for fear of leaks, expertise is lost, the lower ranks feel shut out, and press guidance is uninspired or sterile.

• Reporters then find little of use on the record and they, too, feel shut out. Ill-informed reporters then find ill-informed bureaucrats and ill-informed stories ensue. Alternatively, inner-circle dissenters gain disproportionate influence because, in a world of small circles, a dissenter who disagrees with an option can torpedo it by leaking it to reporters.

• Since stories built on misinformation or self-interest often present an incomplete or unbalanced view of the issues and stakes in a given policy discussion, the concern about leaks is reinforced, as is the inclination to restrict information to small circles.

A number of senior diplomats commented that the lion's share of leaking in Washington is usually done on "the political side," although it is also a time-honored custom for the political leadership to suspect the Foreign Service. In his book *The Government/Press Connection,* Brookings analyst Stephen Hess made the same point. He noted that "the leak is rarely a tool of press offices," which deal with "formal channels of information," or of the lower-level bureaucrats whose "world faces inward." Rather, he identified Congress and political appointees in the executive branch as the primary leakers. "Perhaps the greatest frustration for presidents is when they are forced to realize that most executive branch leakers are their own people—political appointees—rather than the faceless bureaucrats they campaigned against." [5]

Ambassador Pickering conceded that "some diplomats, Foreign Service officers, have driven the political establishment nuts thinking their role is the purveying of private information, whether on the record or on background, in order to influence policy." In his seasoned view, however, "the Foreign Service is actually pretty responsible and doesn't take an issue outside the system when it doesn't like something." Foreign Service officers feel that they would lose access if they did, he said. "The use of the press, when the Foreign Service has failed inside with logic and rationality, is not common." But it is what "gives the political leadership the most concern—with the result that they sometimes become almost catatonic, and given to restricting information and keeping things in small compartments. The trouble is, when you do this, you lose expertise."

This is not to say there will not be issues where the need to know will be very limited. Neither the press nor midlevel bureaucrats expect to be told everything all the time. But they both know when they are being shut out and deprived of information they need to do their jobs. On major issues in the public domain, both deserve to have at least a general sense of what the leadership is aiming at.

There is really only one way out of the downward helix, at least as far as officials are concerned. It is for policy makers to strain, wherever possible, to be *in*clusive rather than *ex*clusive. If bureaucrats and journalists cannot be told everything all the time, the leadership can at least project the sense that it is *trying* to tell as much as it responsibly can, not as little as it possibly can.

One assistant secretary found his bureau "hermetically sealed" when he arrived on the job. Saying he "couldn't function that way, with Congress or the media," he described how he handled the situation.

In close coordination with Public Affairs, I opened up our public diplomacy in an effort to educate U.S. and foreign opinion. I asked for a more assertive role doing backgrounders and interviews. When [the seventh floor] saw it was done in a responsible manner, we moved forward in a disciplined way to be more open to the press, both on background and on the record. I started to build credibility myself, and I stressed it would be my responsibility if anything went wrong.

At the same time, in the bureau, I worked to extend the information base. Except in the most sensitive matters, all members of the bureau should be clued in to what is happening—with the caveat that the first time there is an unauthorized disclosure of sensitive, classified information, it will cost the confidence of the seventh floor in me, and through me, in the bureau. I made a contract with my bureau: I said, "I need your full support and substantive knowledge in order to give the secretary the best possible foreign policy advice. Therefore, I will need to keep you informed, and I will. But we need discipline. There must be no unauthorized disclosures, and interaction with Congress and the press must be coordinated."

And we did it. In the past sixteen months, there has not been one press leak that I am aware of. Why? Because our officers are involved in the work of the bureau, and that brings good morale. No one has a personal agenda to leak.

The assistant secretary added, "Discipline is important. There is a full airing of views in policy discussions, but when I make a decision, that's it."

Looking Ahead

In the twenty-first century it will not be classified cables but unclassified and publicly available information that will have the greatest impact on the course of international events. The efficacy of individual diplomats as instruments of national policy will hinge on their skill as communicators and as suppliers of information, whether to their own government or to the public via the media.

Diplomats should take stock of, and update if necessary, their ideas about the role of the media and of diplomacy. They should accept not only the inevitability, but the desirability of engagement with the press, and prepare as carefully as possible for the encounter. The essential precondition for any media contact is to understand the policy, what it aims to achieve, and what the diplomat's part is in communicating it. In direct dealings with reporters, officials should recognize that the process is not risk-free, but that risks can be minimized by understanding a few basic rules of the road.

On the field of engagement, they should remember the Bohlen Rules: Take the press seriously; never tell the press an untruth; don't feel the need to tell them everything; never discuss an "iffy" proposition; never deal with a question that is in the process of being settled in the executive branch; never denigrate a fellow worker in the executive branch; and, if you don't know the answer to a question, don't be afraid to say so.

Finally, diplomats should be professional about procedure as well as substance. Ground rules should be set clearly, and up front. Officials should recognize that no one, whether diplomat or journalist, is perfect and that mistakes will be made on both sides from time to time. When this occurs, it is rarely the end of the world, even if it seems so at the time. If there seems to be a clear violation of agreed ground rules or some other serious misunderstanding, the diplomat should not leave the matter to fester but should get back to the reporter as soon as possible and clear the air.

Within these general limits, there can be considerable scope for diplomats to help journalists and vice versa. What most foreign affairs professionals fear is not the reporter but themselves, and not knowing when to stop. But diplomats should trust that as foreign affairs professionals, buttressed by careful preparation, they will be able to judge where to draw the line. For their part, good reporters will understand and respect, even if they do not like, the limits imposed on diplomats by duty. What no journalist will respect or understand is being shut out or deliberately misled.

In his book *Diplomacy,* Harold Nicolson observed, "A satisfactory adjustment between the needs and rights of a popular Press and the requirements of discretion has yet to be found."

But recognizing challenge is no reason to avoid it.

"My own advice to the junior diplomatist," Nicolson went on to say, "is not to confine himself lazily to the easy circle of his own embassy but to cultivate the society of journalists both foreign and native. It is from them that he will derive useful advice and commentary. When I look back on the years before Hitler that I spent in the British Embassy at Berlin, I am grateful for the hours I devoted talking to journalists at the Adlon Bar. I learned more from them than I did from any other form of social relations." [6]

APPENDIX

Overview
The State Department and the Media

The Spokesman/Assistant Secretary for Public Affairs

The Assistant Secretary of State for Public Affairs is also the Spokesman of the Department and is the focal point for the Department's relations with the media. The Spokesman is also the principal adviser to the Secretary and the Department on all media and public affairs issues.

The major responsibilities of the Spokesman include briefing the press on foreign policy and other matters and coordinating media policy with the Spokesman of the White House and other government agencies who play a role in foreign affairs.

The Office of Press Relations

The Press Office is the Spokesman's operational staff, and its officers are authorized to serve as spokesmen for the Department of State in answering questions from journalists.

The Press Office's major responsibilities include:

• Help prepare the Spokesman for the daily briefing;
• Task and coordinate the production of press guidance;
• Respond to reporters' questions as quickly and succinctly as possible (the Press Office maintains a duty officer system to take calls after hours);
• Coordinate photo opportunities and coverage of events in the Department involving the Secretary and other principals;
• Advise the Secretary and other Department principals on media interview requests;

Source: "Fact Sheet," U.S. Department of State, Bureau of Public Affairs, Office of Public Communication, October 1990.

• Issue appointment schedules, transcripts of briefings, and statements by the Secretary and other principals;

• Coordinate arrangements for US journalists to accompany the Secretary on trips abroad.

Appendix 2

Ground Rules for Attribution

Ground rules for attribution should be established at the beginning of conversations between Department officials and reporters. Normally, government officials take the initiative to determine the ground rules.

Ground rules can be mixed—[some] information ON BACK-GROUND, some ON THE RECORD—but each time, it must be made clear *at the outset.* The discussion should proceed only after both parties are clear on exactly how the reporter can use or attribute information.

Over the years, the following ground rules have developed and are adhered to by reporters who cover the Department regularly.

- ON THE RECORD—Information may be quoted directly and attributed to the official by name and title.
- BACKGROUND—Attribution is to State Department or Administration officials, as determined by the official. The officials may be paraphrased or quoted directly.
- DEEP BACKGROUND—No attribution is permitted and no direct quotes. The reporter may use the information to help present the story or to gain deeper understanding of the subject, but the wisdom is his, not his source's.
- OFF THE RECORD—The information may not be used in any form whatsoever and is meant only for the education of the reporter.

Source: U.S. Department of State, Bureau of Public Affairs, Office of Public Communication, October 1990.

Public Affairs Clearance Process

Fm SecState WashDC
To All European Diplomatic Posts Immediate
Info Live Oak Immediate
    Joint Staff WashDC Immediate
    USIA WashDC Immediate
    USMission USUN New York Immediate
Unclas[sified] State 145628
Subject: PUBLIC AFFAIRS CLEARANCE PROCESS

1. Summary

EUR [European Bureau] would like to remind posts of the need for Department clearances before accepting certain types of speaking engagements and media interview requests, and before submitting articles or opinion pieces for publication. The need for clearance applies to all personnel for both domestic and overseas events. To avoid confusion and delay, EUR is designating EUR/P [Public Affairs] as the bureau's contact and conduit for clearance requests for public affairs activities.

Please note that EUR/EX [Executive Director] will continue to process other invitational travel requests in close cooperation with L [Office of the Legal Advisor]. (End Summary)

2. Speaking Engagements

The Bureau of Public Affairs [PA] is responsible for reviewing, evaluating and approving requests for speakers. It is also the only bureau in the Department legally authorized to accept reimbursement from sponsoring organizations. In addition, the Office of the Legal Advisor is responsible for certifying that there is no conflict of interest involved in accepting invitations that are funded in whole or part by sponsoring organizations.

To comply with the Department regulations and to speed the approval process, we are asking posts (and Washington offices) to submit one request for each engagement which can serve EUR, PA and L/EP [Ethics and Personnel] in meeting their various responsibilities.

Source: Department of State cable to posts in Europe, 7 May 1990.

Please note: In submitting requests, posts are asked to use judgment. We do not want to be swamped with cables for every officer invited to speak to a local high school or routine businessman's luncheon. The Department's concern is to avoid conflict of interest, to coordinate public affairs activities so as to maximize audience contacts on major foreign policy issues, to minimize expenditures of funds and resources to the extent possible, and to handle reimbursement requirements properly.

Requests should be submitted by cable in the following format to EUR/P, which will pass information copies to relevant desks and coordinate with PA, L/EP and EUR/EX. Those offices have promised a quick turn-around on clearances.

For PA:

1. Name and title of person who will speak.
2. Organization's name, address and telephone/fax numbers (time permitting, PA would appreciate having a copy of the invitation).
3. Date and title of the event.
4. Topic of speech/remarks.
5. Is the event open to media coverage?
6. What portion, if any, of travel/per diem is a sponsoring organization prepared to pay?

For L/EP:

(Note: Before completing this section, employees are encouraged to carefully review the provisions of 3 FAM [*Foreign Affairs Manual*] 620 sections).

1. How would funded travel further the post's or USG's interests?
2. Are post funds available to fund the trip?
3. If post had unlimited funds, would it pay for this trip in light of other priorities?
4. Is the duration of the trip limited to official purposes and commensurate with the official benefit received?
5. To what degree do(es) the private firm(s) offering the travel have business interests before or affected by the post?
6. Would a reasonable person believe that the firm(s) was (were) obtaining improper influence over the post by funding this travel?

3. Funding for Speaking Engagements

PA criteria: Posts should be aware of steps PA is taking on the domestic side in an effort to make the most out of diminishing resources.

These include stricter criteria for the kinds of speaking programs the Department will fund.

In general, PA will consider funding only those engagements which support overall Department goals and foreign policy initiatives, and only those speakers willing to increase the impact of their trips through outreach to media, business, academia and state and local government representatives. As a general rule, PA will not provide funding for those appearances accepted directly and for which there has been no opportunity for prior review.

If all expenses are not covered by a sponsoring organization and PA determines the engagement does not meet its criteria, the officer will have to request funding from his or her bureau or post, or pay out of pocket.

Reimbursement: No employee, domestic or foreign, should accept money (honoraria or travel funds) directly from a private sponsor. We emphasize that PA is the only bureau in the Department legally authorized to accept reimbursement from a private sponsor. PA maintains a fund for that purpose, and can bill any organization which indicates it wishes to reimburse the Department. In such cases, the traveling employee should, after obtaining appropriate PA and L/EP clearances, be issued official US orders specifying the arrangements made, e.g. "no cost (or partial cost) to USG, Department to be reimbursed."

In-kind payment: Employees may accept in-kind travel (meals, prepaid travel, hotels) from private sponsors, as long as travel is done on official US Government orders specifying the arrangements made. Orders should not be issued until receipt of appropriate PA and L/EP clearances.

4. Media Contacts

No one should accept on-the-record domestic interview requests with major media without prior PA clearance. These include TV network news shows and weekend talk shows, major newspapers, national radio shows and weekly news magazines.

It is not necessary to obtain clearance for backgrounders, but PA is interested in knowing of any editorial backgrounders with major media, and of any other backgrounders which may be noteworthy.

PA clearance is also needed for similar overseas major media contacts.

Media interview requests should be cabled, or in the case of time constraints, faxed (202 647-4088) or telephoned (202 647-6926) to EUR/P. PA has promised a quick response on requests.

5. Public Communication Content

Texts of public speeches, statements, articles or op-eds on matters of official concern which have not been previously cleared must be submitted to PA for review at the end of the clearance process. PA especially needs to be alerted to public communications which represent changes in policy, may be controversial or relate to priority issues. A declaration to the effect that the opinions expressed are the writer's own and not necessarily the Department's does not obviate the need for clearance.

We would like to remind posts that Washington and the field must speak to the public with one voice, particularly on sensitive subjects. We understand and sympathize with the need for posts to be able to respond promptly to breaking stories, but post-drafted statements and guidances on politically sensitive events or issues should have Department clearance before use.

Texts of speeches, statements, articles, press guidances should be submitted to relevant desk officers for necessary clearances before submission to PA through EUR/P.

Relevant guidelines for the above include:

FAM 628.5-2 and .5-3;

April 19, 1989 memo by the executive secretary for all assistant secretaries and bureau directors;

January 29, 1987 Bureau of European and Canadian Affairs administrative memorandum on invitational travel to all administrative counselors/officers;

May 3, 1989 memorandum on coordinating public and media appearances through PA, from the executive secretary to all principal officers, assistant secretaries, special assistants, office heads, executive directors;

February 5, 1990 memo from the assistant secretary for public affairs to all Department public affairs advisers;

3 FAM 620 Appendix A; and

December 16, 1988 Department notice to all employees on holiday gifts and the Department's standards of conduct.

[James A.] Baker

Media Contacts in the Field

Dear PAO:

What follows is a short course in foreign relations. It stems from discussions by the Area Directors which ultimately found their way onto paper. You might find it useful.

Increasingly, USIS officers with little or no press background find themselves thrust into situations where they must conduct media relations on behalf of the U.S. government. The price we pay for such on-the-job training can be high when measured in the potential for misunderstanding of U.S. policy or even damage to our interests.

While the training the Agency provides junior officers and those designated to assume press functions overseas has improved, the press of business and the timing of transfers often prevent officers from being able to take full advantage of these opportunities here in Washington. This letter offers some guidelines for those assuming the duties of information officer for the first time; they're designed to be useful reminders for more experienced officers, as well.

We must bear in mind that the relationship between press officer and journalist works most successfully when it is clearly defined; when misunderstandings arise it breaks down, calling into question the reliability of the information provided, the ground rules under which it was offered or the motives behind its transmittal.

Since we deal in information, an intangible commodity, the quality of the product is often judged by the impression left by its purveyor. We are most likely to gain the confidence of journalists when we show ourselves to be well-informed, honest and professional. We must not lose sight, however, of the fact that journalists very often regard the relationship between themselves and press officers as essentially adversarial. Indeed, our interests as representatives of the U.S. government and those

Source: Memorandum from a U.S. Information Agency regional bureau to public affairs officers in the field, 8 July 1988.

of the journalist can differ significantly. Awareness of this tension is a healthy element in our professional relationship, providing a point of reference from which we would be ill-advised to stray too far.

Establishing clear ground rules for press briefings can greatly reduce the risk of misunderstanding. This is especially true when dealing with American correspondents and sophisticated foreign journalists who can be counted on to comply with these rules of engagement. In many parts of the world, however, establishing ground rules is little more than a formality, since local journalists routinely ignore such constraints. In these instances, press officers must brief cautiously, relying on the advice of their local staff and their own judgment and knowledge of the media environment in which they operate.

In an effort to standardize the rules under which we brief the press here and abroad, we offer the following definitions, developed in cooperation with other Area Offices and a number of experienced press officers:

- *On the Record:* At this level, the journalist is free to quote anything you say and to identify you by name and title. Press officers should go on the record only in public fora: speeches and formal press conferences, for example.
- *Background:* In this case, you are not to be quoted and identification must be limited to more general terms, such as "U.S. officials" or "diplomatic sources," or whatever you and the journalist agree to at the outset of the conversation. Background is the most common basis on which press officers brief the press; it permits us to speak more freely than we could on the record and also allows the journalist some level of attribution for the assessments we offer. We must bear in mind, however, that remarks quoted in the press without attribution may be as damaging as on-the-record comments.
- *Deep Background:* Under these rules, the journalist cannot attribute the information, even in general terms, but must couch sourcing in language such as: "it is understood that . . ." or "it has been learned that. . . ." This ground rule allows you even more room for candor. It also asks the journalist to assume a greater personal burden of responsibility, since there is no visible source for the information.
- *Off the Record:* Technically, this means that the journalist can't use the information you provide. It is offered to improve his understanding of an issue and not for publication. Obviously, this is a very tricky area, and one which merits extreme caution, since nothing ever stays off the record. Giving a briefing in this manner puts everyone in an awkward position: the journalist, whose job it is to publish, not withhold, information, and the briefer, who may well be pointing a reporter in the direction of a story we would rather

not see in print for the moment. As a general rule, if you can't say something without going off the record, then you probably shouldn't say it at all.

A reminder: even the best ground rules serve no purpose unless they are clearly established at the beginning of a conversation. As the press officer, you alone bear this responsibility.

The following points address other situations and issues press officers often face in their work.

- If it's not your problem, don't discuss it. The juicy quote uttered in an unguarded moment can make a journalist's day while ruining your own. An additional cautionary note in this regard concerning queries from local media: reporters may attempt to draw U.S. spokesmen into commenting on essentially internal developments which do not fall within the scope of our bilateral relations. We must refrain from remarks that might be construed as interfering in the host country's domestic affairs.

- Do not, under any circumstances, misrepresent yourself or allow employees of yours to do so, even if you come under pressure from the Ambassador or others. Your credibility comes from the unambiguous perception of your role in a given country. To blur this distinction, even for the ostensible purpose of furthering Mission goals, can be extremely damaging.

- To the extent possible, control the environment in which you deal with the press: chaos, crowds and lack of control are anathema to the clear transmittal of information. Convene formal press conferences rather than engage in hit-and-run situations on the street or in foreign ministry corridors which are usually most memorable for the shouting and shoving they generate.

- Be responsive to phone calls from reporters. This does not mean that you have to take every call. Sometimes it is better to take an extra five minutes, assemble any background information you think you might need, prepare yourself and call back than to take the call and find yourself unprepared and fumbling for answers. By returning phone calls—even in those cases when you know you won't be able to provide the answers sought—you also may be able to turn off a story which is wrong or potentially damaging.

- You are under no obligation to go on tape for U.S. radio and television networks which inevitably call during breaking news events looking for a sound bite for their next broadcast.

- Don't be afraid to say you don't know; no one has all the answers. If in doubt, you can always take the question and call back with an answer.

Whatever inconvenience a reporter endures having to wait for accurate information pales in comparison to the damage which might result from your providing misinformation because you were reluctant to appear uninformed. If you don't want to admit that you don't know the facts, simply say that you're "not in a position to talk about" the subject at hand.

• Don't allow yourself to be pressured into trying to answer every question. If you don't feel you can safely enter into a certain area, say so. Within these constraints, be as helpful as possible; we can usually find a responsible way to assist journalists with legitimate inquiries, particularly in helping to determine if information they have unearthed is reliable or if they are headed in the wrong direction. A reporter rarely makes up a bad story but is often given bad or misleading information.

• Establish the kind of working relationship with the principals at your Mission that allows you access to all the facts, so that you can brief from a position of knowledge, not ignorance. The more fully you understand a situation, the better you can explain it to others, even when you are not at liberty to discuss everything you know.

• Reach agreement with your Ambassador and other principal officers so that the PAO or IO becomes the initial point of contact for all media queries. In this manner the Mission will be more likely to speak with one voice. By ensuring that all requests for interviews and information come through the same office, we can better guarantee that journalists understand Mission rules on attribution and we can serve as better sources of information regarding reporters' reliability. The PAO or IO should sit in on all briefings by the Ambassador or other principal officers; depending on local sensitivities, you might even wish to tape all interviews.

• Ask yourself: "Will I be comfortable if this information shows up on tomorrow's front page?"

When we are accessible to journalists, responsive to their inquiries, direct and honest in our replies and professional in our demeanor, we do a great deal to improve understanding between the United States and other countries. As press officers, no one can ask more of us; as professionals, we should be satisfied with nothing less.

The Consular Function and the Media

Unclassified State 095068
Inform Consuls
Subject: THE CONSULAR FUNCTION AND THE MEDIA

1. Events in recent years have forcefully demonstrated the impact of the media on consular issues, problems, and policies (i.e., Jonestown, the arrest of Americans in Iran, the killing of four nuns in El Salvador, the issuance of visas to South African military officers, etc.). As the Bureau which provides important and visible services to the American public, CA [Bureau of Consular Affairs] plays an important role in determining U.S. public and congressional attitudes toward the Department and its policies beyond consular affairs. Public support for the Department is often influenced by media reporting of consular assistance provided to Americans abroad in times of trouble. The purpose of this cable is to offer a few reminders and hints concerning the relation between the consular function and the media.

2. The Department encourages consular officers to be aware of public and media interest in how CA performs its responsibilities at home and abroad. CA and the Department's press office receive dozens of media inquiries daily on consular responses to specific problems around the world. These are often extensions of congressional queries where concerned members have communicated with the press. The more dramatic or serious ones are covered at the Department's daily noon briefings by the spokesman (subject to sensitive political implications or privacy act considerations). Notwithstanding these constraints, CA/PA and the press office disseminate information (to the extent possible) on consular policies, problems, and decisions. Many cases, although never the focus of the "national" press such as the *Washington Post* or *New York Times*, are followed closely by regional or local papers. This [is] particularly true in arrest and certain visa cases.

3. Consular officers abroad can help CA and the Press Office meet our responsibilities by:

Source: Department of State cable to consular officers, April 1981.

- Becoming more aware of media interest in consular matters;
- Keeping the Department fully informed on a timely basis of potential consular cases of media interest;
- Providing brief comment on significant local media inquiries and reaction on consular cases, as the American press often picks up information through foreign press reports;
- Determining Privacy Act applications as soon as possible;
- Becoming familiar with how to deal constructively with the press and establishing guidelines with post PAO (or the designated post spokesperson) for handling consular press inquiries received at post; and
- Keeping in mind that possible media interest is one repeat one of many factors in handling any consular problem.

4. We believe that these suggestions and reminders will help to improve the already frequently good responses from posts and will allow us and the posts to take better advantage of the "accountability factor" to the Congress and public.

5. Posts are encouraged to provide comment on these suggestions and/or any other aspects of the press role in consular affairs. CA/PA is the office in CA responsible for answering press inquiries on consular matters. Posts are encouraged to cable or call [647-1488] whenever you believe we can be of assistance.

[Alexander M.] HAIG

Guidelines for VOA
Foreign Correspondents

Preface

On June 28, 1978, the Director issued new guidelines and operating procedures for VOA foreign correspondents that substantially altered their existing relationships with U.S. missions. Under the new guidelines, the correspondents became administratively separated from missions, to the maximum extent allowable under U.S. government regulations. As a result, the correspondent no longer receives full mission administrative support. The correspondents have been functioning in much the same manner as U.S. non-governmental news correspondents. In order to implement the new guidelines, a VOA task force, in consultation with [U.S. Information] Agency and State Department officials, developed the procedures that have been in existence since 1978.

Effective August 10, 1987, the VOA foreign correspondents' guidelines have been revised. The revision was necessary due to changing regulations, the opening of the State Department's finance centers worldwide and the addition of new allowances. All references contained in these guidelines have been provided to the correspondents and are updated as revisions are issued.

Guidelines and Operating Procedures
for VOA's Foreign Correspondents

Foreign correspondents of the Voice of America stand at the important and highly visible juncture of journalism and diplomacy.

While VOA journalists are government employees, subject to all laws and regulations which apply to the conduct of everyone in the federal

Source: VOA Foreign Correspondents Revised Administrative Guidelines, Voice of America, Washington, D.C., 1987.

service, they are required at the same time to perform with a high degree of journalistic professionalism and integrity. The work and status of VOA overseas correspondents are identical to those of correspondents for other American press and broadcasting organizations, except as specifically noted in these guidelines.

The primary task of the VOA foreign correspondent, in fulfillment of the VOA charter's requirement that Voice of America news be accurate, objective, comprehensive, and consistently authoritative, is to give depth and perspective to the broadcast file. Bearing in mind the special interests of audiences around the world, the correspondent transmits actualities, eyewitness reports, backgrounders, interviews and advisories designed to assist the foreign listener in understanding the news. VOA correspondents broadcast the news; they do not present their opinions nor do they editorialize in their reporting.

VOA correspondents are supervised directly by the chief of the VOA News Division in Washington and receive assignments exclusively from the Voice of America. All material submitted by correspondents is reviewed before usage to ensure that it meets VOA Charter standards.

VOA correspondents will travel with regular fee (not official or diplomatic) passports; they will enter a country with journalist visas; they will register and be accredited as journalists; they will be subject to local laws and regulations applicable to foreign journalists; they will not have access to classified information; they will use post exchange or commissary facilities on the same basis as non-government U.S. journalists are permitted to use these facilities; and they will not depend on U.S. embassies or USIA posts for offices or residential space, secretarial services or other administrative support except as specified in these guidelines.

They will use commercial, not USG, communications channels. (Embassy communications will be available only in cases where emergency conditions cause the establishment of "press pool" services available to other American journalists.) U.S. embassies will be neither more nor less helpful to VOA correspondents than to other American journalists in giving or facilitating interviews, supplying information, aiding in travel, making other arrangements, or assisting with any difficulties.

Since the VOA is an official broadcasting service, it cannot, as a practical matter, divorce itself in the minds of many of its listeners from an identification with the U.S. government. Therefore, a VOA correspondent will not seek an interview with a head of state or other politically prominent or controversial personality, either in or out or government, without the prior approval of the News Division in Washington. If the News Division agrees to the interview, the correspondent will inform the PAO or the mission of the assignment as much in advance as possible. In the event that the chief of mission objects to the assignment, the correspondent will refer the matter to VOA Washington for resolution.

Foreign correspondents on temporary Washington assignment are reminded that it is also VOA policy that a correspondent not ask questions of a U.S. president at a formal news conference.

The same steps, i.e., prior approval from VOA Washington and prior notification of the PAO or mission, will be followed in covering any story which can reasonably be deemed sensitive.

Similarly, should a story require travel in a war zone or other dangerous area, VOA correspondents will consult in advance with VOA Washington and will keep the embassy informed of their plans. The VOA correspondent has a general obligation to inform the PAO of his [or] her presence in the country, and of the general nature of his or her assignments. But PAOs will not supervise the work of a VOA correspondent, and the correspondent has no obligation to clear copy with anyone before transmitting it to VOA Washington. Missions, therefore, bear no responsibility for the content of material broadcast by the Voice of America.

If requested by the chief of mission, VOA will promptly provide a copy of the story after it has been filed.

Any comments, criticism or questions from the chief of mission regarding correspondent activities or copy should be directed to Washington through Department channels with an information copy to USIA/VOA.

The above guidelines are intended to define and clarify the status and responsibilities of VOA correspondents working abroad.

Appendix 7

Press Guidance Drafting

MEMORANDUM TO: All EUR Deputy Assistant Secretaries and
 Office Directors
FROM: EUR/PA
SUBJECT: Press Guidance Drafting

Press guidances are a special breed, as much art as science. To be useful, they must be logical, succinct and—most importantly—answer the posed question and presage the follow-on question.

The following is offered to assist in the drafting of EUR press guidances. [EUR/PA] would appreciate your making copies available to members of your staff and emphasizing to them the importance the Bureau places on cooperating with PA in the press guidance process.

Hints to Drafters

Before you start writing:

• Think about the topic from the Secretary's point of view. What U.S. policy objectives can be advanced by what we say?

• Think about the topic from a journalist's point of view. What is of interest TO THE PRESS? Is background needed to place the event in perspective?

• Consider that while the complexity of the topic dictates the format of the guidance, in general a writer should start by recounting what the Department knows about the subject, provide context for where the day's story fits, and conclude by giving U.S. policy on the issue.

As you write:

• Have the President or Secretary commented on the issue? Should excerpts from those remarks be included?

Source: Department of State, Bureau of European Affairs, Office of Public Affairs. This memo dates from late in the Bush administration.

185

- Is there a Hill or White House angle that requires comment?
- Common State parlance means nothing to the press; don't use lingo, do spell out abbreviations.
- Use clear, plain English, no 25¢ words when nickel words will do.
- Any uncommon foreign words or names should be followed by a phonetic pronunciation.
- Work around an issue if you don't want to address it head on. Don't say that "We don't discuss the content of diplomatic exchanges." (PA comments on diplomatic exchanges all the time; that's the nature of the work.)
- Be succinct but give enough detail to answer the question.
- Don't be coy. Stonewalling is like a red flag to a bull: We are trying to get OUR point across, not keep information from the press.
- Press guidances are the public face of U.S. policy. If a drafter is dissatisfied with certain policies, he should advance his arguments behind the scenes, not by inserting his preferences into the guidance process.
- Press guidances are not the place to embellish the facts.

Finally:

- Has the original question been answered?
- What is the logical follow-on question that a good journalist would ask? Has THAT question been answered?

And keep in mind:

- The Administration is very sensitive to the press and sees it as a foreign policy tool. EUR plays its part by supporting PA and the Secretary in these efforts.
- EUR/PA may on occasion ask that a guidance be rewritten because we don't feel that the answer responds to the question, or because we are aware of PA sensitivities on an issue. We appreciate your cooperation when this happens.

Notes

Preface

1. Interview with Lawrence Eagleburger in his Washington office, March 1993.
2. The secretary of state, deputy secretary, and various under secretaries have their offices on the seventh floor of the Department of State. Many assistant secretaries of key regional and functional bureaus work on the sixth floor. In State Department jargon, therefore, a reference to the "sixth and seventh floors" means the *policy-making* level of the building.

Chapter 1   Diplomatic Sources

1. Bernard C. Cohen, *The Press and Foreign Policy* (Princeton, N.J.: Princeton University Press, 1963), 268-69.

Chapter 2   Opening the Closed Shop

1. Sir Harold Nicolson, *Diplomacy*, 3rd ed. (Washington, D.C.: Institute for the Study of Diplomacy, Georgetown University, 1988), 53.
2. Quoted in Hans N. Tuch, *Communicating with the World: U.S. Public Diplomacy Overseas*, Martin F. Herz Series on United States Diplomacy, Institute for the Study of Diplomacy, Georgetown University (New York: St. Martin's Press, 1990), 26.
3. Jefferson to John Tyler, June 28, 1804, *The Political Writings of Thomas Jefferson*, ed. Merrill D. Peterson (Woodlawn, Md.: Wolk Press, Thomas Jefferson Memorial Foundation, 1993), 152.
4. William B. Macomber, *The Angels' Game: A Handbook of Modern Diplomacy* (Briarcliff Manor, N.Y.: Stein and Day, 1975), 31-32.

Chapter 3   Media Democracy and Media Diplomacy

1. James Reston, *Deadline: A Memoir* (New York: Times Books, Random House, 1991), 105-6.
2. Don Oberdorfer, "Lies and Videotape: Watching Journalism Change in an Age of Suspicion," *Washington Post*, Sunday 18 April 1993, C1.
3. Stephen Hess, *The Government/Press Connection: Press Officers and Their Offices* (Washington, D.C.: Brookings Institution, 1984), 65-66.
4. Appendix 1 describes the responsibilities of the State Department spokesman and the Office of Press Relations.
5. Michael J. O'Neill, *Terrorist Spectaculars: Should TV Coverage Be Curbed?* (New York: Twentieth Century Fund, Priority Press, 1986), 80.
6. Interviews with CNN vice presidents Eason Jordan and Peter Vesey, 15 April 1993. Vesey observed that the U.S. market had matured and could not grow much

faster than the overall growth of the domestic cable market, a couple of percentage points each year. By contrast, he said, the future outside the United States—in Asia, the Pacific, the Middle East, Africa, and South America—was very bright, and in places like China and India "the growth potential is explosive."

7. Molly Moore, "Satellite TV Shows Asia a World beyond Reach of State Censors," *Washington Post,* 10 April 1993, A12.

8. Philip Shenon, "A Race to Satisfy TV Appetites in Asia," *New York Times,* 23 May 1993, Business, 12.

9. John Rockwell, "The New Colossus: American Culture as Power Export," *New York Times,* 30 January 1994, sec. 2, 1.

10. Report McCrum, William Cran, and Robert MacNeil, *The Story of English* (New York: Viking, 1986), 48.

11. Rockwell, *New York Times,* 31.

12. Quoted in Aljean Harmetz, "China's Appetite for U.S. TV Is Increasing," *New York Times,* 28 May 1988, 50.

13. *Tehran Times,* 5 April 1994, 1. (*Tehran Times* is an English-language newspaper published in Iran, and considered by many observers to reflect the views of President Ali Akbar Hashemi Rafsanjani.)

14. *Iran Times,* 8 April 1994, 16. (*Iran Times* is an English- and Farsi-language newspaper published in Washington, D.C., for the Iranian expatriate community in the United States. It draws on Iranian press reporting for much of its news.)

15. Ibid. The debate remained unresolved in late 1994 as this book moved toward publication.

16. John Naisbitt and Patricia Aburdene, *Megatrends 2000: Ten New Directions for the 1990s* (New York: Avon, 1990), 140.

17. Gary R. Orren, "Thinking about the Press and Government," in Martin Linsky, *Impact: How the Press Affects Federal Policymaking* (W. W. Norton, 1986), 10. Orren, a professor at Harvard's John F. Kennedy School of Government, coined the term "media democracy," considering it a third stage in our democratic evolution, after "classical" democracy and "party/elite" democracy.

18. Richard Harwood, "The Growing Irrelevance of Journalists," *Washington Post,* 23 October 1992, 21.

19. Richard Nixon, "His Final Words," *Time,* 2 May 1994, 36.

20. Timothy J. McNulty, "In Gulf War, TV Was Both Friend, Foe," *Chicago Tribune,* 23 December 1991, 1.

21. Timothy J. McNulty, "Decisions at the Speed of Satellite," *Chicago Tribune,* 22 December 1991, 1.

22. Jim Hoagland, "Policy from the Top Down," *Washington Post,* 7 October 1993, A23.

23. Burleigh was Coordinator for Counter-Terrorism at the time of an October 1992 interview.

24. Linsky, *Impact,* 128-129.

Chapter 4   *Desks and Deadlines: Print Media*

1. "Deadline Every Minute" is the title of Joe Alex Morris's history of the former United Press, which later merged with the International News Service to become United Press International. In it, Morris relates the following story:

> "Yes, young man," a famous statesman said to a reporter who sought to interview him some years ago, "I'll be glad to prepare a statement for you. Just tell me when is your—what do you newspapermen call it?—your deadline."
>
> The reporter sighed. "I'm from the United Press," he replied. "Our deadline is now. Some place around the world at this instant a newspaper is going to press. We've got a deadline every minute." (Joe Alex Morris, *Deadline Every Minute* [New York: Doubleday, 1957], 15-16)

2. I found this quote on page 6 of the AP employee handbook, *Your AP*, given to me when I joined the agency in 1973.
3. James Reston, *The Artillery of the Press: Its Influence on American Foreign Policy* (New York: Harper and Row, for the Council on Foreign Relations, 1967), 15.
4. A United Press World War II correspondent, Reynolds Packard, even wrote a novel by this name. It seems, however, that the milkman originally hailed from Omaha. According to Joe Alex Morris, the milkman reference originated with a World War I-era UP reporter named William G. Shepherd, renowned for his simple, factual telling of a story. Asked how he did it, he would say, "Why, there's nothing to it. I just write for the milkman in Omaha. I figure if he can understand what I'm writing, then everybody can understand it" (Morris, *Deadline Every Minute*, 42).
5. After Scripps-Howard sold UPI in 1982, the agency fell on hard times, its ownership changing hands several times. Reuters continued to provide AP with stiff competition worldwide, however.
6. The audience is fairly select—mainly senior officials in the front offices of the regional and functional bureaus, and seventh-floor policy makers. In April 1993 the print run for the press clips was 106 copies. The mix of newspapers that are excerpted changes somewhat from one administration to another. If the secretary of state is from Texas, for example, the Dallas, Fort Worth, and Houston newspapers might be clipped.
7. Such news services are "supplemental" in the sense that they supplement a broadly based service like AP.
8. The "slot" is the chief copy editor. The name comes from the tradition of this editor's sitting in the inside "slot" of a U-shaped desk and farming stories out to copy editors sitting all around him on the "rim," or outer side of the desk.
9. The "lead" story is the top item, usually starting in the upper right-hand corner of the front page. The "off-lead" is an item that starts opposite, in the upper left-hand corner.
10. Sunday and Monday tend to be better than Saturday, because Sunday papers (prepared Saturday) are often largely filled up with previously planned features.
11. The circulations used as 1995 advertising rate bases by the major weeklies were: *Time*, 4.0 million; *Newsweek*, 3.1 million; and *U.S. News and World Report*, 2.15 million (source: *Media Industry Newsletter*, 27 March 1995).
12. A 13 May 1993 *Wall Street Journal* story quotes Walter Shapiro, an *Esquire* writer who moved from *Newsweek* to *Time* in 1987, as saying *Newsweek* editors were much more likely than *Time*'s leaders to discard Monday or Tuesday story lists and assign writers to cover late-breaking items. At *Time*, he said, the list "didn't change much as the week went on."

Chapter 5   Desks and Deadlines: Television

1. Reuven Frank, *Out of Thin Air: The Brief, Wonderful Life of Network News* (New York: Simon and Schuster, 1991), 405-6. Italics are mine.
2. Kiku Adatto, *Soundbite Democracy: Network Evening News Presidential Coverage, 1968 and 1988* (Cambridge, Mass.: Joan Shorenstein Barone Center on the Press, Politics and Public Policy, John F. Kennedy School of Government, Harvard University, 1990), 4.
3. Quoted in Edward Jay Epstein, *News from Nowhere: Television and the News* (New York: Random House, 1973), 4-5.
4. Frank, *Out of Thin Air*, 406.
5. Av Westin, *Newswatch: How TV Decides the News* (New York: Simon and Schuster, 1982), 57.
6. There is quite a sizable literature on war coverage, and especially postmortems on the Gulf War. Although there is no space here to do the discussion justice,

suffice to say it will be an ongoing issue. As Ed Cody, deputy foreign editor of the *Washington Post*, remarked, "The press has probably learned a lesson. Next time, there will be a two-pronged effort. There will be the people who will go to the pools, take the handouts, and file those kinds of stories. But there will also be free agents, people whose job it will be to do other things, to get away and not work within the system. The military will try to prevent it, but they can't."

7. As noted at the beginning of the chapter, there is a rather theological debate in television reporting about whether the story should come before the pictures or the pictures before the story. Without prejudice to either side, I elected to put the pictures before the story in this illustration.

8. Frank, *Out of Thin Air*, 411-12.

9. A Canadian citizen, Champ in 1993 became the host of the Canadian Broadcasting Corporation's national breakfast program, *This Morning on CBC*.

10. Liz Trotta, *Fighting for Air: In the Trenches with Television News* (New York: Simon and Schuster, 1991), 329-30.

11. Benjamin Weiser, "Does TV News Go Too Far?" *Washington Post*, 28 February 1993, A1.

12. As quoted in William A. Henry III, "Where NBC Went Wrong," *Time*, 22 February 1993, 59.

13. David Schoenbrun, *On and Off the Air* (New York: E.P. Dutton, 1989), 12.

14. Dan Rather, "From Murrow to Mediocrity?" *New York Times*, op-ed page, 10 March 1987. Ken Auletta describes in detail the changes and budget cutting that occurred at the networks in the 1980s in his book *Three Blind Mice: How the TV Networks Lost Their Way* (New York: Vintage Books, Random House, 1992).

15. In the early 1990s the three networks together were spending about $1 billion a year on news, compared with roughly $200 million for CNN (Auletta, *Three Blind Mice*, 569).

16. Richard Zoglin, "The Magazining of TV News," *Time*, 12 July 1993, 51.

17. There were nineteen bureaus when I spoke to Jordan in April 1993 at CNN headquarters in Atlanta. A twentieth, in Johannesburg, was added in early 1994.

18. Lewis A. Friedland, *Covering the World: International Television News Services* (New York: Twentieth Century Fund, 1992), 7.

19. George F. Kennan, "If TV Drives Foreign Policy, We're in Trouble," letter to the editor, *New York Times*, Editorials/Letters page, 24 October 1993.

20. David R. Gergen, "Diplomacy in a Television Age," in Simon Serfaty, ed., *The Media and Foreign Policy* (New York: St. Martin's Press, 1991), 48-49.

21. Quoted in "For the Record," *Washington Post*, 27 April 1994, A22.

Chapter 6   Patterns of Coverage

1. Mort Rosenblum, "Special Correspondent Quixote," *Gannett Center Journal*, fall 1989, 5, 8.

2. According to one 1990 count, there were 1,734 full-time staffers—reporters, editors, producers, and photographers—working for various U.S. news organizations overseas, 820 of them Americans. This contrasted with 676 in 1975, including 429 Americans. (Ralph E. Kliesch, "The U.S. Press Corps Abroad Rebounds: A 7th World Survey of Foreign Correspondents," *Newspaper Research Journal*, winter 1991, 26.) The April 1994 *American Journalism Review* published a list of U.S. news organizations and their bureaus around the world.

3. A 1991 study by the Chicago Council on Foreign Relations provided some evidence for the view that interest in international affairs was on the rise. It showed that the number of people professing to be "very interested" in news about the relations of the United States with other countries rose from 45 percent in 1982 to 53 percent in 1990. Similarly, the percent "very interested" in news *about* other countries rose from 28 percent to 36 percent in the same period. (Freedom Forum

Media Studies Center Research Group, *The Media and Foreign Policy in the Post-Cold War World* [New York: Freedom Forum Media Studies Center, 1993], 37).
One problem with such data, media analysts point out, is that some people tend to answer positively because they feel they *should* care about foreign affairs. Bernard Gwertzman, foreign desk editor at the *New York Times* and a former State Department correspondent, commented that "at any given time, there are only about two million people in this country who are really interested in foreign affairs" (ibid., 20).

4. These concerns were outlined by Eugene L. Roberts Jr., former executive editor of the *Philadelphia Inquirer*, in a speech at the National Press Club in November 1993. See "Nothing Succeeds Like Substance," *American Journalism Review*, December 1993, 3-4.

5. Paul Taylor, *See How They Run: Electing the President in an Age of Mediocracy* (New York: Alfred A. Knopf, 1990), 259.

6. Byron T. Scott and Ann Walton Sieber, "Remaking *Time, Newsweek*, and *U.S. News and World Report*," and David Gergen, "Commentary," in Philip S. Cook, Douglas Gomery, and Lawrence W. Lichty, eds., *The Future of News* (Baltimore, Md.: Johns Hopkins University Press, 1992), 201, 207-8.

7. Howard Kurtz, *Media Circus: The Trouble with America's Newspapers* (New York: Times Books, Random House, 1993), 364.

8. Joseph Ungaro, "First the Bad News," *Media Studies Journal*, fall 1991, 103-4.

9. *The Age of Indifference: A Study of Young Americans and How They View the News*, Times-Mirror Center for the People and the Press, Washington, D.C., 28 June 1990, 20.

10. Lucas A. Powe Jr., *The Fourth Estate and the Constitution* (Berkeley: University of California Press, 1991), 201; Ungaro, "First the Bad News," 103-4.

11. U.S. Bureau of the Census, *Historical Statistics of the United States: Colonial Times to 1970*, Part 2, Washington, D.C., 1975, 855-56; and idem., *Statistical Abstract of the United States: 1992* (112th ed.), Washington, D.C., 1992, 559.

12. The number of daily newspapers declined from 1,748 in 1970 to 1,611 in 1990.

13. According to the *Media Industry Newsletter*, newspaper ad revenues vaulted from $14.8 billion in 1980 to $32.4 billion in 1989—an increase of 119 percent—but then fell to $30.7 billion in 1992. The 6 percent drop between 1990 and 1991 was the worst single-year drop since data began to be compiled in 1949. California State University journalism professor Michael Emery did a content analysis of ten leading U.S. newspapers in late 1987 and early 1988. He found they devoted only 2.6 percent of their nonadvertising space to news from abroad: 8,245 foreign stories taking up 89,395 column inches of space. See Michael Emery, "An Endangered Species: The International Newshole," *Gannett Center Journal*, fall 1989.

14. Though this discussion refers specifically to the desking of a story by combining input from several vantage points, the term "triangulation" is also used in a more general sense to connote cross-checking. "Professional newspeople use two devices when informing themselves," writes AP special correspondent Mort Rosenblum. "They absorb any account with some skepticism; this is suspended belief. It is not so much the messenger who is in doubt as the message itself. Facts and impressions are then tested against another account—and then a third; this is triangulation." See Mort Rosenblum, *Who Stole the News?* (New York: John Wiley and Sons, 1993), 56.

15. Reston, *Deadline*, 335.

16. James D. Squires, *Read All About It! The Corporate Takeover of America's Newspapers* (New York: Times Books, Random House, 1993), 218-19, 226.

17. Howard Kurtz, "What's Wrong with Newspapers?" *Washington Post Magazine*, 18 April 1993, 24-25.

18. Auletta, *Three Blind Mice*, 227 (see chap. 5, n. 14).

19. The giveaway on voice-overs is the sign-off. If the correspondent does a piece from Somalia, he will usually do an on-camera stand-upper at the end and sign off, "Joe Smith, XBC News, Mogadishu." If he does it over a piece assembled in London

from agency material, the item might carry a straightforward "Joe Smith, XBC News, London." But if there is no stand-upper and the sign-off is simply "Joe Smith, XBC News"—no mention of a place—then the piece, however stylish, is a voice-over, done in London or some other hub bureau. There is an element of sleight-of-hand in this, and many broadcast professionals are not comfortable with it.

20. See Tal Sanit, "The New Unreality: When TV Reporters Don't Report," *Columbia Journalism Review,* May-June 1992, 17-18. He quotes CBS's Betsy Aaron as saying: "I don't believe that buying footage and looking at it secondhand is a substitute for going there yourself. I do know that when I look at the tape and I don't see what's beyond that tape, I am not seeing the story. I'm relying on someone else to gather that story for me. I have no idea what the person's agenda was— and there always is an agenda. And we're putting that on the air with the CBS label or the NBC label or the ABC label and we're doing it in a cavalier fashion that we never would have done twenty . . . or ten . . . or even five years ago."

21. Auletta, *Three Blind Mice,* 565.

22. Friedland, *Covering the World,* 11 (see chap. 5, n. 18).

23. CNN maintains an around-the-clock "satellite desk" at CNN Center in Atlanta, with specialists who do nothing but juggle and book time on domestic and international satellites. This is a high-tech area subject to frequent change, but as this was being written, CNN employed twelve satellites to deliver its service.

24. *American Journalism Review,* April 1994, 29.

25. Turner has such strong views about CNN's international role that in 1988 he banned the use of the word "foreign" at the network and threatened violators with fines. "Sometimes, we go through the damnedest convolutions to avoid using it," said Stuart Loory.

26. Writing a five-minute radio newscast is tough; the script must be clear, concise, and inclusive. As a graduate student at Ohio State University's School of Journalism in 1973, I put together and announced a newscast at WOSU in Columbus. Later that year, I got the best training I probably ever had in AP's Columbus bureau—boiling down long items from the main news wire into two-paragraph summaries for the broadcast wire that went to radio and TV stations all over the state.

  In 1976-79 I wrote and voiced spots from Portugal and Beirut for the UPI Audio network. At WOSU and with UPI, a thirty-second spot was considered ideal; forty-five seconds was pressing the outer limits of what was usable. That's about twelve lines of copy. Anything over a minute was extremely rare. Local radio stations preparing five-minute newscasts simply do not have time for more, and a thirty-second spot gets twice as much play as a forty-five second one.

  My scriptwriting formula centered on conveying an idea, not detail: Tell them what you're going to tell them, tell them, then tell them what you told them. (There was fighting today in Beirut. The fighting was between Palestinians and Lebanese militias. It was the worst outbreak of violence in three months.)

Chapter 7   Ground Rules

1. See appendix 2, "State Department Ground Rules for Attribution," U.S. Department of State, Bureau of Public Affairs, October 1990.

2. William Safire, "Off the Record," *New York Times Magazine,* 28 October 1989, 16.

3. When UPI sent me to Beirut as bureau chief in 1976, I was twenty-six years old. Almost immediately, my authority was tested by one of our best employees, a Lebanese journalist who refused to work night shifts, arguing two junior women on the staff should do all nights and he, by virtue of seniority, only days. Beirut was dangerous at night: an employee had been kidnapped and murdered on his way home from work the previous year. I said the schedule stood as it was. He replied, "In that case, I quit." I told him to draft his letter of resignation and I

would forward it to London. He did not quit, and he worked his fair share of nights. We also became, and remain, fast friends. The limits had been established.

4. See appendix 2, "State Department Ground Rules for Attribution."

5. A May 1990 instruction, known informally among State Department and USIA officers as the "leash law," spelled out the guidelines:

> No one should accept on-the-record domestic interview requests with major media without prior PA clearance. These include TV network news shows and weekend talk shows, major newspapers, national radio shows and weekly news magazines.
>
> It is not necessary to obtain clearance for backgrounders, but PA is interested in knowing of any editorial backgrounders with major media, and of any other backgrounders which may be noteworthy.
>
> PA clearance is also needed for similar overseas major media contacts.

The guidelines were renewed early in the Clinton administration with a 20 February 1993 cable of instruction to all diplomatic and consular posts that said: "With the personnel turnover at the beginning of the new administration, it seems appropriate to remind everyone that all speaking engagements and high profile media interviews with senior Department officials should be cleared in advance through the Bureau of Public Affairs. This has been the policy for several administrations." The cable then recapitulated the standing guidelines for department officials in Washington and at overseas posts, adding: "The bottom line is the same as it always has been. If it makes news here, we want to know about it in advance."

See appendix 3 for text of the May 1990 instruction.

6. See appendix 2, "State Department Ground Rules for Attribution."

7. One experienced State Department correspondent defined "senior official" as assistant secretary on up. Thus, Oberdorfer's phrase, "a senior official high in the European Bureau," would be tantamount to naming the assistant secretary for that bureau. A reasonable argument might also be made for starting with deputy assistant secretary, the lowest rung of the policy level. In practice, however, the number and variety of deputy assistant secretaries argues against this. While some deputies are very senior indeed in terms of their responsibilities, others with this rank are comparatively less so. Thus, for purposes of journalistic attribution if not bureaucratic standing, assistant secretary is probably the lowest level where all in the category can definitively be said to have senior policy-making responsibilities.

8. David D. Newsom, *Diplomacy and the American Democracy* (Bloomington and Indianapolis: Indiana University Press, 1988), 63.

9. See appendix 2, "State Department Ground Rules for Attribution."

10. Safire, "Off the Record," 18.

11. From the author's own 1980 copy of the ground rules memo, which appears to date from the late 1970s (possibly from Hodding Carter III's 1977-80 tenure as spokesman), and to have been recirculated internally a number of times since. The full text of the same memo, put out again in 1982, has been published in Hess, *The Government/Press Connection*, 118-21 (see chap. 3, n. 3). It remains a good shorthand set of guidelines.

12. Safire, "Off the Record," 16.

13. Ibid., 18.

14. See appendix 2, "State Department Ground Rules for Attribution."

Chapter 8   *Preparations: The Five P's*

1. The Democratic Front for the Liberation of Palestine, a Marxist-Leninist group led by Nayef Hawatmeh.

2. Abu Mazin (Mahmoud Abbas), a senior official in PLO chairman Yasir Arafat's

Fatah organization, played a central role on Palestinian-Israeli dialogue issues. Abu Iyad (Salah Khalaf), also a Fatah member, was generally considered the number two person in the PLO after Arafat until his assassination in Tunis on 14 January 1991. A PLO report later accused a member of the dissident Abu Nidal organization of carrying out the killing.

3. The Commerce Department publishes a number of useful reports with statistics and economic background information on various countries. The State Department's Country Reports on Human Rights contain not only information on the human rights situation of particular states but also considerable detail on the workings of their political and legal systems. USIA's Wireless File supplies the embassy with unclassified official texts from Washington of speeches by U.S. officials. Finally, the post sometimes has on hand, or knows where to find, a variety of other country-specific material, such as factbooks put out by the central bank or local chamber of commerce.

Chapter 9   The Reporter: "Forester" or "Strip Miner"?

1. The identification that distinguishes between a staff writer and a stringer often appears in the small-type "agate" line under the byline. Nomenclature varies, but in the *Washington Post*, for example, a staff foreign correspondent would have "*Washington Post* Foreign Service" in the agate line, whereas a stringer's copy would have "Special to the *Washington Post*."
2. ABC now has an 80 percent share in WTN and worked closely with UPITN back then.
3. A reporter talking to diplomats at the State Department's Foreign Service Institute said that when he mentioned some of these considerations, an FSO asked a good question: What do I do when a columnist—a one-night stand, but an important, powerful actor—shows up? Go on sick leave, another FSO suggested. The only answer, really, is that this is just one of those occasions when ambassadors exercise their judgment and earn their money.

Chapter 10   Field of Play

1. Howard Kurtz, "Why the Press Is Always Right," *Columbia Journalism Review*, May-June 1993, 35.
2. Macomber, *The Angel's Game*, 32-33 (see chap. 2, n. 4).
3. Erik Tarloff, "Innocents in Washington," *Washingtonian*, August 1993, 23.
4. It should be noted that in all cases involving the arrest and detention of Americans overseas, the Privacy Act of 1974 prohibits officials from divulging any information that is not in the public domain without the express written permission of the affected individuals. It also provides for criminal sanctions against government officials who willingly and knowingly disclose information to an unauthorized recipient about a person entitled to protection under the Act.
5. Oakley explained that although she was a spokeswoman, her *title* was "deputy spokesman."
6. Quoted in Leon V. Sigal, *Reporters and Officials* (Lexington, Mass.: D.C. Heath, 1973), 114.

Chapter 11   Read It and Weep

1. Former secretary of state George Shultz offers a version of this in his memoirs, noting that President Ronald Reagan often told the story, too. See Shultz, *Turmoil and Triumph: My Years as Secretary of State* (New York: Charles Scribner's Sons, 1993), 227.
2. Camarena was kidnapped and killed while working in Mexico in 1985.

3. In Washington the U.S. Information Agency is USIA, but its overseas arm is the U.S. Information Service (USIS).
4. See discussion of "deep background" and "not for attribution" in chapter 7.

Chapter 12   *In the Embassy*

1. See appendix 4, a USIA memo on field media contacts; appendix 5, a State Department cable on consular work and the media; and appendix 6, VOA guidelines on relations between VOA correspondents and U.S. missions abroad.
2. The Wireless File, sent to posts daily by USIA, is the primary vehicle for transmission of official texts and statements between Washington and embassies overseas.
3. Subsequently, in September 1989, Bazoft was arrested by the Iraqi government for spying after allegedly collecting soil samples near an Iraqi military installation where an explosion had occurred. He was executed on 15 March 1990, in a case that caused a significant international outcry and became a major issue in relations between Iraq and Britain.
4. A related point: If a diplomat knows and trusts a reporter, he might consider granting the journalist permission to "clean up" quotes. This allows the correspondent limited editorial license to reduce awkward or wordy sentences without ellipses. If the diplomat has his own tape, it is a measure of insurance against distortion. If a journalist is unsure about the propriety of a change, he should check back through the PAO.
5. Tuch, *Communicating with the World*, 47 (see chap. 2, n. 2). This book is a useful overview of the work of USIA and of U.S. public diplomacy.
6. Ibid., 47-48.

Chapter 13   *Washington: Eunuch Games*

1. Nagorno-Karabakh is the predominantly Armenian enclave in Azerbaijan, scene of recurring fierce clashes between Azeri and Armenian forces.
2. Oberdorfer, "Lies and Videotape," C4 (see chap. 3, n. 2).
3. This interview took place in June 1993.
4. Linsky, *Impact*, 203 (see chap. 3, n. 17).
5. Ibid., 221-22.
6. Ibid., 204-5.
7. For an extended review of the noon briefing, the coordination of guidance, the agendas of journalists attending, and follow-up by department officials, see Hess, *The Government/Press Connection*, 61-74 (see chap. 3, n. 3). Although researched in 1981-82, the Hess study was still accurate in its essentials as this was being written in 1993. See appendix 7 for an internal State Department memo outlining the basics of good press guidance.
8. Jim Anderson, "Administration of Silence," *Foreign Service Journal*, July-August 1982, 22.
9. Robert J. McCloskey, "The Care and Handling of Leaks," in Serfaty, ed., *The Media and Foreign Policy*, 119 (see chap. 5, n. 20).
10. George Kenney, "Truth as a Policy Casualty," *Washington Times*, 7 October 1992, G2.
11. Ibid.
12. In 1993 Marshall Harris and Stephen Walker, Bosnia desk officers, and Jon Western, an analyst in the Bureau of Intelligence and Research, also resigned over Clinton administration policy toward Bosnia and the former Yugoslavia.
13. For an elaboration of this view, see Kenneth I. Juster, "The Myth of Iraqgate," *Foreign Policy*, Spring 1994, 105-19.
14. There is a considerable literature on the terrorism-media-government triangle. Two good discussions are Robert B. Oakley, "Terrorism, Media Coverage, and

Government Response," in Serfaty, ed., *The Media and Foreign Policy*, 95-107 (see chap. 5, n. 20); and O'Neill, *Terrorist Spectaculars* (see chap. 3, n. 5).

15. *USIA: New Directions for a New Era* (Washington, D.C.: Institute for the Study of Diplomacy, Georgetown University, 1993).
16. Linsky, *Impact*, 212 (see chap. 3, n. 17).
17. Anderson, "Administration of Silence," 23.
18. Hodding Carter III, "Decompressing Information," *Foreign Service Journal*, July-August 1982, 27.

Chapter 14: Looking Ahead

1. Jules Cambon, *The Diplomatist*, quoted in Nicolson, *Diplomacy*, 29 (see chap. 2, n. 1).
2. The State Department's use of computers and technology, to put it kindly, has lagged far behind available technology, whether in word processing, use of local area networks, fax and e-mail, compatibility with other U.S. government agencies, cable processing and filing, or visa issuance. To give but one example: As this book was being written, only two of the five State Department geographic bureaus had electronic data links with USIA. This presumably should be a priority communications concern, since USIA's Wireless File is *the* prime source for policy updates each morning at missions all over the world. But a public affairs officer told me in early 1993 that the fastest way he had of getting a speech by his assistant secretary over to USIA for transmission to embassies by Wireless File was to send it by courier.
3. In 1973 a "National News Council" was launched to review complaints concerning the accuracy and fairness of news reporting. Conceived by the Twentieth Century Fund and tracked in the *Columbia Journalism Review*, the council was handicapped from the start by the opposition of major news organizations, including the *New York Times* and *Washington Post*, who reportedly saw it as the first step on the road to more organized censorship. The council expired in 1984.
4. In the fall of 1993 the Foreign Service Institute was moved to a new site in Arlington, Virginia, and renamed the National Foreign Affairs Training Center.
5. Hess, *The Government/Press Connection*, 76 (see chap. 3, n. 3).
6. Nicolson, *Diplomacy*, 51, 142-43 (see chap. 2, n. 1).

Suggested Readings

Hess, Stephen. *The Government/Press Connection: Press Officers and Their Offices.* Washington, D.C.: The Brookings Institution, 1984.

Linsky, Martin. *Impact: How the Press Affects Federal Policymaking.* New York: W. W. Norton & Company, 1986.

Macomber, William. *The Angel's Game: A Handbook of Modern Diplomacy.* New York: Stein & Day, 1975.

Newsom, David D. *Diplomacy and the American Democracy.* Bloomington and Indianapolis: Indiana University Press, 1988.

Nicolson, Sir Harold. *Diplomacy.* 3d ed., 1963. Reprint. Washington, D.C.: Institute for the Study of Diplomacy, Georgetown University, 1988.

Index

DATE DUE

DEC 3 0 1997			

DEMCO 38-297